Home Again,
Home Again

ALSO BY THOMAS FRONCEK

AS AUTHOR
Take Away One, 1985

The Emergence of Man: The Northmen, 1974

AS EDITOR
Sail, Steam and Splendour: A Picture History of Life aboard the Transatlantic Liners, 1977

The City of Washington: An Illustrated History, 1976

Voices from the Wilderness: The Frontiersman's Own Story, 1974

The Horizon Book of the Arts of Russia, 1970

The Horizon Book of the Arts of China, 1969

Home Again, Home Again

A SON'S MEMOIR

THOMAS FRONCEK

ARCADE PUBLISHING · NEW YORK

FIRST EDITION

"Riders in the Sky (A Cowboy Legend)" by Stan Jones copyright © 1949; copyright © renewed 1977 by Edwin H. Morris & Company, a division of MPL Communications, Inc. Used by permission.

Library of Congress Cataloging-in-Publication Data

Froncek, Thomas
  Home again, home again / Tom Froncek. —1st ed.
   p. cm.
  ISBN 1-55970-332-6
  1. Family—Wisconsin—Case studies. 2. Sons—Wisconsin—Biography. 3. Home—Wisconsin—Psychological aspects—Case studies. 4. House construction—Wisconsin—Case studies. Aging parents—Wisconsin—Case studies. I. Title.
  HQ536.15.W6F76 1996
  306.85'09775—dc20   95–53074

Published in the United States by Arcade Publishing, Inc., New York
Distributed by Little, Brown and Company

10 9 8 7 6 5 4 3 2 1

Designed by API

BP

PRINTED IN THE UNITED STATES OF AMERICA

When my son Jesse was a small boy of four or five, I would often take him for long rides on my bicycle. With him buckled into a yellow plastic seat behind me, we'd ride around town or out into the countryside, enjoying the scenery and each other's company.

Returning from one such outing, I discovered that his mind had been occupied with more than the scenery, for as I unbuckled him from his seat and lifted him down to the ground, he presented me with a breathtaking image of the generations of which he and I were a part. "When I grow up," he told me, "I'll take my boy riding on my bicycle. And he'll take his boy on his bicycle. And that boy will take his boy. And we'll all go riding together."

I was stunned then, as I still am, by the breadth of his innocent imagining. Bending to hug him, I told him how wonderful that would be. And I meant it from the bottom of my heart. In the nearly twenty years since then, I have not encountered a more hopeful vision of harmony between fathers and sons.

This book is for Jesse,
who's next on the bicycle.

The world owes all its onward
impulses to men ill at ease.

—Nathaniel Hawthorne

Part I

If we could make contours in hearts, as we do in maps, to see their love, we should learn what strange, unexpected regions attain the deepest depth. Often we might discover that a place rather than a person holds the secret.

— Dame Freya Stark

1

HOMECOMING

I WAS LOOKING FOR THE HOUSE AGAIN. It happened every time. The minute the plane began its descent over the lake, I'd be glued to the window, watching for the approaching shoreline and wondering if I'd be able to spot the place.

The chances were not good. Once over land, the plane would have to come in on the right course, plus I'd have to be sitting in the right place to get a view. It was always a long shot. Still, I always looked. One of these trips I might just get lucky.

"Ladies and gentlemen, we are beginning our final approach to Milwaukee. Please make sure your seat back is in an upright position. . . ."

We crossed the shoreline just north of downtown. Off the left wing tip, a cluster of gleaming glass-and-steel skyscrapers jutted from their drab surroundings like quartz crystals sprouting from a field of gravel. There weren't many of them: enough, no doubt, to swell the hearts of the chamber of commerce, but not so many that ordinary folks were likely to lose sleep worrying that the evils of big city life might be creeping north from Chicago.

Off to the south I could make out the grimy docks, freight yards, and factories of the industrial south side. Just beyond, fading into the wintry haze, stretched the old Polish neighborhoods that had once supplied those factories with laborers, including my father and his father before him. This had been their heartland: the place where they scraped by and made do; where they came home at night exhausted; where they let off steam in their local taverns on Saturday nights and got up on Sunday mornings to sing in their church choirs.

The churches were still down there. I could see their steeples. Probably the taverns were there, too, as well as the miles and miles of close-packed, two-family houses. But nowadays, I knew, most of the factories were closed, and the old neighborhoods were in ruins. The taverns had Spanish names, and the churches were called *iglesias*.

The plane banked left, straightened, then banked again, tipping my side toward the ground. Looking out, I realized what was happening: we'd been looping around the city from the north and west and were now approaching the airport from the south — exactly the right direction to bring us within range of the house I was looking for.

Surprised by my own excitement, I began searching the ground for landmarks. I got my bearings as soon as I caught sight of the double ribbon of concrete that marked old Highway 41. After that it was easy. As the plane continued its steady descent over the suburban sprawl, I spotted a familiar water tower, then a park, then a particular red barn. I knew there would be a certain crossroads coming up soon. Yes, there it was! And there was the little white church I remembered. Now, if I just let my eye follow that crossroads a little to the east —

All at once the plane pivoted again on its wing tip and suddenly there it was, directly below me: the place I was always trying to find, the place I kept coming back to in my dreams and my memories: the house my father built.

What amazed me was how easily I could pick it out from the other houses that lined that road. It was the only one that wasn't set close to the pavement, the only one that wasn't centered squarely on its lot. Turned at an angle to its neighbors and to the passing traffic, it stood apart. Isolated. Off center. Out of place. Like the man who built it, it faced the world obliquely. Yet compared to the lock-step conventionality of the houses nearby, it projected a certain stubborn independence, a kind of quirky originality. And those things, too, were like the man himself.

Now, as the plane slid toward its landing and the house passed from view, I found myself wondering what it was about the place that kept haunting me and drawing me back. Why did it keep turning up in my dreams? Why, whenever I made one of these rare visits home, was I always so hungry to catch a glimpse of that small rectangle of wood and shingles set so rakishly on the midwestern prairie? What was it that drew my eye and my imagination back there again and again? It didn't make sense. After all, we lived there so briefly. And so long ago.

My mother was waiting in the crowd at the arrival gate. At first I wasn't sure it was she. The woman I saw waving in my direction from the other side of the barrier was dressed in a smart wool coat. Her hair was carefully permed, and she had obviously taken time with her powder and lipstick. Yet she looked so much smaller and frailer than the woman I had kissed good-bye at this same gate a little over a year ago. Despite the makeup there was no disguising the haggard look, the dark circles around her eyes.

I shouldn't have been surprised. Over the last few months she had filled our Sunday evening phone conversations with wearying accounts of how she had not been sleeping well, how she had been worrying too much, doing too much. Still, I was shocked by the way she looked. How had she suddenly got so old?

I set my face in a smile and made my way over to where she waited. With my valet bag slung over my shoulder, I bent to kiss her cheek and caught a hint of rose water. "Hello, Mom," I said.

She reached up and hugged me to her. "Hello, dear. Oh, it's good to see you." Her eyes were misty behind her tortoiseshell glasses. "It's been so long."

I ignored the implied rebuke. If it had been up to her, I would never have left home at all, much less moved a thousand miles away and made a life and a family of my own.

I stepped back. "You look terrific," I said.

She brightened. "Do you really think so?"

"Absolutely. And I love the coat. It's new, isn't it? The blue is just right for you."

She drank in my compliments like lemonade on a hot afternoon, and as we made our way through the terminal and out toward the parking garage, she was almost giddy with excitement.

Then I spoiled it.

"How's Dad?" I asked.

It was as if I had turned out the lights in the toy store. Her face immediately clouded over.

"About the same," she said. "I haven't seen him yet today. But yesterday the therapist had him sitting up by himself."

"Well, that's an improvement."

She shrugged indifferently. "A little."

"That's great. I'm glad." I was trying hard to salvage the situation, to sound upbeat. But I had to wonder: improvement to what end? My father had been ill for years. The stroke he'd suffered the previous month was only the most devastating in a series of setbacks. For him, any real life had ended long ago. Yet somehow he kept hanging on. Usually I made a joke of it: "He always was a stubborn son of a bitch," I'd say, making it an offhand tribute to his fighting spirit. But sometimes I had a feeling he was hanging on out of pure spite. It would have been just like him.

My mother unlocked the trunk of her car. I set my bag inside.

"Want me to drive?" I asked.

"If you like."

She handed me the keys with what I imagined was a sense of relief at having at least that one small responsibility lifted from her shoulders.

In the past, it was my father who had done the driving for the two of them, just as it was he who had paid the bills, kept the car repaired, caulked the windows, strung the clotheslines, fixed the leaky pipes, unstuck the storm doors, replaced the cracked bathroom tiles, mowed the lawn in summer, and shoveled the sidewalks in winter. Now she did it all, or had to find someone else to do it for her. And that was in addition to keeping up with her usual routine of cooking, cleaning, washing, ironing, grocery shopping, plus nursing Dad when he was at home, feeding him, cleaning him up when he soiled himself, making sure he got his pills on time, and telling him when to get up, when to take a walk, and when to just sit still until she could get to whatever it was he needed.

Part of her relished her new role. After years of deferring to his wishes, she was discovering strengths and abilities she never knew she had. Best of all, she was calling the shots. If she said go, they went. If she said stay, they stayed. But there was another part of her that hated every minute, that wanted nothing more desperately than to have him take care of her again.

I opened the passenger door for her, then went around to the other side and slid into the driver's seat. His seat. To my surprise, I did it without a qualm. There was a time, not too many years ago, when I wouldn't have dared.

To get to the small town where my mother was now living, we had to drive south on the interstate. Along the way, I knew, we would pass within a mile of the house I had seen from the air.

"Like to stop by and have a look?" I asked.

"Well, I don't know." My mother glanced at her watch. "They usually have him down for therapy at four. I thought you'd like to be there for that."

"Oh. Sure. Right."

"I hope you don't mind."

"No, no. That's fine. Maybe we'll get a chance on the way back."

"Maybe," she replied now. "If there's time."

I was not surprised by her lack of enthusiasm. The truth was that no one else in the family seemed to be drawn to the place the way I was. Neither my sister nor my brother had ever talked about going back to visit the house or driving by just to have a look. As for my mother, she tended to brush off my obsession as a tedious waste of time, an irrelevant bit of self-indulgence or even dementia. Well, I wasn't going to argue. I'd already done enough to spoil our reunion.

The nursing home where my father was staying did not look anything like the gloomy asylum that I had expected. A sprawling two-story brick building, it was as cheerfully bland as a turnpike motel. The windows had no bars on them, and the curtains were pulled back to let in the pale January light. Obviously there was nothing to hide here: no abusive attendants, no starving or raving inmates. It seemed blessedly ordinary.

Inside, the atmosphere was much the same. A receptionist smiled and exchanged cheerful first-name greetings with my mother, then went back to her typing, leaving Mom to lead the way along a series of well-lit corridors. On the walls were framed dime-store prints of sunlit meadows and mountain streams. An old man in a baseball cap shuffled past, leaning on a cane. A nurse, gliding by on crepe-soled shoes, offered a pleasant smile and said, "Hi, there," as if we were old friends. Farther along, in a sunny alcove, a group of white-haired men and women were quietly playing cards and smoking cigarettes. A soap opera flickered on the television in the corner, but no one was watching it. There were potted plants on the window ledge, a couple of parakeets twittering in a cage, a bookcase full of Reader's Digest Condensed Books. Ordinary. Safe. Reassuring.

Still, as we came to an elevator and stood waiting for the doors to open, I could not shake the growing dread I felt as we drew closer to wherever it was they were keeping my father. The last time I saw him he was still living at home and capable of making his way around the house with the aid of a walker. All I knew of his present condition was what Mother had been telling me over the phone: loss of the use of his left arm and left leg; inability to stand or walk; general lack of responsiveness.

"I hope they got him to therapy on time today," my mother said as the elevator doors opened. We stepped inside and she pressed the Down button.

"Don't they usually?"

"Sometimes they wait too long. If they get him there too late in the day, he's too groggy to do anything."

"Oh," I murmured. My courage was faltering.

The elevator doors parted, and we stepped out. After walking along a corridor, we came to a doorway that opened onto a large, bright, busy room, where we were greeted by a chirpy young woman with a clipboard. She had dusty yellow hair, a plain face, and a pleasant smile. Was everyone here trained to smile that way?

My mother introduced us. The nurse's name was Jackie, and after shaking my hand, she informed us that the therapist would be ready for Dad in just a few minutes. "In the meantime, I'm sure Walter would be happy to see you. He's just over there." She nodded vaguely toward the far side of the room.

I looked in the direction of her nod but saw no one who looked like my father. What I did see reminded me of a geriatric version of a workout room in a health club. On one wall, under the windows, were a couple of raised platforms covered with mats. At one of them, a young man in a green hospital jacket was helping a white-haired codger raise and lower his legs. At a nearby table sat an old woman in a wheelchair; as a young nurse looked on encouragingly, the woman used her clumsy arms to push

8

around what appeared to be a set of multicolored children's blocks. Elsewhere, a frail creature in a housedress and slippers sat on the edge of an exercise machine, tugging at a pair of weighted ropes. Nowhere did I see my father.

"There he is," my mother said, starting across the room.

I followed her over to a long table on which an old man lay staring at the ceiling. He was fully dressed in a short-sleeved shirt, plaid slacks, and slippers, and he was held to the table by broad straps, which encircled his chest, hips, and legs. Were the straps there to keep him from rolling off, I wondered, or to restrain him in case he turned violent? Repelled in either case, and embarrassed for him, I averted my gaze. Only when my mother bent to kiss the man's forehead did I realize with a jolt that this pale, wasted shell was all that was left of my father.

"Hello, Walter," my mother said. "Look who came to visit you today." She spoke to him as if to a child, in a high, singsong voice.

Automatically, I bent to kiss his cheek. "Hello, Dad." I felt the scratch of his whiskers, saw the blue veins on his bald head, felt his hot breath on my cheek. With unfocused eyes he peered up at me, a small frown wrinkling his forehead as if he were trying to place who I was.

An attendant came and raised the top end of the table so that Dad was almost vertical. The "tilt table," my mother explained, was designed to use the pull of gravity to help restore the circulation in his legs. With the strap across his chest holding him upright, he hung from the table, arms dangling, head lolling. I took one of his hands, lifted it, felt the bones beneath the skin. The skin itself was as thin as the paper of a hornet's nest.

"Hello, Dad," I said again.

"Do you know who this is, Walter?" my mother asked.

He stared at me, uncomprehending.

"It's me, Dad. It's Tom."

Still staring, he moved his lips. "Tom," he whispered. It was as if he was trying out a word he had never used before. "Tom," he repeated.

"That's right, Dad. It's me. Your son, Tom."

I tried to sound cheerful. But I heard my voice catching in my throat.

For years I'd had to stay away, unable even to be in the same room with him without my insides getting tied in knots. At times, I had hated him. At times, I had longed for the day when I would see him utterly helpless and me triumphant in my youth and vigor. I thought I would dance for joy should such a day ever come. Yet now that it was here, dancing was not what I wanted to do. This was not the kind of triumph I had envisioned.

This sorry creature, this ravaged shell that hung from the upright table like the shrugged-off carapace of a cicada stuck to the side of a tree — this was no victory of mine. It was the cold, corrosive victory of age and disease, of chemical imbalance and neurons gone awry.

Standing there, looking down at him, I could feel nothing of anger or hatred but only a terrible pity at seeing what he had become. His life had once been full of hope and promise and brave beginnings; full of dreams and the stubborn will to make those dreams become reality. Seeing him now, yet thinking back to those other times, I felt as if I were looking through binoculars and struggling to match the disjointed images in the two sets of lenses. But try as I might, I could not bring the picture into focus. How had it happened? I wondered. How was it possible that my father's life had gone so very wrong?

2

PICNIC

"When are we going to be there?" my sister asked from her corner of the backseat.

Joyce would be turning seven in April. In my child's view of things, this meant that until my birthday in July, my sister would be two years older than I was instead of just one. I still remember how it irked me. Not only was I not catching up with her, I was actually losing ground.

"Not far now," my father answered cheerfully. "Hold your horses."

Just where my father was taking us we had no idea. The only thing he'd been willing to tell us was that it was a surprise and that we were going to have a picnic when we got there.

Nor was my mother any help. Although she must have known what my father was up to, she had been doing a fine job of pretending not to know a thing. It hadn't yet occurred to me that she might be as good at keeping secrets as he was.

"It must be a park if we're going to have a picnic," I said, thinking I could trick my father into telling us more.

"Nope, it's not a park."

"Is it . . . a playground?"

"Nope, it's not a playground either."

"Yeah, but —"

"Don't say yeah," my mother chided. "It's not good English."

"Okay, but if it's not a park and it's not a playground, how can we have a picnic?"

"Well," my father said, "I guess you'll have to wait and see." Then he laughed a sneaky kind of laugh, and I thought I saw him wink at my mother. But from my seat in the back I couldn't tell for sure.

One thing I was sure of, though: my father was having the time of his life. His brown fedora was pushed back on his head, his elbow was hanging out the car window, and now he was even singing, giving us a top-of-the-lungs rendition of "Finicule, Finicula," with lots of emphasis on the la-la-la-la-la parts. Whatever his big secret was, it was making him very happy.

It was a Sunday afternoon in the early spring of 1948. Since this was still a couple of years before my brother Michael came along, there were just the four of us breezing along in the black seven-year-old Chevy coupe, plus Beauty, our collie, who lay on the seat beside me with her chin on my lap.

As we drove, the air that came rushing back from my father's open window was heavy with the smell of wet earth and last year's moldering leaves and grass. Here and there, where the stubbled cornfields rolled down to a stream or stopped at the edge of a stand of trees, patches of snow still littered the ground, like fugitive clumps of laundry blown off a clothesline by the March wind. The winter-bare trees were penciled against the brilliant blue sky like an artist's sketch waiting to be filled in. But in the sunny places on the hilltops and up against the sides of farmhouses and barnyard fences, little tussocks of green were beginning to show.

"Almost there now," my father said as we stopped at a crossroads and waited for the light to change.

We were at a broad four-lane highway, and as we rolled across it I got up on my knees so I could see better. Beauty, too, rose to her haunches. Pushing in front of me, she stretched her black snout toward my father's window, filling her lungs with the damp wind. She, too, seemed to sense that something was about to happen.

And it was. My father was slowing the car now. It seemed to me that he was even getting ready to stop, although for what reason I could not

12

imagine. As far as I could tell, there was nothing to distinguish this place from any of the other places we had been driving past. On the left, fields of last year's grass, pressed flat by winter snows, stretched to a distant stand of trees. On the right, a string of houses lined up parallel to the road. But nowhere could I see anything that looked like a spot for a picnic.

Yet now — what was this? — my father was turning off the road onto a muddy track that led out into a grassy field. Ahead, a long earthen ridge, freshly excavated, rose like a miniature mountain range.

"Why, Walter, where in the world are you taking us?" my mother asked with exaggerated wonder.

If I had been a little older and a little less gullible, my mother's play-acting would probably have tipped me off to the fact that she had been in on my father's secret all along. But I still trusted everybody, especially my mother.

"Is this it?" I asked.

"Are we there?" asked Joyce.

"Well, we're somewhere, aren't we?" my father answered. "Hold on, now. It gets a little bumpy here."

Then, as he circled around to the other side of the mound of earth, an amazing thing happened. It was as if the ground had opened up in front of us, and my father was transporting us down into it, down below the stringy roots of the prairie grasses, down into the earth itself. To my child's eyes, it looked as if he was driving us into one of those box canyons I was always hearing about on the radio, the ones where the holdup men went to hide when the Lone Ranger was chasing them. Earthen walls rose sheer on all sides. The sky was a sharp-edged square of blue overhead.

"Well, here we are," my father announced as he slowed the car to a stop. "All out."

Only then, after Beauty had bounded out ahead of me and my feet had touched the dirt floor of the canyon, did my father tell us where we were: in the basement of what was going to be our new house.

New house? I didn't understand. Until that moment neither of my parents had said a word about a new house, at least none that I ever heard.

I try now to imagine what it must have been like for me, at not quite six, to be the recipient of such earthshaking news. We had been living in the same place for almost as long as I could remember. To me, it seemed as secure and comforting as the sound of my mother's voice when she sang me to sleep at night, and I had no reason to think that we wouldn't go on living there forever. Yet here was my father telling us that everything was now going to change.

My head was suddenly full of questions. What would become of the house we were living in now? Would somebody else live there after we left? And what about school? I was in kindergarten at Mill Valley. Was I going to have to start all over again someplace else? What puzzled me most of all was how my father was going to get a house out of this hole in the ground. Where would it come from? How would it get here? How big was it going to be? What would it look like?

My father had anticipated my questions. Reaching into the car, he brought out a long tube of rolled-up papers. When he spread them over one of the front fenders of the car, I saw that they were drawings of a house, each sheet showing a different view. The front showed steps leading up to a fancy door that had a little roof over it. A side view showed a wide brick chimney — "That's the fireplace," my father explained. Across the back of the house stretched a broad porch.

"What's that?" I asked my father, pointing to an oversized door beneath one end of the porch.

"That's the garage," he said. "That's where we're standing now."

I was mesmerized. The house, it seemed, was going to be built into a slope of the earth, with a garage on the basement level.

The really intriguing drawings were the ones that showed the different floors of the house as they would look from above, with the roof taken off and all the rooms opened to the sky. There were doors and closets, steps to the basement, appliances in the kitchen, and not one but two bathrooms, one upstairs and one down, each with its own little toilet and sink and tub drawn in.

Even today, whenever I hear anyone talk of drawing a tub, I find myself smiling as the pun brings back the memory of the day I first saw my father's dream laid out on paper, and of how, like Scheherazade spinning her wonderful tales, he enchanted us with visions of the house — or was it a sultan's palace? — that would one day be ours.

With the drawings in one hand and a stick in the other, my father led us around the excavation, scratching lines in the earth to show us where the rooms were going to be: kitchen in one corner, living room in another, dining room in between, his and Mom's bedroom off in the far corner.

"Where will we sleep?" my sister asked.

"Your rooms will be upstairs," my father said.

I stopped. Had I heard him right? "Do you mean I'll have my own?" I couldn't believe it. Until now Joyce and I had always shared a room. This seemed too good to be true.

My father looked serious. "Don't you like that idea?"

"Oh, boy. Yeah — I mean, yes, I do. I like it a lot."

"Because if you don't we can always use that space for a closet. Or maybe a sewing room for Mom."

"Walter, don't tease," my mother chided.

My father grinned. "Aw, he can take it." He rolled up his drawings. "Well, how about it? Now that we've all seen the new house, how about that picnic? Anybody hungry?"

"I am," I piped up.

Joyce looked uncertain. "You mean here?"

"You betcha," my father said. "We'll set it up right over there in the kitchen. Come on."

He tucked the drawings under his arm and strode down the hallway that he'd marked on the ground, taking exaggerated care not to step across any of the wall lines. Giggling at this fine new game, Joyce and I followed carefully in his footsteps. Beauty, oblivious to "walls" and "doors," scampered wherever she pleased, her nose to the ground.

That afternoon we had our first meal in the new house.

Using rocks unearthed by the bulldozer that had gouged out the excavation, my father built a cooking hearth in one corner of our box canyon, where it would be sheltered from the March wind. While my mother began rummaging through the trunk of the car for the food and paper plates, my sister and I went off with my father to gather dry sticks from the edge of the woods.

Before long, a lively fire was dancing in the hearth, beneath a metal grill that my father had balanced on the rocks. Upon this improvised stove my mother set a kettle full of beans, then laid out a bunch of hot dogs. While these were cooking, she spread a red-checked oil cloth on the ground for a kitchen table, then had Joyce set out plates and utensils.

Our kitchen chairs were pieces of cardboard that my father had torn from an old packing carton he found in the trunk.

"Okay, pardners," he said when everything was ready. "Time for chow."

I remember looking at him with something approaching awe. He sounded just like a trail boss in a Hopalong Cassidy movie.

"Wahoo!" I cried, slapping a hand across one knee.

Even my father laughed out loud. Clearly he was having as much fun pretending as I was.

That blustery March afternoon, as I sat huddled with my mother and father and sister at the foot of those canyon walls, I doubted that even Hoppy himself had ever had such a tasty supper of hot dogs, beans, and my mother's homemade potato salad. It was, I thought, the best picnic ever.

Exactly why we needed a new house I had no idea. As far as I could tell there was nothing wrong with the place where we were living.

Where we were living was on the edge of a small subdivision near Little Muskego Lake, amid the rolling farm country south and west of Milwaukee. Today, freeways have brought the area within easy commuting distance of the city, and a multitude of subdivisions and tract houses dot the countryside. But when we lived there, the land was still mostly open fields. It was a world away from the factories and breweries and the sour smokestack smells of the industrial south side where my father had grown up and where we still returned on holidays and weekends to visit various aunts and uncles and grandparents. Our house was at the end of a quiet dead-end street called Gem Drive. Acres of corn grew just on the other side of our hedge — a rustling, restless sea of green that stretched in row after endless row all the way up to the brow of a distant hill.

I liked our house. It was a small, solid brick building with two dormers that protruded from the green roof like the eyes of a bullfrog. Our backyard had a white picket fence around it and a sandbox and a swing and an apple tree with branches low enough for me to climb on. There was a garden where my father grew vegetables, and even a muddy pen where he kept a small flock of ducks. "Muscovies," he called them, and I never tired of watching them. But what I liked best was lying on my back on our front lawn and smelling the grass and watching the puffy white clouds go drifting across the sky. And if an airplane came buzzing lazily into view, I would lie there and wonder where it had come from and where it might be going.

I was happy where we were. Which was why it made no sense to me that my father wanted to live someplace else.

"Why do we have to?" I asked my mother one day after school.

"Why do we have to what?"

"Move to another house?"

We were in the kitchen. My mother was peeling potatoes for supper. Joyce was setting the table. I was sitting cross-legged on the floor beside Beauty's box, running my hands through the silky white fur that circled her neck and shoulders like a luxurious scarf. Her full name was Sleeping Beauty, since sleeping was what she mostly did.

"Because Daddy's new job is so far away," my mother said. "He has to drive a long time to get to work. The new house will be much closer."

"But I don't want to live anyplace else," I said.

"Me either," said Joyce.

"I know," Mom said. "I like it here, too. But sometimes we have to do things that we don't really want to do."

"But why?"

"I already told you why." There was an edge to her voice that I missed but that my sister picked up on.

"She did," Joyce said. "She already told you."

"Who asked you?" I shot back.

"Tommy! That's no way to talk to your sister."

"She started it!"

"I don't care who started it, I want you to stop."

I stopped.

Joyce waited until Mom's back was turned and then made a face, a snotty grin of triumph.

I sulked. I turned to Beauty, whom I knew I could rely on to be nice to me. I lifted her ear and examined its insides. I was intrigued by the swirl of pink ridges surrounding the dark hole that sank so deep into her head I couldn't see where it stopped. I waited. I did not look up, but I could hear Joyce at the table setting out the glasses and the knives and forks. My mother's knife clicked on the chopping board as she sliced the potatoes into little pieces. Finally, I tried again.

17

"How come if we have to move we don't just buy a new house?" I asked. "How come we have to build one?"

My mother did not reply right away but kept clicking away with the knife. She seemed to be concentrating very hard on what she was doing, and for a moment I wondered if she'd heard me. "It's something your father wants to do," she said at last. Her voice sounded ragged, the way it did when she had a cold and had to clear her throat.

Joyce scowled at me. Mom was upset and it was my fault. It wasn't like her to get upset. She was usually so calm, so steady. We waited, not knowing what was coming next.

Then, as if she had suddenly decided something, she put down the knife. As we watched, she rinsed her hands and wiped them on a towel. Then she pulled out a kitchen chair and sat down, carefully tucking back a lock of hair that had fallen loose over her forehead.

Reaching out an arm, my mother folded Joyce close to her side. But it was me she was looking at. She had gentle blue eyes and light brown hair with lots of waves in it, and she always took care that each wave was in exactly the right place, just as she made sure that each spoon was in the right place at the table and each sock in the right place in our dresser drawers. It was one of the ten thousand things about her that made me love her.

She gave Joyce a kiss on the cheek. To me she said, "You know how sometimes you really want to do something and you just won't be satisfied until you've done it?"

I stroked Beauty's head. "I guess so."

"Well, that's the way it is with Daddy about building a house." Her voice was calm, reasonable. "It's something he wants to do very, very much."

I thought about that for a moment, while I stroked the top of Beauty's head and she looked up at me with her big brown eyes. "Then I guess he should do it."

My mother smiled just a little. "That's what I think, too."

3

STRANGERS

*T*he therapist was ready now. His name was Joe, and I was all set to dislike him. For weeks my mother had been telling me what wonderful things Joe had been doing for my father. During our regular Sunday evening phone conversations, while I sat at my kitchen table a comfortable thousand miles from the front lines, she gave me glowing reports of the progress Joe was making in the battle to keep my father moving, his muscles from atrophying.

"Joe got Dad to lift his legs," she would say. Or: "Joe has been trying some new exercises. Dad responded so well. I wish you could have seen it."

I was grateful, of course. But I couldn't help feeling a little annoyed that a stranger was doing more for my father than I was. Never mind that I had no training as a physical therapist. Never mind that I lived half a continent away and had my own family to look after. Part of me still felt that I was the one who ought to have been shouldering the burden. This was what a son did for a father. This was family business. And it was private. Shades should be drawn. There should be no strangers here.

Yet I also knew that where my father was concerned, any efforts I might have made on his behalf, had he been aware of them, would certainly have come up short in his estimation. He had never been an easy man to please. So probably it was best for someone else to step in now, even if that someone was a stranger.

Joe joined my mother and me beside Dad's tilt table. Joe was not tall, but he looked as solid as a hundred-year-old walnut. His skin was just about the same color as that tree's wood. From the way his shoulders and biceps bulged beneath his T-shirt, I imagined he kept in shape by juggling cinder blocks and bench-pressing Ford pickups. He extended a hand the size of a baseball mitt, and I braced for pain. But the man's grip was surprisingly gentle.

"Good to meet you," I said. "I've been hearing about all the good things you've been doing."

He shrugged off the compliment. "Your dad's the one who's been doing all the work. Say, I'm glad you're here. Maybe you can give me a hand getting him off the table so we can get started. How about it, Walter? Ready to go to work, my man?"

My father, hanging from the straps that bound him to the table, lifted his head. His whispered yes was barely audible. It was pathetic, I thought. What kind of work could he possibly do? But Joe seemed to see with different eyes and to hear with different ears.

"Aw right!" he exclaimed, full of enthusiasm. "That's what I like to hear."

From a corner of the room Joe retrieved a high-backed wheelchair and wheeled it over to the tilt table. As I helped him undo the straps that bound Dad to the table, I found myself feeling grateful that I was finally getting an opportunity to actually do something for my father. I was pleased, too, to see that Joe treated him not as a helpless child, but as a normal adult who had all his faculties. It was an illusion, I knew, but it worked, helping Dad — and the rest of us — preserve some sense of his human dignity even in these humiliating circumstances.

With the straps undone, we eased Dad into the chair. It took surprisingly little effort. In his later years, my father had grown so obese that the mere thought of picking him up and moving him without the help of at least two other people was almost enough to induce a hernia. Now he had shrunken to a fraction of his former size. Lifting him, I felt the way amputees are said to feel about their missing limbs: as though the ghostly remnant was still there, still as weighty in my mind as he had once been in real life.

Having got Dad settled in the wheelchair, I took the handles and pushed him across the room, following in Joe's wake while my mother walked alongside. The padded wooden platform to which Joe led us was twice as wide as a king-sized bed and nearly as high off the ground. While I steadied the wheelchair with my foot, Joe bent down, wrapped his arms around Dad's torso, and lifted him to his feet. Then, pirouetting like a dancer with a rag doll, he eased Dad into a sitting position on the edge of the platform.

"Ouch," my father said, wincing. And again, "Ouch."

"Sorry," said Joe.

"What hurts, Walter?" my mother asked.

Dad had slumped forward on the edge of the platform. His head drooped to his chest. He seemed to have no backbone or muscle and would have fallen over if Joe had not been there to hold him up. He mumbled an answer.

"Speak up, dear, I can't hear you. What hurts?"

"Penis," he said. Then, looking up at her, he gave a mischievous grin. "Too much screwing around," he said.

"Walter!" My mother flushed. "What a thing to say!"

In better times, he had often delighted in pricking her starchy sense of propriety with bawdy jokes and off-color comments. But now, despite her prim rebuke, not even she could resist a smile. His ribaldry was gratifying proof that at least some faint spark of his old vitality survived. His mind was not a total blank after all. He was still in there somewhere, thinking, maybe even laughing.

What had caused Dad's discomfort, Joe discovered, was the catheter that ran from his urethra to the plastic bag that was strapped to his calf, beneath his plaid trousers. Discreetly, my mother adjusted the catheter for him. When she was done, Joe was ready to put Dad through his paces.

"Let's get that head up now, Walter," he said. Grabbing Dad's shoulders in his big hands, he straightened Dad's back fore and aft, while I did my part by sitting beside Dad with an arm around his waist and trying to keep him from slumping sideways.

"Come on now," Joe said, coaxing Dad along with all the gung-ho authority of a high-school gym teacher. "Lift that head up, Walter. That's it. Good work."

I was amazed. Dad was actually following Joe's instructions. Never in

21

my life had I known my father to let anyone tell him what to do. He was a man who made up his own mind, did what he decided to do, and brooked no contradictions or challenges. Certainly not from anyone in the family. Certainly not from me.

For a moment or two he managed to hold his head upright, so that he was able to look at Joe through his glasses instead of over the rims. Then, either because he forgot what he was supposed to be doing or because his neck muscles got tired, he let his head sink to his chest again. Ever patient, Joe reminded him to raise it again, and then again, until he was keeping it up for ten or fifteen seconds at a stretch.

"Good," Joe repeated. "That's very good."

Next, Joe began working on his legs.

"How about it, Walter? Are you going to lift that right leg now?"

Without either of us helping him, my father did as Joe said.

"Good. That's great," said Joe. "You're doing much better than you did the other day." He turned to me. "I think your being here is really making a difference. He wants to do well for you."

"You think so?"

"I really do."

I gathered I should have been pleased, and I made an effort to look it. But privately I was skeptical. That my father might strive to do well for my sake seemed highly improbable. Illness may have softened him, but I doubted that it had changed his character as much as that. More likely what was pushing him on were remnants of his old cantankerous pride and bullheadedness. He wasn't going to give anyone — me least of all — the satisfaction of thinking that he couldn't do the job.

"Okay. Now let's try the left leg," Joe was saying. "Raise your left leg, Walter. No, that's the right leg. Raise the left one."

But it was the right leg that responded. The left one stayed still, moving only when Joe used his own strength to make it move, raising and lowering it, massaging it, pulling it, pushing it, talking to Dad quietly the whole time, urging him on, reassuring him.

"What we want is for him to be aware of that left side," Joe explained. "The exercise and stimulation should help restore the muscles and also some of the nerve connections in his brain. Often, when one part of the brain is damaged by a stroke, the body compensates by rerouting the circuits and finding other channels."

I nodded.

"Look, let's try this. What if you come around to the other side and hold the right leg down, while I see if I can get him to lift the left one."

It sounded easy, but for all Dad's seeming frailty, he was still amazingly strong. When Joe asked him again to lift his left leg, I had to push down hard to keep the right one from popping up. But the exercise had the desired effect. After half a dozen tries, he was able to lift his left leg on command.

Joe grinned, showing teeth. "Aw right. That's the way. Good goin', Walter, my man."

We then tried the same thing with Dad's arms and hands.

Starting on Dad's right side, Joe prompted him to raise his arm, to bend his elbow, to squeeze his hand into a fist. Then Joe moved to his left side while I held down his right, and we repeated the process. The three of us were working together now, Joe, my father, and me. We were a team.

"Look at that," Joe said as Dad managed to squeeze his left hand. "That's a good strong grip you got there, Walter. Here, feel that," Joe told me. "Your old man's got a grip like a heavyweight."

"Is that right, Dad?" I asked. "Let me see. Give a good squeeze. That's it."

Sure enough, I could feel the pressure. This hand, once so formidable at building and fixing, so artful at drawing, so fearsome in anger, now clenched faintly, the thin skin loose and wrinkled over the web of blue veins. I asked Dad to repeat the motion again, then again, and was rewarded each time with a squeeze of his hand on mine. It was then I began to wonder if Joe wasn't right after all. Perhaps my being there really was having some effect. In just this short time, I had seen a definite improvement in his alertness and abilities.

I was impressed. Until now, having heard about my father's therapy sessions only indirectly via my mother, I had been unable to see any sense in putting Dad through such an empty ritual three times a week. What was the point? It was obvious that he was never going to recover and that the only road left for him was all downhill. Even if he improved a little, the same fate awaited him in the end. Between his strokes, diabetes, and Alzheimer's, it was pure fantasy to imagine that he would ever again lead a normal life. But now I saw that the exercises themselves really had nothing to do with ultimate ends. They had nothing to do with past or future, with history or dreams or ambitions. All that mattered was the simple fact that just now my father had managed, if only for a moment, to squeeze his seemingly lifeless left hand into a fist. A change had happened. A minuscule step had been taken. It wasn't a walk on the moon, but progress had been made.

Was it enough? Not nearly. In my mind, real progress would have meant nothing short of Dad lifting his head, straightening his back, getting to his feet, putting his arms around me, and saying, "Hello, Tom, good to see you," and then walking out the door with my mother and me and getting behind the wheel of the car and driving all of us off to a diner for a cup of coffee and a Danish.

That wasn't going to happen, of course. All we had of him now were the small gestures, the tiny triumphs. But I saw now how even those could seem as momentous as a sunrise.

Eventually Joe announced that Dad had done enough for one day. I was relieved. The intensity of the session had left me drained. Reaching for Joe's massive hand, I thanked him for his efforts. Then, taking the handles of Dad's high-backed chair, I wheeled him around and followed my mother out of the therapy room.

Dad's room was on the second floor, near the end of a long corridor. The oldsters we passed along the way were in various stages of mobility and decrepitude. Some shuffled along under their own power, leaning on walkers. Some sat in wheelchairs and stared blankly at nothing. Others glanced up at us with faint curiosity. We were, at least, something new to look at.

Passing a doorway, I heard a feeble voice. "Help me," it called. "Help me."

Looking in, I saw a tiny and very wrinkled old woman propped up in her bed, staring back at me with hollow eyes. "Help me. Come here and help me please," she begged.

I stood there with my hands glued to the handles of Dad's wheelchair, uncertain what to do. A nurse passed by and kept going. An aide, carrying an armload of towels, passed in the other direction, also without stopping.

"Help me," the old woman called again.

My mother, who hadn't slowed her pace, looked back to see what was keeping me.

"Shouldn't somebody do something for her?" I asked.

"Oh, she's always like that," my mother said. "Come on."

I was startled by her indifference. Apparently, though, this kind of thing went on here all the time.

Did it happen to Dad, too, when we weren't here?

Would it happen to me one day?

My father's room was a wintry cell whose only concession to cheerfulness was a set of orange draperies open to the snowy day outside. The floors were dull linoleum, and the furnishings were minimal: two beds separated by a folding screen, two dressers, a couple of chairs, a television set high on the wall facing the beds. There were no pictures on the walls, only a small bulletin board over Dad's dresser. A motley collection of Christmas cards was tacked to the desert-brown cork, which was festooned across the top with a single swag of metallic green-and-red tinsel. I was pleased to see my own card there ("To the best dad ever. Merry Christmas"). There were also photographs of the children and grandchildren he surely did not remember. To him, I imagined, we were like the characters in the soap opera that played on the television overhead: a revolving cast of strangers.

I helped Mom get pillows tucked against his sides so he would not slump sideways.

"How's that, dear?" she asked. "Comfortable now?"

My father murmured something that sounded like a yes.

"That's good. Now do I get a thank-you at least?" She was prodding him, trying to keep him engaged, to keep him from slipping away again. But I could see he was fading.

Another faint response, even murkier than before, escaped his lips.

My mother shrugged. It was all she was going to get. "You're welcome, dear," she said, and kissed him on the forehead.

"Good-bye, Dad," I said, as if we had been carrying on a perfectly normal conversation. "It was nice to see you. I'll be back again tomorrow."

He looked at me blankly, but I didn't even try to prod a response from him as my mother had done. Me prod him? Me dare to suggest what he should do? He never would have stood for it when he was healthy. Now, even though he was beyond protesting, I could imagine all too easily what he'd have said if I had tried such a thing:

"Just who do you think you're talking to, huh? You think because I'm stuck in this goddamned wheelchair and can't move and can't talk — you think you can stand there and say any damn thing you want, don't you?"

"That's not true."

"Think you're pretty smart, don't you? Think you're better than everybody else, just because you're still young and healthy. Well, you've got another guess coming, mister. You hear me?"

"Yes."

"Yes, what?"

"Yes, sir."

Even now as I stood looking down at the helpless, inarticulate creature who was my father and held his featherlight hand in mine, its blue veins as vivid as the highways on a road map — even now, after all these years of being on my own and making a life for myself separate from his petty tyrannies, I was astonished and depressed to realize what a hold he still had on me and how quickly I could be confounded by the old fear, the old helpless fury.

4

FRONTIER

*M*y father began visiting the building site every chance he got. On Saturdays he'd leave our house early in the morning and not get home until after dark. We didn't find out what he was doing there until one weekend a month or so after our first visit. He had loaded the trunk of the car with tools and advised Joyce and me to bring toys and books to keep ourselves occupied while Mom helped him do whatever it was he was going to do. Both of them were dressed in work clothes — my father in overalls, my mother in denim pants and an old shirt, her hair tied back in a scarf. Both wore heavy shoes and brought work gloves, but from their high spirits they could have been going off to play rather than to work.

As we breezed along the country road, past greening fields and rolling hills, the sunshine and the rhythmic thrumming of the tires as they rolled over the joints in the pavement seemed to inspire my mother and father to song, and soon Joyce and I were joining in on a lively version of "She'll Be Comin' Round the Mountain." This was followed by several choruses of "Jimmy crack corn and I don't care — my master's gone away."

Then a romantic mood seemed to overtake my parents, and they began singing what I thought of as mushy stuff: songs from the amateur operettas they had been in before they were married. The songs were from shows like *Katinka* by Rudolf Friml, *The Red Mill* by Victor Herbert, and *Maytime* by Sigmund Romberg. Since the days when my parents had performed those songs on the stage of Milwaukee's Pabst Theater, they had not forgotten a single word or melody. Now, as my father drove, he launched into a bravura rendition of "On the Road to Mandalay (Where the Flying Fishes Play)." Next we heard my mother's velvety alto blend with my father's resonant baritone in "Ah! Sweet Mystery of Life (At Last I've Found You)." And after that came their favorite, "Sweethearts":

> *Sweethearts make love their very own,*
> *Sweethearts can live on love alone.*

It was the title song from the operetta they had been in when they first met, and I always loved listening as they crooned it to each other. Their voices would become dreamy and they would start throwing moony looks back and forth, and when they were done singing, my mother would remind us once again that it was "our song," hers and Dad's.

At the time, I did not have a very clear idea of what an operetta was, but from the clippings in my mother's scrapbook I could tell that it must have been fun. Everyone dressed like characters out of storybooks. They got to be pirates and princesses, knights and fine ladies. The picture I liked best showed my parents at a cast party, wearing gypsy costumes. My mother wore a flowing skirt and fancy blouse with a big floppy collar and puffy sleeves edged with embroidery. Big hoop earrings dangled from each ear. Around her neck she had an array of beaded necklaces. Three bracelets adorned each of her wrists. My father, leaning close, was dressed in a flowing white shirt, baggy pantaloons, a sash around his waist, and a piratical bandanna around his head of slicked-back black hair. From his sidelong, seductive smile, it was clear that he was very pleased indeed with his Gypsy girl, his bright-eyed, Bohemian sweetheart.

"That was before I was born, right?" I always asked whenever I saw the picture.

"That's right," my mother invariably replied. But despite her assurances, I still could not imagine that there had been such a time. If I wasn't there yet, where was I?

Arriving at our driveway, my father turned in at the muddy track and drove out into the field. To me, it looked like the wild frontier. True, there were signs of civilization nearby. On one side of our property the wall of a neighbor's garage stood right next to our fence. On the other side sat the first in a string of drab bungalows, which were lined up along the road like sparrows on a telephone wire. But the site for our house was set so far back that the neighboring houses intruded hardly at all on my child's-eye view of the world. To me, our two and a half acres of weeds and spring wildflowers were an endless prairie, a sprawling, untamed wilderness.

Others might see houses nearby; when I noticed them at all, I saw distant frontier settlements, so far off they may as well have been in the next territory. Others might see holsteins grazing in the open field across the road; to my eyes they were a herd of buffalo.

At the building site not much had changed since our last visit. Weeds had begun to sprout on the mountains of dirt that surrounded the basement excavation. But the sprawling hole itself still sat empty. My box canyon, rough and rock strewn, was still open to the sky.

The big change had happened nearby. Not far from the excavation stood what looked to me like a pioneer cabin. Unfortunately, it was made not out of logs but of ordinary boards and two-by-fours. There was nothing picturesque about it. The outside walls were covered with black tar paper, and the roof was pitched to one side, making it look less like a house than like an overgrown rabbit hutch. In other ways, though, it wasn't much different from the boyhood home of Abraham Lincoln — the one pictured in my Little Golden Book. It had only one room, and the way it stood all by itself on one side of our property made it seem as isolated as the wilderness home of any trapper or cowboy.

"Temp. frame dwelling, 12' x 16'" is the way the cabin is described in my father's papers. In other words, it wasn't much bigger than an average-sized dining room. It had openings for a door and a small window on the side facing the driveway, and an opening for a large window on the side facing the hole in the ground where the new house would someday be built. The windows and the single door were salvaged from a junkyard. A stack of secondhand cinder blocks served as steps up to the door.

What the neighbors must have thought, seeing this shabby little black box standing in what had formerly been a pristine field, I can only imagine. Seen from the road, it might easily have been mistaken for a construction shack — one of those places where the foreman keeps his blueprints and where the workmen come in to get warm and have coffee from a thermos bottle. The cabin, however, was designed to house neither a family of giant rabbits nor a work crew. It was meant for the four of us. This was where my mother, my father, my sister, and I were going to live until the new house was finished.

Although the financial realities of house building were not explained to me at the time — nor would I have understood them if they had been — the fact was that my father could simply not afford to keep up payments on two properties at once. To build the new house he first had to sell the old one. In the meantime we needed a place to live. The "temp. frame dwelling" was my father's solution. By living on the property while the new house was being built, he could avoid paying two mortgages. Then too, since he himself intended to do much of the construction work, he'd be able to squeeze in a few hours on the job whenever he had a chance and still be home in time for supper.

As for me, I had no trouble at all imagining what it would be like to live in that single room in the middle of that big open field. Having gorged on the frontier stories I heard on the radio and read about in my storybooks, I thought pioneer life sounded fine. I knew just what it was supposed to be like: the father out working in his garden, his musket always within arm's reach in case of an Indian attack; the mother in her apron, making clothes out of deer hide or stirring a kettle of soup on the fire; the kids playing hide-and-seek along the edge of the woods, tempting a passing Iroquois warrior to grab them and carry them away. At night, assuming everyone got back alive, the family would gather around the hearth telling stories and singing songs, while the boy of the family, who was always the hero of the story, would sit carving pieces of wood with a pocket knife.

But first the cabin had to get finished.

Covering the tar-papered walls with clean new siding was the job that my father had in mind for today, and from where I stood, it looked easy enough. The boards piled nearby had ridges along one edge and grooves along the other. When you set the grooved edge of one board over the ridge of the board beneath it, the two locked together. Then all you had to do was nail them to the framework underneath. Easy.

30

"Can I help?" I called up to my father. He was perched on top of a ladder and was trying to set one of the long boards in place while my mother, on another ladder, held up the far end of the board. My father had a hammer in one hand and about six nails clamped between his teeth, and he was reaching far to one side, trying to wedge his end of the board into place. "Can I help? Can I?"

"Nmm-mm," he said.

"Can't you see we're busy?" my mother said.

"But if I help, you won't be so busy."

"Mmmm," my father growled around his mouthful of nails.

My mother, ever sensitive to his moods, rushed to intervene before he got angry. "Why don't you go and play," she said. "You shouldn't be around here anyway. Something could fall and you'll get hurt."

"'Nd take dog wif uh," my father managed to mumble as he eyed Beauty over his shoulder. She was sniffing around the bottom of his ladder.

Defeated, I turned and trudged away. "Come on," I said to Beauty, and to my satisfaction she followed along happily. At least *she* did what I wanted her to. Behind me I heard the rhythmic tattoo of my father's hammer driving home the nail: thock-thock-thock, thock thock.

I headed for the car, intending to climb inside and sit by myself and sulk. But when I got there, I discovered that my sister was already arranging her dolls on the backseat. Ignoring her, I went to the trunk, hauled out the box of toys I had brought, and started walking away.

"Where are you going?" Joyce called after me.

"None of your beeswax."

"Can I come too?"

"No."

"Why not?"

"Because I said so."

The box I carried contained my collection of cowboys and Indians: plastic figures about three inches high. Some of the Indians were aiming rifles, and others had bows and arrows, with the arrows in place and the strings drawn back ready to fire. Most of the cowboys carried six-guns; others held rifles or lariats. Some of them — the bowlegged ones — were meant to sit on the plastic horses that came with the set. My collection also included a stagecoach that was pulled by its own team, and a one-horse buckboard that could be made into a covered wagon by arching a piece of paper over the top. There was even a little cowboy dog — a German shepherd.

I lugged my toys over to the basement excavation, with its dusty desert floor, its hidden valleys and towering mountain ranges. While Beauty stretched out nearby, her chin resting on her paws and her eyes half closed, I set to work laying out a ranch for my men. The Circle Bar, I called it, and it was the biggest spread in the territory, its boundaries extending as far as a man could ride in three days. With the blocks I found at the bottom of my toy box, I built the outline of a bunkhouse for the men. A few sticks arranged in a circle made a perfect corral for the horses.

The main job of the boys of the Circle Bar was to drive cattle back and forth. Some of them also broke wild horses. It was a happy place, where the skies were not cloudy all day. But the ranch was in for trouble. The neighboring Sioux were on the warpath, and as soon as a few cowboys set out across the valley with their buckboard and covered wagon (they were on their way to town for supplies), they ran smack into an ambush.

The battle that ensued was terrible. A few cowboys died in the first assault and were immediately scalped and hacked to pieces by the Indians. The others took cover behind the wagons and tried to hold off the redmen until help arrived. But their efforts were doomed in the face of the overwhelming numbers and clever tactics of the Sioux. Eventually the cowboys were overrun. They were slaughtered to the last man. Only their horses were left alive. And their dog.

Yet the sweet taste of victory was brief. Somehow, the hacking and scalping was not very satisfying — not when all I was doing was pushing little plastic figures around in the dust. What I needed was more challenging quarry.

From my toy box I dug out the feathered headdress and the rubber tomahawk I had been given the previous Christmas. The handle of the tomahawk was a real tree branch, with real bark on it and real feathers tied to it with a piece of real rawhide. Donning my headdress and sticking the tomahawk in my belt, I began prowling over the dirt ridges in search of enemies.

I didn't have far to look. In the distance I heard a suspicious sound: thock-thock-thock, thock thock. With my wolf dog at my side, I crept to the top of a ridge to investigate. What I saw was a family of settlers hurrying to finish their cabin before the winter snows began to fly. The father, in his T-shirt, was nailing siding over the tar-papered outside walls, while the squaw woman was holding the other end of the board in place. But what was this? The settlers' pigtailed daughter had stepped away from the safety of the settlement. And now, even as I watched, she was approaching the wilderness. My wilderness. She seemed to be looking for something or someone, calling out in the strange tongue that was used by white people, "Beauty! Where are you? Come here, girl!"

It was a foolish thing for her to do. I grabbed my wolf dog's collar and held it tight. Fiercely clutching my tomahawk, I lay in wait for my unsuspecting quarry. Then, just as the girl appeared around the corner of the ridge, I jumped up and let out a terrifying war whoop. The girl shrieked. Waving my tomahawk, I went charging down on her. My vicious dog was close behind, bounding and barking ferociously.

My intention was to knock the girl down, grab her pigtails, and hack off her scalp. I wasn't quick enough, though. The settler's daughter was older than I was and had longer legs, and I never got close enough to get a swipe at her. Probably it was just as well. Deep down I knew that I couldn't have done the job properly. Certainly not with a rubber tomahawk. Besides, the girl was a well-known tattletale, famous throughout the territory, and I knew that if I'd succeeded in scalping her she would have run and told my mother. Then I would have been in real trouble.

It was early summer before the cabin was livable: the siding finished, the roof shingled, the windows set in place, the door hung on its hinges. Inside the empty room our voices sounded hollow. The sun, streaming in through the picture window, made a bright patch of light on the floorboards, and Beauty promptly stretched out in it as if she were claiming the spot for herself.

"Look at that," said my father. "She's made herself right at home. Haven't you, girl?" He bent to scratch her behind the ear.

My mother frowned. "She better not get too comfortable. There's hardly going to be enough room for the four us without her living in here too."

"Aw, we'll be fine," my father said, straightening. "Anyway, it won't be for all that long. Just until the house is finished. Then we'll have all the space we'll need."

"And I'll have my own room!" Joyce said with glee.

My father reached out and put his arm around her. "You sure will," he said. He hugged her to him, and as he did she looked at me with a smirk.

I didn't know which was more annoying, that hug or that smirk. I did know I was surprised to see her so delighted at the prospect of having her own room. Anxious as I was to get away from her, it had never occurred to me that she might also want to get away from me.

"Can I have the top? I want the top."

"No. I get it," my sister said.

"You always get everything," I said.

"That's because I'm older."

"That's no fair."

"And anyway, I'm the girl."

"Itsnofair, itsnofair, itsnofair."

"Hey!" The shout was like a gunshot in the woods. It came from my father. Just one word, but it shut us up fast. My father could be frightening when he got angry. Usually he would just glower, which was scary enough. But when he raised his voice, he boomed like thunder.

His shout put an end to our squabbling. But he also gave us a way out. He would toss a coin, he said, to see which of us got to sleep in the top bunk first. After that, Joyce and I would alternate, one of us on top for a week, then the other.

The bunk stood in one corner of the cabin. My father had found it in an army-surplus store. It was a drab gray green, and you got to the top by climbing up the slats of the footboard.

Joyce won the coin toss. But after spending only a couple of nights on the top bunk, she decided she liked the bottom better. I suspected it had to do with something I said a few days after we moved in. I told her how easy it would be for things from outside to find their way into the cabin in the dark.

"You know, snakes and spiders and stuff," I said.

"Don't be dumb. Nothing like that can get in here."

"Betcha."

"How would they do it?"

"All they need is a little hole somewhere. You know, like up there in the corner, over the top bunk, where the roof and the wall come together."

"That's dumb. There aren't any holes up there."

She refused to believe me, or at least pretended to. But she suddenly stopped wanting the top bunk. I hid my satisfaction: sometimes things worked out just fine. Having the top bunk was almost like having a room to myself. Besides, from up there I could spy on everything going on below.

My father had bought the bunk especially for the cabin. Joyce's and my real beds, like most of the other household furnishings, were now in storage in the attics and garages of various relatives. But even with our possessions whittled down to the bare necessities, our "temp. frame dwelling" was still cramped. On the left when you came in the door was a small refrigerator, a sink, a stove, and a metal storage cupboard for dishes, pots, and pans. The kitchen table and chairs took up most of the room in the middle of the floor. The bunk bed and my parents' double bed stood along the back wall, and the rest of the wall space around the cabin was taken up by two chests of drawers and a wobbly metal clothes rack. Tucked in near the door was a small space heater, for when winter came.

What my father referred to as "the facilities" were outside, down a muddy path on the far side of the driveway: a single-seat outhouse with a half moon cut in the door. We called it Mom's House because it was mostly her handiwork. My father had dug the hole and built the frame. But my mother had done all the rest. It was she who cut the siding, nailed it on, and tacked down the shingles. I never knew anyone else's mother who was as good with a hammer and saw. Thanks to her, we could now say we had a two-room house — even if we did have to go outside and across the driveway to get to the second room.

The cabin had electricity, but for a time there was no running water. Before a well was dug and pipes were hooked up, water for drinking, cooking, and washing came from jugs that my father filled at work. But even after the water was hooked up, the only place we had to take baths was a washtub, with water heated on the stove and blankets hung around the tub for privacy. For a real bath we had to wait for the weekend, when we packed towels, washcloths, and dirty laundry and drove over to my mother's parents' house, where there was a real bathroom with a door you could lock, a toilet you could flush, and a bathtub that you could fill with hot water right from the faucet.

"How can you live like this?" I heard my aunt Helen ask when she came to visit us in the cabin. My mother smiled a tight smile, then lifted her chin a notch or two. "We manage," she said.

How proud she made me feel! *We* manage, she had said, which meant all four of us. *We* were brave. *We* were tough. *We* would be all right.

But one night I suddenly was not so sure. As I lay asleep in the top bunk, I was awakened by strange sounds. At first I couldn't tell what it was. I opened my eyes. The room was pitch black except for a pale square of light that showed where the quarter moon was shining through the large window. I lay perfectly still and listened. One of the sounds was a kind of mewing, like a kitten crying for milk. The other was a low gravelly rumble. And then I realized what it was. Somewhere out there in the darkened room, down beyond the foot of my bunk where my parents' bed was, my mother was crying softly and my father was saying comforting things. I heard him say "sweetheart" in different ways and "don't cry" and "it won't be for so long," and I knew from the way he spoke that what was making her so unhappy had to do with him and with what my aunt had said.

I squeezed my eyes shut and pulled my blanket over my head to shut out the sounds, but they still came through. I coughed and turned over. Instantly my parents were silent, waiting, listening to see if I was up or just turning in my sleep.

I think I must have gone back to sleep then. But I did not forget what I had heard, or how angry I was at my father for making my mother so unhappy.

5

REUNION

*D*inner that evening was at Joyce's house, across town from the nursing home.

As I pulled up to the curb I was struck by how little anything seemed to change here over the years. When my sister and her husband first moved to this development tract twenty-five years ago, the trees that lined the bone-white concrete streets were no more than saplings set hopefully against the bleak monotony of rows of brand-new suburban ranches. Since then, the saplings had flourished, spreading their branches wide over sidewalks. In that time, too, Joyce's kids had grown to adulthood. But from the fresh, well-scrubbed look of the place it was hard to see that anything much had ever happened to disturb the neighborhood's somnolent tranquillity. No gutters drooped, no paint flaked, no shingles were out of place. It was frighteningly tidy. It gave me the creeps. I couldn't imagine how my sister had endured staying in such a place for so long.

During the years that Joyce and the trees had taken root, I had been on the move almost constantly. London, Paris, New York, London again, back to New York — my pursuit of a career and of a life in the wider world had landed me in so many rented rooms, flats, bed-sitters, studios, pied-à-terres, house-sits, and sublets that a clever broker could have housed a whole neighborhood in them and still have had rooms left over for company. It was true that my wife and I had now been settled in the same house for a dozen years: a creaky old Victorian in a pleasantly shabby little river town just north of New York City. I had been around long enough to know the neighbors. Nino at the pizza parlor recognized my voice on the phone. Lenny at the hardware store wrote up my charges without having to look up my name in his files. I sat on local boards and chaired committees. And whenever I walked down the street with my son, I was always surprised by the number of kids who called out to him. Still, I couldn't help feeling it was all temporary, a place where my wife and I were merely passing through until the time came — as I was sure it would — when we'd be moving on.

The odd thing was that although Joyce and I had shared the same dislocated, disjointed upbringing, we had reacted to it in such different ways, she cleaving to roots and stability — almost desperately, it seemed to me — while I, perhaps with equal desperation, had been repeating the footloose pattern of our childhood. Why this should be so I could not fathom. Maybe it was one of those "mysteries of the faith" that the nuns always cited when we asked questions they couldn't answer.

Joyce greeted me at her front door with tears in her eyes.

"Oh, it's so good to see you!" she said, opening her arms for my hug.

It was always this way. Months, even years, could go by without us having any direct contact. Phone calls at Christmas, quick notes on the backs of birthday cards — usually that was the extent of our contact. Yet our reunions invariably brought forth a gush of emotion, as though I were some long-lost prodigal, sorely missed and now safely returned to the bosom of the family.

Still, I wasn't about to complain. Being fussed over was one of the advantages of visiting infrequently and never staying long enough to be taken for granted. And now, as Joyce's husband Dick pulled away from the television and came to shake hands, and as my brother Michael and his wife, Dee, came out of the kitchen to welcome me, I felt a rush of family warmth that was all the sweeter for being so rare.

Michael was the baby of the family: younger than I by eight years, younger than Joyce by nine. Coming onto the scene as late as he did, he had missed the early part of our family odyssey. As children, Joyce and I had done things and been places that he knew nothing about. As a result, he had always been something of an outsider whenever the talk turned back to those early years. On the other hand, after Joyce left home to get married and I went to college, Michael had suddenly had Mom and Dad to himself. He had become an only child.

My parents' last and youngest, he was pampered and, I sometimes thought, over-indulged. Maybe I was just jealous, but it always seemed that he enjoyed a special place in my parents' lives. That he could sit hip to hip with my father on the sofa, as I had once seen him do, with an arm thrown casually around Dad's broad shoulders, suggested a depth of affection and intimacy that I simply could not imagine between my father and me. At best, Dad and I had always been guarded with each other. At worst we had verged on open warfare.

Once the welcoming hugs and handshakes were over, Dick offered beers all around. "Here, have some of the good stuff," he said, handing me a bottle. "Made in Milwaukee," he added, in case I'd missed the point. "Not one of those foreign imports."

To Dick, "foreign" meant anything east of Lake Michigan. Dick was an unabashed Wisconsin chauvinist. Aside from his four years at the state university and a stint in the army, he had spent his whole life in the same small town. He loathed big cities, shunned any food more exotic than Chinese, and never missed a chance to get in a dig at effete easterners, of which he seemed to consider me a prime example. Once he went so far as to greet me at the door wearing a T-shirt that trumpeted his exact sentiments: I Hate New York.

"Gee, Dick," I had said, "you sure know how to make a guy feel welcome."

But tonight there was no edge on Dick's hospitality. As we stood sipping the local brew and catching up on each other's news, I felt embraced by genuine warmth and conviviality.

We weren't left standing for long. Supper was almost ready, and Joyce was soon calling us in to eat. The combination dining-and-family room was a cheerful, autumn-colored space furnished in modern Early American. The maple dining set featured reproduction ladder-back chairs; the windows were dressed in half-shutters and ruffled valances. The magazine holder on the hearth, a decorative copper coal scuttle, had obviously never been insulted by a chunk of coal. The overall effect was one of New England on the prairie: make-believe tradition. Was this another way Joyce had found to anchor herself? Or was I reading too much into her taste in decoration?

Taking our places at the table, we sat down to a meal of steaming lasagna, garden salad, and the inevitable Jell-O mold. The Jell-O was a tremulous two-tone concoction in orange and green, within which bits of fruit cocktail were suspended like fossils in amber. The whole thing was topped with a spiraled heap of Reddi Wip. I loved it. Although my Connecticut-born wife referred to Jell-O with affectionate disdain as "midwestern caviar," I had never lost my taste for the stuff. I still considered a well-made Jell-O mold to be among the glories of the domestic arts, a cherished reminder of Sunday afternoon dinners at Gramma Raniszewski's house, when my mother's sisters would try to outdo one another with their gelatin extravaganzas.

I was sitting there savoring the golden aura of hearth and home, when Mike and Dee joined hands and bowed their heads. A hush fell over the table. I stiffened. Uh-oh, I thought. Here it comes.

Years ago, my brother had adopted his wife's evangelical Lutheranism. He seemed to have found strength and comfort in his new faith, and I certainly did not begrudge him any of that. Having long since left Catholicism behind, and having eventually embraced Judaism, I had no reason to fault my brother for the new direction his life had taken. What set my teeth on edge was that he wore his religion like the neon-bright blazer of a carnival barker. A natural-born salesman and a gifted mimic, Mike had made a career as a voice for hire. Radio listeners all over the southeastern part of the state knew his voice from countless commercials for grocery chains, men's underwear, automobiles, and banks. He was good at what he did. But my hackles rose whenever he felt called upon to sell the elixir of righteousness to all and sundry, including his own poor benighted family, whose souls he presumed to be teetering on the brink of damnation.

Now, as Mike and Dee bowed their heads, I was afraid we might be in for a burst of religious flamethrowing. But Joyce was quick. Before Michael could get started, she jumped in with her own more or less ecumenical version of grace. With that, the uneasy moment passed, and the steaming dishes were soon making the rounds of the table.

"Everything is just great," I said. "Love the lasagna."

Joyce was beaming. "It's just so nice to have you all here," she said, her eyes filling again. "It's too bad Dad can't be here, too. And Ellen, of course," she added, including my wife in the afterthought.

Such intimate gatherings were indeed rare between us. What few family get-togethers I had attended over the years had usually been crowd scenes, with lots of kids around and no chance for anything but small talk. By now, though, all of Joyce's kids were either away at school or busy with jobs. And since my own family had been unable to accompany me on this trip, it was just the few of us at the table tonight: Joyce and Dick, Mike and Dee, me and Mom.

We were a family once again, and enjoying it. But as we sat side by side, passing dishes back and forth, bantering and teasing, I realized that the conversation was just a little too light-hearted, a little too strained. Time and distance had come between us, and we hardly knew how to speak to each other anymore. Perhaps we never did. Perhaps our once-upon-a-time closeness was only a nostalgic illusion. For too many years we had been not one family but four, each of us caught up in lives so different from one another's that it was hard to believe we were even acquainted, much less related. For years now, Mom's life had been bound by the demands of caring for an invalid. Her days had been measured out by meal times, bathroom times, medication schedules, and, most recently, by trips back and forth to the nursing home. Joyce and Dick's world had centered on their home, their kids, their neighborhood, their careers — his as personnel director of a small electronics firm, hers as a math and computer teacher in a local high school. Mike and Dee were wrapped up with their media consulting business and their church. They lived hardly more than an hour's drive from Joyce's house, but their lives, too, revolved in a different orbit.

And I? I lived farther away than anyone else. Restless, nosy, wanting to be where big things were happening, I had hurried away as soon as I finished college, determined to make a life of my own, beyond my father's critical gaze. By now I had been living out east for more years than I had lived in the heartland. My family connections had been reduced to those Sunday-evening talks on the phone with my mother, a visit once a year, and exchanges of holiday gifts and birthday cards. And that was all — that, plus a headful of memories and an odd obsession

41

with that time, almost forty years ago, when we were still a family and Dad was building us a house.

The odd thing was how vivid those memories seemed, even after all that time, and how insistent they had recently become, popping up not just in my dreams, but anytime, anywhere. I might be taking a shower or driving to work or sitting in a meeting. Someone would say something, or I'd catch a whiff of new-mown grass on a damp breeze, or I'd notice the way the sun slanted across a rug. Then suddenly it would be there: a flash of memory that seemed more startlingly real than whatever objective reality I happened just then to be inhabiting.

Sometimes it was embarrassing. I'd be having lunch with colleagues, or dinner with friends, or standing around in a crowded room with a cocktail glass in my hand. Everyone else would be sticking to nice, safe, impersonal subjects like politics or the price of real estate. And there I'd be, spewing out stories about when I was a kid and my father was building us a house. Afterward I'd wince, realizing how bizarre I must have sounded. Obsessed even. But like a drunk at a bar or a diabetic in a pastry shop, I couldn't help myself.

And now, here it was, happening again, as we sat around the supper table in Joyce's family room. What took me by surprise, though, was that this time I wasn't the one who was bringing up the subject. It was Joyce.

She and Dee had got up to clear the dishes and bring out coffee and a chocolate layer cake. As she refilled our cups and sliced a second helping of cake, she began talking about how she had recently gone out of her way to drive past the house on Rawson.

"You know, just to have a look at the place," she said. "It's funny. Sometimes I just get this urge to see it. I don't know why. It's almost like there's a magnet that pulls me back there."

"You're kidding," I said, startled by this revelation.

She gave an embarrassed laugh. "I know. It's silly."

"No, no, that's not what I meant. It's just that I do the same thing."

"Really?" Now it was her turn to look startled.

"Absolutely. Whenever I come out here, I always want to drive past the place. I even have dreams about it."

She laughed, delighted. "That's amazing." She turned to her husband. "See," she said. "I'm not crazy."

42

"Oh, yeah?" Dick said, grinning. He was a relentless tease and never missed an opening. "Maybe it just means you're *both* crazy."

Before I could protest, Michael spoke up. "In that case you better make it three of us. Because the same thing happens to me."

We all looked at him in astonishment.

"He's right," Dee said. "He brought me to see the house even before we were married. He pointed it out to me and said, 'My dad built that.' He was just so proud."

All this time I had been thinking that I was the only one who was so weirdly obsessed with the place, who kept being drawn back to it as if to some sort of holy shrine. Now I discovered that I had company. Despite our differences, despite the varied directions our lives had taken, my brother and sister and I had found common ground. Dick may have been right. When it came to that house, maybe we were all a little nuts.

Comparing notes, we soon realized that lately each of us seemed to be thinking about the place more than usual.

"That's funny. Why is that?" asked Joyce.

"Maybe it has something to do with Dad getting sick," Michael suggested.

I nodded. "And also realizing that we're all getting older."

"Speak for yourself," Joyce said.

I laughed. "No, I mean it. You start looking at your own life and wondering what you've accomplished and you think, hey, when Dad was my age, look at what he'd done. He'd built a house. He had something tangible he could point to and say, 'I made that.'" I shook my head. "I don't know what it's like for the rest of you, but about all I have to show at the end of a year's work is a few more pieces of paper to stick in a file drawer."

Mike nodded. "And nowadays, with computers, you probably don't even have that."

"That's right. Just a few more megabytes worth of electronic impulses. Just . . . air. See what I mean? It wasn't like that for Dad. The house he built is still there. It's as real and solid as the day we moved into it. And it's still got people living in it."

"And we've got a lot of memories," Joyce said, gazing into her coffee cup.

We talked about those memories then, and I discovered that Joyce's were as vivid and immediate as mine. She had not forgotten the picnic in

43

the basement excavation, or the cowboy and Indian games we played on our miniature Rocky Mountains, or taking baths in the washtub in the cabin, or making flashlight trips at night to the outhouse.

"Mom's House, we called it," I said, grinning. "Remember, Mom? You built it yourself."

"Really?" said Michael. "I didn't know that."

"Well, Dad built the frame," Mom conceded, modest as ever. "But I did everything else. I built the platform for the seat and nailed on all the siding. The shingles, too. *And* I painted it!"

Clearly she was still proud of her handiwork.

"Remember the snow piling up outside the cabin that winter?" Joyce said. "It was over the top of the steps."

"And how about the night it got so cold that the milk froze in the gallon jug that we'd left outside?" I said. "The glass shattered and left the milk standing there in the shape of a jug."

"Why was the milk outside?" Mike asked.

Mom grimaced at the memory. "Because our refrigerator was so small there was no room inside."

Michael hung on our words. Born too late, he knew the cabin and the house building only from the photographs in the family album. But over the years he must have heard us talk about them so often he had formed an attachment to the place that was as strong as Joyce's and mine. In some essential, lifeblood way, the story of those years had become as much a part of him as if he had been there himself.

In the back of my mind the question echoed once more: Why? What was it about that place that it could still exercise such a powerful pull on all of us, luring us back again and again like some inexorable tidal force? But there was no time for the question to find form. I was too caught up in the moment, talking, reminiscing.

Neither did I notice that Mom was not joining in. For the most part she sat quietly, saying little. But that changed when we began talking about what happened after we left Rawson Avenue. Our tone grew sardonic as we remembered all the moving we did in the following years. We joked about what experts we all became at packing and unpacking, and about how some boxes never even got unpacked before we had to move again. Michael, too, remembered that part, and laughed.

He turned to Mom. "How many houses did we live in anyway?

Sometimes I try to count them up for Dee, but I'm never sure I've got them all, especially the early ones. How many were there? Fifteen? Twenty?"

"Oh, who cares how many there were?" she snapped.

The rest of us exchanged startled glances.

"Sorry," Michael said. "I just wondered . . ."

"It's all over and done with," she continued. "Why keep raking it all up?"

Usually undemonstrative and mild-mannered, she seemed suddenly overcome with bitterness. A nerve had been touched. But what nerve? Why was she so upset?

There was no way to find out. Not then. Embarrassed, not wanting to upset her further or to intrude on her pain, we conspired by some unspoken mutual consent to turn our eyes and thoughts away, as you would from an accident victim's open wound.

"Anybody want more coffee?" Joyce asked, getting to her feet.

Dee pushed back her chair. "I'll clear the cake plates."

"So how's the job these days?" Dick asked me.

It was amazing how quick we were to dodge the slightest display of emotion. Funny stories, easy sentimentality, nostalgia — those were things we could deal with.

Soon afterward Mom and I got ready to leave. I hugged my sister and brother and sister-in-law, and shook Dick's hand and said, "Thanks, it was great." A few minutes later my mother and I were on our way to her house. As we drove, the streetlights made puddles of brightness in the dark streets. My mother sat in morose silence, staring straight ahead.

"What is it, Mom? What's wrong?"

She shook her head. "Oh, nothing. I just — I guess I shouldn't have said anything. You were all having such a good time until I got everyone upset."

"You said what was on your mind, that's all. I was surprised, though. What happened anyway? What was so upsetting?"

Slowly then, as though with a great effort, she told me how unhappy it had made her — all the moving and the repeated disruptions, the packing and unpacking, never knowing when Dad would want to pull up stakes again and move on. What hurt the most, though, was having to leave the house on Rawson.

45

"I loved that place," she said. "We were so happy there. And then for him to just walk away the way he did, after all the work we put into it. . . . Oh, I was so angry at him. And now to hear you all talking about it again, like it was some kind of joke —"

I said nothing for a moment, just drove, thinking how empty these quiet suburban streets were at nine thirty in the evening. Houses all around, but no one out, everyone closed in behind tidy front lawns and blank front doors. "Is that why you never want to go back and see the place?"

She nodded. She had a handkerchief out and was wiping her eyes. "It hurts too much." She straightened herself and took a deep breath. "I'm sorry," she repeated, embarrassed by her tears. "I get carried away."

We drove the rest of the way in silence. When we arrived at her house, I went to her pantry, took down the bottle of Scotch she kept there for me — it had been untouched since my last visit — and poured myself a drink.

"Would you like anything?" I called after her as she disappeared down the hall.

"Oh, sure," she called back. "A glass of wine would be nice. I'll be right there."

As I settled myself at the kitchen table, I heard her stop in the bathroom, then come out again. But she didn't return to the kitchen right away. I could hear her rummaging around somewhere in one of the bedrooms. I thought she was probably changing her clothes, but when she came into the kitchen she was still dressed as she had been before. In her hand, though, was a manila envelope.

"You might be interested in this," she said, setting it on the table in front of me. I recognized Dad's scrawl along one side: "Rawson Ave Plans."

I glanced at her. Was this what I thought it was? With eager fingers, I undid the rusty clasp, opened the brittle envelope, and tipped it on end. A cascade of paper fell out onto the table. Pink and yellow receipts. Materials lists. Bills from lumberyards, plumbers, carpenters, electricians. Sketches, drafts, and blueprints. Here was the step-by-step documentation of the house that had been my father's obsession all those years ago. I felt I was being given a glimpse of my father I had never seen before. And it was coming to me in his own hand.

A healthy hand had made these drawings and kept these notes — a steady hand, full of vigor and confidence. His materials lists and specifications were done in a rounded, flowing script, with a certain theatrical flair. The words were written quickly, in sketchy phrases and half sentences, as though his thoughts were racing ahead of his pencil. His sketches were tangled masses of lines and erasures, while his finished drawings displayed all the precision of the professional draftsman, with neatly drawn arrows and carefully printed notes and dimensions.

Sitting there at my mother's kitchen table, with my father's notes and invoices and diagrams spread out before me, I felt all the exhilaration that an archaeologist must feel when uncovering the evidence of a long-lost civilization. What was taking shape before my eyes, however, was no obscure culture from ages past. It was something much more immediate and personal. Amid that clutter of papers was the record of my father's dream being born: the dream of the house that was to become so much a part of all of our lives that, although decades had passed since our leaving of it, in our dreams we lived there still.

6

HOME GROUND

*T*hat fall my father seemed to spend every spare moment thinking about the new house. In the evenings, as soon as supper was over and my mother had cleared the table, he would set up his drafting board and spread out his graph paper and his sketch pads on the red-and-white checked oil cloth. With a fresh cup of coffee at his elbow and his slide rule and pencils in hand, he would spend the rest of the evening drawing and redrawing his plans.

The house was on his mind even when we were away from home. During our Thanksgiving visit to my grandparents' house, while all the women were in the kitchen cleaning up the dishes and all of the men were dozing in easy chairs in the living room, I found my father down on his hands and knees in the bathroom. He had a steel tape measure in one hand — the kind that snapped back into its case when you pressed a button — and he was checking the dimensions of the toilet and the bathtub.

"Just in time," he said when he saw me. "Here, you can give me a hand."

I pressed my knees together. "But I gotta go."

"You can hold it. This will just take a minute. Here, take the end of the tape and hold it right there."

He indicated a spot in the corner behind the toilet. I got down on my knees and concentrated hard on holding the end of the tape measure, telling myself not to think about the pressure building in my bladder. But the more I tried not to think about it, the more I felt the pressure. I squeezed my muscles hard, until I was sure I couldn't hold it any longer.

"Dad —"

"Hang on. Almost done." He jotted a note on his pad.

"But Dad —"

"Oh, stop your whining."

I squeezed harder, tightening every muscle from my toes up to my eyelids. My teeth were clenched so hard they hurt. Behind the lids of my clamped-shut eyes bright white and red lights exploded like flashbulbs.

"Okay, that's it," my father finally said, getting to his feet. "You can let go now."

Did I dare? I was afraid that if I let go of the tape, I'd let go of everything else, too.

"Didn't you hear me?" my father asked. "I said you can let go now."

Against every instinct I lifted my hand. The tape whipped away on its spring. I doubt it had wound all the way back into its case before I had the toilet seat up and my pants down around my knees and felt the glorious release of the waters pouring forth.

Just when my father would finish his measuring and begin the actual building, I had no idea. Months had passed since the day in spring when we had our picnic, but the house itself existed only on paper and in my father's imagination. The hole in the ground and the weed-covered hills that surrounded it were beginning to seem as if they had been there forever, like the line of trees on the horizon and the cornfield across the road. Then, one afternoon in early December, Joyce and I stepped off the school bus at the end of our driveway to find two enormous trucks parked near the edge of the excavation. My father's car was there, too, which was another surprise. What was he doing home in the middle of a weekday afternoon?

"Come on," I told Joyce. "Let's go see." And I ran ahead, my lunch box banging against my hip.

I was almost to the cabin steps when my father came out. He had on his work boots, an old paint-spattered jacket, and a cap. He had an eager look in his eye, as if he couldn't wait to tackle whatever the project was.

"What're the trucks here for?" I wanted to know.

49

"Trucks? What trucks? I don't see any trucks." He looked every-where except where the trucks were.

"Over there. Those trucks."

He turned to where I was pointing and gave a look of exaggerated surprise. "Well, what do you know! There's a couple of trucks all right."

"But what're they for?"

"That's a good question. I guess we should go and find out."

Joyce and I dropped our books and lunch boxes on the steps of the cabin, then followed him to the excavation.

Looking down into the hole, we saw a group of men who were busy with hammers and saws. Despite the chilly weather, the men were in their shirtsleeves. Just what they were doing down there did not make any sense to me. Along the outside edge of the excavation floor, at the base of the dirt walls, someone had gouged a shallow trench. Inside the trench the men had built a kind of frame, using two parallel rows of thick boards that they had stood on edge and braced together. The two rows of boards were staked out carefully so that they were absolutely parallel and a precise distance apart. Another double line of boards was set into a trench that ran right across the floor, dividing the area into two sections.

"What're they making?" I asked my father.

"Those are going to be the footings for the basement walls."

"What're footings?"

"Well, they're like the foot at the bottom of your leg. They're the feet that the house will stand on."

I was still puzzled, but my father promised that we'd soon see how it was all going to work.

The next day, when Joyce and I got off the school bus and walked up our driveway, we were greeted by Beauty barking hello from the end of her chain. There was a new sound, too: the deep-throated growling of some machine. The sound was coming from the excavation. And over in the same direction we could see puffs of smoke rising mysteriously from behind my Rocky Mountains.

"What's that?" Joyce asked.

"Indians," I said.

"That's dumb," she said. For her, everything was either real or it wasn't. And if you didn't see things the way she did, she told you that you were dumb.

We set our books on the cabin steps, shouted hello to my mother, who was inside doing housework, and ran over to the rim of the excavation. The noise and smoke, we discovered, were coming from a cement truck. The enormous cylinder on its back was turning slowly, and as it turned, a river of heavy gray cement oozed down a metal chute that hung off the back of the truck. At the bottom of the chute, a workman was directing the gray mess into the wooden frames that had been built the day before. Two other men were busy with shovels and rakes and boards, smoothing out the cement as it slid and settled into place.

As the men worked, their gruff voices rose to where we stood, and I noticed something I had also noticed about the men who'd been there the day before: they all worked hard and said little. When they did speak, their words were brief and to the point: "Joe, hand me that board, will you?" or "Over here, Bill. I need more over this way." Not a word or motion was wasted. There was a sureness about them, a quiet confidence. They knew how to do things. They made things happen. Big things, important things. Where before there had been nothing but a hole in the ground, now there was a shape: a strip of still-wet concrete that ran all around the edge of the excavation floor, between the standing boards. When the concrete hardened, a whole house was going to rest on it. And these men were part of that. I was filled with awe and envy, and I wondered what it must be like to be as big and as confident as they were, and to do such important things.

Before the men left, they covered the wet cement with hay taken from bales they had brought with them.

"That's to keep the cement from drying too fast," my father explained later when I asked him about it. "If it dries too fast, it'll crack."

For days afterward, the air around the excavation was sweetened with the musty smell of hay and wet cement. Even today, all these years later, all I have to do is pass a construction site and catch a whiff of that distinctive sweet smell to be carried back to that time, that place.

A week or so later, the men came back. With them came two truck-loads of concrete blocks. While the blocks were being unloaded and stacked in the middle of the basement floor, the workmen removed the straw they had laid down and knocked away the wooden frames that enclosed the now hardened concrete footings. They then began laying the concrete blocks along the top of the footings. When they had laid one row down, they set another on top of it, then another. Each new block was cemented to the blocks below and beside it. To make sure each row of blocks was straight, the men measured it with a level and a length of string that was pulled taut along the line of the wall-to-be. Step by step, over several days, the men raised walls where none had been before. Building with my toy blocks was nothing compared to this.

When the basement walls were finished, other men came and smeared the outside with a thick coating of tar. "Waterproofing," my father explained. "So when it rains the water doesn't seep in through the walls."

One day, I came home from school to find that the job had been finished. A bulldozer had come and leveled most of my Rocky Mountains. The piles of dirt had been pushed in around the exterior of the basement walls. All that was left of my great western landscape was one lonely peak.

School. By now I had been going to Saint Stephen's for over a month, but I still had nightmares about the first day. I'd been terrified.

"I don't feel so good," I told my mother that morning. "I think I should stay home."

I wasn't just making excuses, either. I was sure I had a fever, and my stomach felt as if it had been used for a knot-tying contest. My mother fiddled nervously with the top button of my new plaid shirt. Using her fingers as a comb, she made one last attempt to impose some order on my unruly curls. "You'll be fine," she said. "You're a big boy now."

Caught up as I was in my own misery, it didn't occur to me that she might feel as bad about my going as I did. Ever since we moved into the cabin in June, my mother had had my sister and me to look after while Dad was away at work. Now she was about to be left by herself, in a flimsy shack set out in the middle of nowhere, with only a dog for company.

"Come on," my father called from the car, where he and Joyce were waiting. "Let's get a move on. We haven't got all day."

Resigned to the inevitable, I pulled myself away. I was a big boy now. My mother had told me so, and I was determined not to disappoint her. I got into the car. As my father backed down the driveway, I had a last look at her standing on the cabin doorstep in her apron. Watching us go, she looked small and forlorn as she raised a hand and sent my sister and me off into the world, bravely doing her mother's job: saying good-bye.

My parents had been taking us to Saint Stephen's for Sunday Mass ever since we moved into the area. Probably because it was the first church to make an impression on me, it sticks in my mind as being everything a church should be. Built of cream-colored brick, it had a high-pitched roof, tall windows that rose to graceful Gothic arches, and a lofty spire that seemed to point the way to heaven.

From the first time I followed my parents up the front steps and through the enormous front doors, I was enchanted with the place. Inside, everything was beautiful. Shafts of light streamed in through the tall stained-glass windows, which glowed in every color of the rainbow. To me, those windows looked like gigantic versions of the illustrations in my storybooks. The people I saw depicted there wore fine, flowing robes. Some of the men wore armor, some of the women carried babies or flowers, and they all looked beautiful and stately and good. My mother had explained to me that the golden circles over their heads showed that the people were saints, which meant they had never done anything bad. Being a saint, I decided, must be a wonderful thing if it meant you got your picture up in a beautiful window, where everyone could admire you and see what a good person you were.

But the holy people in the colored glass were not the only ones to be found in Saint Stephen's. On the walls below them were wooden reliefs of the stations of the cross — seven on each of the two side walls. Intricately carved, they told the story of Jesus' last agony as he was tortured and beaten by the Romans, forced to drag his heavy cross through the streets of Jerusalem, then nailed to it while his mother looked on. I was fascinated by the drama of the story and the horribly realistic details of cruelty and death. My favorite seat in church was the one nearest Station Eleven, which showed a nasty-looking Roman driving nails into our Lord's hands. I winced to look at it; yet somehow I could not pull my eyes away. Blood dripped from the crown of thorns on Jesus' head and from the wounds made by the spikes. It looked so real that I wouldn't have been surprised to see puddles of blood on the floor below the carving.

In the front of the church was a carved wooden altar rail, beyond which stood the altar itself, a magnificent piece of work with a wooden base depicting scenes and figures from the Bible. But it was the screen behind the altar that most often drew my attention. A soaring wall of sculpted wood, it was a veritable forest of Gothic spires, niches, and crannies, into which were set scores of statues of saints and angels. As with the altar and the stations of the cross, all the figures were exquisitely wrought, and the niches and their statues rose tier upon tier, higher and higher, in an Everest of saintliness that soared right to the vaulted ceiling, where golden stars gleamed in a deep blue sky.

With so much to look at, I was never bored during Mass. There was always something new to discover: a figure I hadn't seen before, a carved bird or flower tucked away in a corner. Then, too, the service itself could be interesting. The priest, who wore silken robes that swirled and shimmered like moonlight on water, seemed to exude mysterious powers as he intoned magical words in a strange language. Sometimes he would raise a golden cup, and one of the two boys assisting him would ring a set of golden chimes while the other swung a silver basket from which billowed puffs of sweet-smelling smoke. The boys wore long white shirts with elaborate fringes on the bottom and sleeves. To my child's eyes it was wonderfully dramatic and theatrical, and I only wished that I was going to Mass this morning instead of to school.

No such luck. Today we headed around the church to a big, ugly brick building sitting behind it. Although I had never seen a prison, I had no trouble imagining that this was what one looked like. I was sure all kinds of horrible things happened inside — tortures and beatings. Other parents and children were converging on the building, too, and before I knew it, my father, my sister, and I were being drawn into the swirling crowd. The worst part was, I didn't see one face I recognized. My sister and I were strangers here, and I was convinced that we were the only ones who were.

"Come on," my father said, "this way." Holding our hands tighter, he guided Joyce and me through the surging crowd and up the front steps.

Once through the door, we found ourselves inside a high, echoing hallway, where we were carried along by the crowd, buoyed by the noise of voices and shuffling feet. My father didn't seem to know where he was going any more than we did. But finally, after asking a priest for directions, he found his way to a door that led to Joyce's classroom. He let go of her hand, and I was impressed by how calm and brave she seemed as she stepped inside and disappeared from view. I knew I wouldn't be as brave when my turn came.

And I wasn't. When we reached the door of what was to be my classroom, my hand froze in my father's. It simply would not come loose, no matter how hard I tried. My father finally had to pry it from his hand before it would let go.

Cast adrift, not knowing whether my knees would hold me, I took a shaky step through the open door. Inside I found myself facing a roomful of strangers. And all of them were staring at me. Glancing back, I wondered if there was still time to run. But my father was gone. I turned to face my fate.

"Well, what are you standing there for?" said a deep voice behind me. "Find a seat and sit down."

I knew the gruff sound of authority when I heard it. Without pausing to turn around, I hurried to the first empty chair I could find. Only then did I look up to see who had spoken.

To my surprise, the voice did not belong to a man. But I wasn't exactly sure it belonged to a woman either, for the only features I could see were a round pale face and two thick white hands. The rest of the creature was completely hidden beneath the voluminous folds of a black dress that reached to the floor and a black veil that cascaded from the top of the head to halfway down the arms. Beneath the veil, the head was wrapped in what looked like a white bandage, leaving only the white face exposed. So cold were the gray eyes that peered down at us and so pinched was the mouth that I was sorry the face, too, had not been bandaged over.

A bell shrilled, making me jump. The nun strode to the door and pulled it shut. In the sudden silence of the room her skirt rustled like dead leaves, and the chain of beads that dangled from her belt rattled like stones on a beach.

"Good morning, children," she said in her gravelly voice. "My name is Sister Dennis, and I am going to be your teacher this year. We will begin our day the way all good children should begin every day — by saying our morning prayers. Up, up, up."

There was a scraping of chairs and a shuffling of shoes.

"Now, fold your hands and repeat after me: 'Our Father, Who art in heaven . . .'"

As we prayed she walked among us, and when she passed me I could see without raising my bowed head that the chain of beads she wore was really a huge rosary. From the end dangled an enormous metal crucifix that looked heavy enough to raise a welt if it happened to swing and hit you.

As Sister led us through the rhythmic cadences of the Lord's Prayer, I began to relax for the first time all morning. Having heard the prayer during Sunday Mass, I was finally on familiar ground — enough so that when I knew Sister wasn't looking I let my eyes wander. For the first time I noticed the crucifix hanging high on the wall, above the blackboard. It was as gory and sad as the one in church.

The only other decoration in the room was a color photograph of a gaunt, bespectacled old man that I later learned was the Holy Father, Pope Pius XII. Dressed in pure white robes and wearing a white skullcap, he had a thin, wizened face and looked stern and remote.

Although I could not have put it into words at the time, something about the two images clashed in my mind. The raw, bloody crucifixion and the distant, untouchable whiteness of the pope's garments did not go together. And yet they were both there on the wall, side by side, both part of what it meant to be a Catholic. It was very mysterious.

There were other mysteries, too. "'And lead us not into temptation,'" Sister Dennis was saying, "'but deliver us from evil.'" As we dutifully repeated the words, I found myself wondering what she was talking about. What was temptation? What was evil? And, more concretely, why on earth did a woman have a man's name?

But I dared not ask. I was not about to draw attention to myself if I could help it.

My caution did no good. Hardly had we finished praying and resumed our seats than Sister asked us to stand one by one and give our names. By the time my turn came I had the jitters all over again. I stood. I felt hot. I tried to speak, but my voice stuck in my throat. When a sound finally came out it was a high squeak. Even I heard it. I sounded exactly like a chicken.

Someone snickered. Sister scowled. Immediately there was silence. I tried again. This time I was able to get the words out and was rewarded by being allowed to sit down. In hopes that no one would take any further notice of me, I did my best to make myself as small as possible. It worked. No one paid any attention to me at all. Which made me feel even worse.

The basement was finished just in time. Hardly had the men come and flattened my mountain range than the first winter storm blew in.

It came quietly: gray sky, whisper of snow, no wind at all. Joyce and I were on our way home from school when it started. By the time we got off the bus and came tramping up our driveway, the ground was covered with a fine white powder. When we stamped our feet in it, it poofed out like dust around our shoes, leaving elephant tracks where we'd walked. Beauty came running to meet us, bounding in and out around our legs. Her footprints were like crazy stitches sewing ours together.

By the time my father got home from work, the snow was over the tops of his shoes. He stomped it off on the porch, came in, buckled on his overshoes, and went back out to put chains on the car tires. Then he began shoveling: one narrow path to the car, another to the outhouse.

The storm kept up all through supper and on into the night. When we pulled back the curtains and looked out, it was as if there was another curtain on the other side, lacy white, endlessly falling.

". . . six to eight inches," said the voice on the radio. "Winds will be picking up to thirty-five miles an hour, with gusts to forty-five. So bundle up and stay indoors. It looks like the first storm of the season is going to be a real big one."

Later that night, when I put on my coat and hat and mittens and buckled on my overshoes and took the flashlight and stepped out into the snowy night for my before-bed trip to the outhouse, I found myself enveloped in a strangely muffled world. The only sound was of my feet crunching in the snow. When I stood still, it was like standing in my grandmother's closet among the coats and dresses: the air thick with silence, so that all I could hear was my own breathing. But no, there was something else, too. I turned off the flashlight and stood in the darkness and lifted the earflaps of my hat, and it was as if there was a whispering all around me — a faint but steady hissing of snow falling on snow.

The wind didn't begin until after I was in bed.

I was already asleep on the top bunk when it woke me up. At first I didn't know what it was. What I heard was a weird moaning, like the sound of some strange animal. I opened my eyes. The cabin was almost completely dark except for a faint yellow glow that came through the little window of the space heater. No one was awake but me. I listened to the wind building, and now, along with the low moaning, there was a kind of howl as the storm flew across the open fields and hurled itself against the walls of our cabin. The door rattled. The windows creaked. From the stovepipe came an eerie wail. And over my head, just an arm's length away from where I lay, I could hear a scraping and clawing at the roof. It was as if the wild creature outside was trying to get in. Beauty, who usually slept by the door, whimpered and moved closer to my mother and father's bed.

"Mommeee." It was Joyce calling, but it might just as well have been me.

"Shh." My mother's voice came out of the dark corner, below the foot of my bunk. "It's all right. Go to back to sleep."

"But I'm scared."

"It's only the wind."

From my bunk I watched as my father pulled on his robe and slippers and went over to check the stove. My mother got up, too. From the rack by the sink she grabbed a bath towel and jammed it against the bottom of the door; then she hurried back to bed. I burrowed deeper under my covers, trying to shut out the scraping overhead, the roaring at the door.

I woke up the next morning to the smell of toast and the bubbling of a pot of oatmeal. The wind had died, and outside the big window the snow was still coming down hard, obscuring everything behind a gray-white veil. The woods at the back of our property were nothing more than a faint gray band. In the foreground, at the construction site, my sole remaining Rocky Mountain had been so softened and rounded that you couldn't tell where the flat land ended and the slope began.

My father was already outside shoveling, and by the time I got dressed and got into my coat and boots and hat and mittens for the trip to the outhouse, he had cleared the path again. The snow was piled up on either side as high as my waist.

Our car had disappeared altogether. Where it had been parked the night before, there was now only a big white hump. But the air was sharp and fresh, and when I'd finished in the outhouse, I was in no hurry to go back inside. Joyce came out, and Beauty, too, and together we forged through the knee-deep snow, falling in it, throwing it at each other, flopping backward in it, then lying there and making angel wings with our arms, while yet more snow fell on our faces from the gray sky overhead. We had all the time in the world. School was closed, the radio said, and even though the snow finally stopped late that afternoon, it was another whole day before a man finally came in his truck and plowed us out.

Winter stayed a long time. The thermometer outside our picture window showed below-zero temperatures for days on end: cold enough to freeze that famous jug of milk that my mother left outside on the steps one night because the small refrigerator was full. More snow fell. It drifted over the top of the snow fence that my father had erected along our driveway. It piled so deep in the corners of our new basement that it was over my head.

Joyce and I built a snowman, which my mother turned into a snowwoman by adding an apron, a babushka, and a broom. We built snow forts in the drifts and had snowball fights, while Beauty tore back and forth in front of us, barking excitedly.

We must have looked as if we were having fun because we were soon joined by a couple of other kids. The boy's name was Tim and his sister was Kathy, and they lived in a house across the road, at the end of a long driveway that ran alongside a wheat field.

Tim was about my age, and Kathy was as old as Joyce. That made it unfair when we divided into teams for a snowball fight, boys against girls, because the girls were bigger. But Tim and I could throw better, so things evened out. When one of my snowballs caught Joyce in the side of the head and made her cry, the victory was sweet indeed. But then Joyce spoiled it by threatening to tell on me as soon as Daddy got home. Only after I fervently assured her that it was an accident and I didn't really mean it and I was really, really sorry, cross my heart, did she finally relent. By then, all the joy had gone out of my triumph.

What was most fun was seeing Tim and Kathy's reactions when we invited them to come inside to warm up with cookies and warm milk.

"Inside where?" Tim asked.

"Inside the cabin, of course," Joyce said, pointing to our little square home.

59

"You mean —" Kathy seemed at a loss for words. "You mean, that's it? That's your house?"

"Yup," I said, proudly.

"You all live in there together?" asked Tim. "Your mom and your dad and everything?"

"Yup."

Tim beamed. "Hey!" he said. "Neat-o!"

7

STRAITS

*S*pring crept in by night that year, as if afraid the winter wind might catch it out in daylight and drive it back into hiding. One morning, after bundling myself up for the icy dash to the outhouse, I was surprised to discover that I no longer needed a heavy coat, cap, and woolen socks inside my overshoes. As I stood at the top of the cabin steps, a warm breeze was blowing, the air was sweet with the smell of damp earth, and the sky was a gentler shade of blue than it had been since the previous summer.

Had the change really happened overnight? It seemed that way. True, there were still patches of snow clinging to the edge of the woods and down in the shady corners of the basement. Out in the open fields the tall grass was still flattened as though some giant animal had slept on it all winter. But things were changing, no doubt about it. There was a new softness in the air. Softness in the ground, too, as I discovered the minute my foot left the bottom step and touched the earth. The path to the outhouse was a quagmire, mud sucking at my overshoes and sticking fast, until my feet felt as heavy as bricks.

My mother sang just one song that day and in the days that followed: "Leave your boots outside!" The words were on her lips whenever she heard one of us coming up the cabin steps. She spread newspapers over the linoleum. A damp mop was always handy near the door.

Rain and continued thawing put the building site beyond reach. The driveway became impassable. After our car got stuck for the second time, my father took to leaving it up near the road and walking back to the cabin.

"I'll have to do something about that," he told my mother one evening at supper.

What he could do about mud I had no idea. But my faith in my father was total. He could fix anything, improve anything. Did the Chevy stall? He'd raise the hood, poke around with pliers and a screwdriver, and get the thing started again. Was a pipe leaking under the sink? He'd get out his tool box, dig out a wrench and some tape, and abracadabra, no more leak. So there was no question in my mind that he would be able to do something about the mud, too.

But how? The answer did not become clear until the following Saturday morning, after he drove off in the car with the battered old trailer bouncing and banging along behind. Usually he used the trailer to haul lumber, furniture, and whatever else was too big to fit in the trunk. Today, when he returned, the trailer was spilling over with a load of gravel, bought, I later learned, from a nearby quarry.

In the meantime, Uncle Tad and Uncle Ray had turned up, having promised to help with whatever the job was going to be. Although the two of them were as different from one another as Abbott from Costello, I liked them both. Uncle Tad was very tall, had a deep, authoritative voice, and was kind to everyone, even us kids. Uncle Ray was always telling jokes, then laughing at them louder than anyone else.

Once, at a family picnic, the person watching the hot dogs on the grill had asked him to pass the tongs.

"The what?" asked Ray.

"The tongs."

"What?" Ray repeated.

"Tongs! Tongs!"

"You're welcome. You're welcome," said Ray, much to his own delight.

I loved it. I knew no other grown-up who had such a good time being silly.

Uncle Ray and Uncle Tad had hardly finished the coffee my mother poured for them when my father returned with his load of gravel. He handed each man a shovel and took a rake and a shovel for himself. Then the three of them set to work leveling the ruts in the driveway and spreading the gravel where the mud was deepest.

They were cheerful when they started, talking and laughing. Uncle Ray sang, "It's a treat to beat your feet in the Mississippi mud." As I watched I could tell they were having a good time. But their high spirits didn't last long. Soon the only sounds I heard from them were grunts and heavy breathing, mixed with the scrape and rattle of the stones on their shovels.

When my mother came out with the camera, the three of them were happy to take a break and pose for a picture. There they are now in her photo album, their peaked caps shading their eyes from the low spring sun: Tad leaning his lanky frame on a long-handled shovel, an easy grin on his face; Ray, a stubby fireplug of a man, looking surprised to find himself standing there with a shovel in his hands; my father leaning on a rake beside the half-empty trailer, no doubt impatient to get back to work.

Behind them stands the cabin, and beyond the cabin are a few bare elms, their branches made blurry by a stiff March wind. Farther back, beyond the elms, lie open fields, broken only by a distant line of trees and — a long way off — a solitary house, the one where my friend Timmy lived. The country looks not much different than it must have looked a hundred years earlier, when it was still wild prairie. The plow has been there, of course. The prairie grass has long since been ripped up and turned under. Season in and season out, the land has been furrowed, seeded, grazed, and harvested. Plows, disks, combines, and hay bailers have been dragged over the earth again and again. But the bulldozers and graders of the developers have not yet appeared. The sprawling housing tracts and condos, with their razor-cut lawns, their decorative plantings, their backyard swing sets and concrete driveways, are still twenty or thirty years away. For now, the fields lie fallow, waiting only for the sun to dry them so that the spring plowing can begin once more. The horizon is wide, the sky is clear, and in the foreground my father and my uncles are ready to get back to work.

When the trailer was empty, my father drove off for another load of gravel, then another. By the end of the day he and my uncles were having trouble straightening their backs. But they got the job done. Now, instead of a quagmire, we had a gravel driveway and a gravel path between the cabin and the outhouse. The car did not get stuck again, and my mother had less cause to complain about mud being tracked all over her nice clean floor. My father had fixed the mud, just as he said he would.

I think it must have been that spring that my father took us to visit the place where he worked. Having left behind the gritty machine shop where he had labored as a tool-and-die man, he had taken a step up and was now something called an "assistant instrument test engineer" at Lakeside Power Plant.

I had seen the place many times before, but always from a distance. Situated on a bluff overlooking Lake Michigan, it was the biggest thing on that flat prairie landscape, and its six enormous smokestacks were visible from miles away, marking the eastern horizon like ever-watchful sentries.

That my father worked in the township's biggest building beneath the tallest smokestacks was no more than I expected. Still, I was awed to see the place up close. Everything about it bespoke size and power: the smokestacks with their great plumes billowing out over the lake; the enormous square powerhouse itself, so big that the few doors and windows around its base looked like nothing more than pinpricks on its vast blank walls. In the yard outside the plant stood mountains of coal almost as high as the building itself. Freight cars on the sidings lay ready to disgorge even more coal onto the looming black peaks. And everywhere around us bristled forests of high tension towers festooned with loops of electric cable, like giant clotheslines.

Driving past the guard at the gate, my father parked, then led us inside, where he showed off the biggest machines I had ever seen, all of them growling and rumbling. There were gigantic furnaces, huge steam generators, pipes everywhere, some of them thicker than a man was tall, and monstrous turbines. As my father led us through the plant, he explained how the furnaces created steam, which turned the turbines, which in turn created the electrical power that went out over the high tension wires, bringing light and energy to homes, stores, and factories all over the south side of the city.

My father's job was to test and keep records of the multitude of instruments and gauges that measured the temperature of the fires in the furnaces, the pressure of the steam generators, the speed of the turbines. He also had to go outside and check that the smoke coming out of the stacks was the right color: not too dark, not too brown, not too light, but just the right shade of gray.

As he was telling us all of this, he led us along a bewildering array of corridors and walkways. He knew his way around, and he seemed to know everyone. Men would wave or nod as we passed, or call out, shouting to be heard over the roar of the generators. "Got some helpers with you today, huh?"

"You betcha," my father shouted back, giving them a grin and sticking up a thumb the way pilots did in war movies.

Clearly my father was an important man, and by the time we left I was absolutely convinced that were it not for him, the furnaces would have stopped burning, the generators stopped generating, the smokestacks ceased to throw their gray plumes into the air, and the lights would have gone out all over the city.

I did not know it at the time, but going to work at the power plant was probably a pleasure for my father that spring. Monitoring his gauges and instruments must have been a relief compared to coping with the crisis that now loomed before him. For during late March and early April of 1949, it began to look as if the house he had begun might never be completed.

In the back of my mind I must have always known that there was a problem. Why else would it have taken so long for the house to get built? Over the years, whenever I leafed through the family album, I could see in the photos the passing not only of months but of whole seasons. I could track the changes in the light and foliage, the transformations of the landscape from bountiful grassland to arctic ice and snow, then to mud and back to grass again. I could see the way our clothing changed from shorts and shirtsleeves to winter coats and back to shirtsleeves. On occasion I was even moved to pull one or two photos out of their black corner mounts to check the date written on the back in my mother's graceful hand. The story was there to be read all along, if I had only bothered to think about it.

Had I done so, I might have mustered the courage to sit down with my father, face-to-face, with no distractions, no one between us, and hear the story from his own lips before it was too late.

At the time, though, and for years afterward, it did not occur to me even to wonder. As a child, I simply took it on faith that whatever my father did must be the way things were meant to be done. If he needed more than a year to build our house, well then, that was how long it was supposed to take. I never imagined there was any other way to do it. By the time I was an adult, the distance between us had grown too great. Neither of us was interested in dwelling on the past. The past was too painful, too full of disappointments and recriminations, while the present was crowded with its own demands, including the vague sense I always had that some questions were simply not meant to be asked.

Only years later, when I began looking through the papers that my mother had dug out of my father's file drawers, did I realize that somewhere along the way his original plans for the house had gone terribly wrong. What was it? What had caused my father to leave us stranded in that little one-room cabin for all that time, like survivors of a shipwreck adrift in a little square lifeboat on a sea of grass and mud?

As I looked through the drawings and the random papers that went with them — our family's own Dead Sea scrolls, our own Rosetta stone — other questions came to mind as well. If the footings and the basement walls were already in place by Christmas 1948, why were most of my father's plans and elevations dated from the spring of 1949? Why was he still designing the house after the foundation had been built? If he didn't already know what kind of house he was going to build, how could he have known how big to make the foundation on which it was going to stand?

For the first time I began to wonder if it was possible that the man I had always seen as being oh so capable might not have done things exactly backward. Was it likely that he, who usually planned everything so meticulously, would have undertaken such a major project in such an offhand manner? Or was there something else going on, something that I knew nothing about?

The drawings themselves provided hints of answers to my questions. Mixed in among the floor plans and elevations of the modest, single-story house I had always known — the one that kept turning up in my dreams — I found plans for an entirely different house. This was an elaborate, two-story affair. The main floor had a bedroom, a bath, a spacious living room, and a large kitchen. There was even a dining room, something the finished house never had. Upstairs there were two more bedrooms and a second bath. Dormer windows looked out on the yard and the woods beyond. Altogether it was a plan for a much roomier and more comfortable house than the one I remembered. But at the bottom of the drawing my father had written a one-word note and the date: "VOIDED, 4–4–49."

"What's this?" I asked my mother, showing her the drawing.

"What? Oh, that. That was his first idea." She waved a hand dismissively. "More pipe dreams."

"What happened? Why didn't he build it?"

She shrugged. The question did not interest her. "I'm not sure. I think the credit union wouldn't give him the money. Or the builder told him he couldn't build such a big house for what he could spend."

Money. Of course. Everything always came down to money. Once she said it, it seemed perfectly obvious. If I'd had cause to doubt it, which I didn't, I soon discovered written proof of his predicament. Leafing through the other papers in the manila envelope, I found a whole slew of overdue bills and receipts from lumberyards, hardware stores, suppliers, and contractors.

A bill from Banner Lumber Company, dated September 29, 1948, was for thirty-eight pieces of two-by-eight lumber, costing a total of $110. Of that amount, $46.88 was two months in arrears. Less than fifty dollars, yet my father was having trouble paying it.

Then there was the building contract for the basement, handwritten by the contractor, one Allan Ross. In it were spelled out the overall details of the basement construction:

> 10" concrete block basement of dimensions 40 feet by 36 feet. An offset fruit cellar and an offset pump room.
>
> 1. Lay all forms for footings
> 2. Pour 13 yards of concrete for footings
> 3. Lay up all walls with 10" concrete block to the highth of 10 coarses [*sic*]
> 4. Back plaster and tar outside of walls below grade.

The total cost was to be $1,641, payable in three installments, with the final installment due on completion of the work. Yet in the top left corner was a note in my father's hand indicating that, although the work was finished on December 17, 1948, the final installment ($241) was not paid until five months later, on May 18, 1949.

The picture that emerged was painfully clear: my father was in over his head. Not that we kids ever heard about it. There were two things he never talked about in front of us. One was love. The other was money. But the papers in the envelope told at least some of the story. To me, as a child, it might have seemed only natural that building the house should take as long as it did. I could see now that the fact that it got built at all was something of a miracle.

I could imagine my father, in that spring of 1949, with his carefully drawn plans suddenly rendered worthless. I could imagine him standing on the edge of his finished basement and staring at the concrete-block walls for which he still owed $241 and which he had designed to fit a two-story house that would never be built. Clear as day I could see him standing there and thinking: Now what do I do? Just what in the hell do I do now?

"I believe in God, the Father Almighty, Creator of heaven and earth —"

Sister Dennis's eyes swept over us. She was watching our lips, making sure we were all repeating the phrases exactly as she said them.

"— and in Jesus Christ, His only son, our Lord."

I repeated the words along with the rest of the class, our voices rising in a singsong chorus. My hands were pressed together at the palms, the way Sister had shown us, fingers pointed toward the ceiling, sending my prayer directly to Jesus in heaven. At least I hoped so. As I prayed I kept my eyes fixed on the crucifix that hung on the wall over the blackboard. The figure suspended there was naked except for a towel around his waist, and his wounds looked horrible. Blood oozed from around the nails that pierced his hands and feet. In his side was an ugly red gash where a cruel Roman soldier had jabbed him with a spear. His forehead dripped with blood from the crown of thorns his torturers had pressed into his skull. Every time any of us kids committed a sin, Sister told us, we were driving another nail into Jesus's body, another thorn into his head. It made me feel awful, and as I prayed to the figure on the cross I promised with all my heart and all my soul that I would always be good and never ever commit a sin.

Being good meant doing what I was told by my parents and never getting mad. It meant being nice to Joyce and never getting mad. It meant doing what I was told by Sister Dennis and paying attention during Mass and never saying bad words or getting too big for my britches. I wanted very much to be good. I certainly did not want Jesus to be stuck with any more nails or thorns on my account. I wouldn't want that to happen to anybody. Except maybe — But I caught myself. It was bad to think such things, especially about my own sister.

When morning prayers were finished, we moved on to arithmetic, which I was not very good at. There was so much to remember, so many — well, numbers. Joyce, of course, always got A's in arithmetic, as she did in almost everything.

My favorite subject was geography, which we finally got to after I had endured forty-five minutes of addition. Our geography lesson centered on a wooden rack mounted on the side wall of the classroom, above the blackboard. The rack held a collection of wonderful maps that could be rolled up and down like window shades. Unrolled, they opened glimpses on other worlds — exotic, odd-shaped places with tantalizing names like Panama, Madagascar, Norway, the Sahara Desert, and California — places I had heard about on the radio and in movie newsreels but that seemed as impossibly far away as the moon.

The map that Sister unrolled for us that morning was of North America. On it, the forty-eight states were displayed in a variety of colors, artfully arranged so that no two states sitting side-by-side shared the same one. Above the United States lay a huge expanse of land labeled Canada. Below stretched the muscular arm of Mexico.

Sister turned toward the class. "Now, who can tell me which one is our state? Tom?"

"Wisconsin," I said proudly, and had the satisfaction of hearing Sister tell me I was right.

"And can you show us on the map where Wisconsin is?" she asked.

That was easy. Stepping to the front of the room, I took the long wooden pointer Sister handed me and set its black tip on the purple shape that was Wisconsin. You could always tell which was Wisconsin, because it was shaped like a mitten and had one of the Great Lakes running down its side — the one that was shaped like a squash.

According to our geography book, each of the Great Lakes looked like something else. I could see clearly that Lake Superior looked like a wolf's head and that Lake Huron looked like a man bent over with a pack on his back. I wasn't so sure that Lake Erie looked like a beaver or that Lake Ontario looked like an otter. But by now I had learned that I was not supposed to question the assertions made by such authorities as my father, Sister Dennis, priests, policemen, the leaders of our state and nation, or the authors of books, all of whom certainly knew much more than I did.

Pleased with my success, I went back to my seat. So far I had gotten everything right. But it was not Wisconsin that Sister was really interested in that morning. She had something else in mind. Directing our attention to the territory of Alaska, up in the top left-hand corner of the map, she pointed to the Bering Strait. That narrow strip of blue, she told us ominously, was all that separated our sweet land of liberty from that evil and dangerous place called the Soviet Union, which was shown in red on the map and which was ruled by frightening and terrible people called Communists.

We knew all about Communists. Sister talked about them frequently. So did our heroic senator, Joseph McCarthy, whom we often heard on the radio. Communists were evil, nasty people who, Sister said, hated God and children who believed in God. If we were ever caught by the Communists, she had told us time and again, they would do terrible things to us until we promised to give up being Catholic and believing in Jesus.

Until now, my chances of ever being captured by Communists had seemed pretty slim. That's why it was so shocking to see on the map just how close they really were and how easy it would be for them to get to where we were.

"All they have to do," Sister said, tapping the narrow blue place with her pointer, "is to cross the Bering Strait in their airplanes and battleships." Her voice was full of foreboding. In the classroom there was absolute silence. No one rustled a paper, no one shifted in his seat.

"Once the Russians have landed on our shores," Sister Dennis went on, "all they have to do is march across Canada —" her pointer made a great arc across the vast spaces — "and before you know it they will be right here." Her pointer came to rest on our cozy purple mitten. "Right on our streets, boys and girls. Right on our doorsteps."

Sister's small dark eyes bored into the eyes of each of us in turn. "Will you be ready?" she asked. "When you are told to renounce our Lord, will your faith be strong? Will your souls be clean and spotless for our Lord in heaven?"

I lowered my eyes. I knew that if I let her look into them she would know the truth: that my soul was covered with spots, just like the picture of the milk bottle in our catechism book. The picture showed two milk bottles side by side. One represented a pure soul; the milk in it was all white. But the milk in the other bottle was tainted with dark blotches. That was how a sinful soul looked, the book said, and I had no doubt that was the way my soul looked, too. Only the night before, I had argued with my mother instead of setting the table when she told me to. And during Mass that morning, when I was supposed to be praying, my mind had wandered to other things. If the Communists came and killed me then, before I could make an act of contrition, I would go to hell for sure. Well, maybe just purgatory since I hadn't done anything really bad, like killing someone. But the idea of purgatory was still pretty frightening. It had fires, too, although they were not as hot as the fires in hell and, if you died with sins on your soul, you had to remain in purgatory only until someone on earth said enough prayers on your behalf, or one of the saints went to God and told him you were okay. Then maybe you would be allowed into heaven; but that could take years, and in the meantime you'd be bored and miserable and really hot.

"You must pray every day," Sister was telling us. "You must pray to our Lord Jesus to defeat the Communists and to keep our country strong. And you must pray to keep yourselves from doing evil. Ask yourselves every day: what sins have I committed today? How have I hurt our Lord today? Examine your conscience and pray to our Lord for forgiveness. Do you understand, boys and girls?"

A chorus of weak, trembling voices responded: "Yes, Sister."

Her eyes swept over us like searchlights. "I hope you do, boys and girls. For your sakes, I hope you do. Now, let us pray."

I folded my hands and lowered my head. I felt terrible. I wanted more than anything to be good. But somehow the harder I tried, the more I seemed to mess things up. I'd whisper in class. I'd daydream. At home, I'd do things that I knew would rile my father. Like talk during supper. Or dawdle when he wanted me to do something. I didn't know why I did bad things. Something would get into me, and I just couldn't seem to help myself. My only hope was to pray harder.

I squeezed my eyes shut and tried to concentrate. But then I had another thought. I knew that if the Communists tortured me and if they killed me because I refused to give up my faith, then I would go right to heaven, even if I did have spots on my soul, because then I'd be a martyr and martyrs always got in. Not only that, but if I was a martyr, I might even get to be a saint.

I liked that idea. Being a saint was better than being a cowboy. When you were a saint, people said good things about you and everybody liked you. They named churches after you, and in the churches they put up statues of you, and then people came and prayed to your image. If you were a saint you could do all kinds of special things, such as help people get over being sick. You could find things they had lost. You could protect them when they took trips. But you didn't have to do those things unless you felt like it. If you didn't care for the person who was praying to you, you didn't have to do anything for them. And they couldn't get back at you, either. If I were a saint, I wouldn't have to worry about Jimmy, the bully on the playground, who liked to twist my arm until I said "Give," or about the kid on the school bus who liked to stick out his foot and trip me when I walked down the aisle to my seat. If I got to be a saint, I'd be safe forever.

But there was a problem. Being a martyr was by far the worst way to become a saint. That much I knew from the stories in the books Sister read to us. Martyrs were killed in all sorts of horrible ways. One book had a picture of a saint who had been stuck full of arrows, as if Indians had attacked him. In others I heard about saints who had been stabbed to death, or hung upside down on crosses, or clawed and chewed by wild animals in the Roman arena. Still others had been cut into pieces with swords or ripped apart on wheels or burned at the stake.

The effect of the martyr stories on my imagination was surely not what Sister had intended. The more I thought about it, the less I liked the idea of being a martyr and the less I thought I could ever measure up. Oh, sure, it would be nice to go straight to heaven without passing Go. But when I was being absolutely truthful with myself, I knew for a fact that I would never be able to go through with it. I was just too much of a coward. Deep down, I knew that when the Russians crossed over into

Canada with their tanks and their bombs and their thousands of men, and then came thundering across mountains and prairies and pounded on our cabin door, they wouldn't even have to show me a knife or tie me to a stake. All they would have to do was talk about torturing me, and my poor faith would go right out the window.

It was a hard truth to accept about myself, but eventually the realization sank in: I was just not good martyr material. If I was ever going to be a saint, I would have to do it the hard way. I would have to be perfect.

I only hoped I could manage it before the Russians showed up.

My father was stuck.

He now had a basement he could not finish paying for, which had been designed for a house he could not afford to build. He could not see how to go ahead. Yet the longer he did nothing, the longer his family would be cooped up in the cabin.

He knew he had to do something, but what? None of the possible solutions looked very satisfactory. He could scrap the project: kiss his investment good-bye, put the property up for sale, and find someplace else for us to live. But who would want to buy a piece of land out in the middle of nowhere that had a hole in the middle of it lined with the foundation of someone else's abandoned dream?

Besides, he wasn't ready to give up. He was sure there had to be a solution, some way of working out the problem.

The solution he came up with was a reluctant compromise, but an elegant one. After discussing the problem with a builder, he decided he had no choice but to scale back his original design. Using the existing foundation, he would plan the kind of house that the mental dwarf at the credit union thought he could afford.

Night after night that April, while my mother cleaned up the supper dishes and Joyce and I sat at one end of the table doing our homework, my father sat at the other end, absorbed in reworking his drawings, the lamplight deepening the furrows in his brow. Spread before him on the oil cloth was an amazing collection of implements: fine-tipped pencils that he sharpened by scraping their points across a piece of sandpaper, yellow and pink erasers, pads of graph and tracing paper, a ruler, a slide rule, and a whole series of shiny chrome drawing instruments that he kept in a beautiful black box lined with soft blue velvet.

Looking at his drawings now, all these years later, I can almost feel as if I am standing at his elbow as he works. In one of the side-view elevations, you can see exactly where he bore down with the eraser, sweeping away his original vision in a blizzard of rubber crumbs. The walls of the second story have been rubbed out, leaving the roof hovering in the sky as if it has been lifted off by a prairie wind and is about to be blown away. Below it, my father has drawn in a new roof line, this one for his new, more practical vision: a single-story house.

Lowering the roof line was easy compared to reworking the floor plan. What he had to do was somehow squeeze the two upstairs bedrooms into his original first-floor plan. For starters, that meant shrinking the living room and the first-floor bedroom. The dining room had to go completely. To make up for the lost eating space, he did away with the original cozy breakfast nook and made the kitchen large enough to accommodate a full-sized table and chairs. After that, all he had to do was find some way to cram two more bedrooms and a full bath into the remaining floor space.

He went through one draft after another. Crumpled sheets of graph paper piled up at his elbow and on the floor around his chair. He moved walls and doorways. He took a closet from one corner and put it in another. He worked out traffic patterns between the rooms. He studied *Popular Mechanics* and *The Amateur Builder's Handbook*. From them he learned that the best way to arrange the kitchen was to lay out the sink, the stove, and the refrigerator as if they were at the points of a triangle, making each work center easily accessible to the other two. That way, when my mother was preparing meals, she could move around with the least wasted motion. Always my father's calculations were confined by the dimensions of the existing basement, and by the need to keep everything as efficient and economical as possible.

By the middle of April, he finally had what he thought was a workable design. Back he went to the builder, who said yes, he thought this version could be done for a price my father could afford. The only remaining hurdle was the credit union down at the plant, where he handed in his loan application, blueprint copies of his design, carbons of his cost estimates, copies of last year's income tax returns, and copies of his recent pay stubs. Days of waiting then, anxious days, while his application was studied and credit checks were run. What if they said no? He had already taken one loan to buy the land. Would he be able to manage another? What if he got laid off or fired? How would he keep up the payments? He could end up the way his parents did during the Depression. Owners of a boarding house, they had lost everything when the foundry where my grandfather worked went bankrupt. Now my father, too, could lose everything he had worked for.

And all the while he said nothing to my mother. Whatever agony he was going through, whatever doubts or fears must have plagued him, he kept them to himself. A man did not complain. A man did not show weakness or uncertainty. A man did what he had to do. That was all there was to it.

And yet, what a relief it must have been when he finally heard that his loan had been approved and that he would indeed have the money he needed to pay his outstanding bills and to move ahead with the building. He knew that his house would no longer be the house he had dreamed of. He knew that he would have to do much of the work himself and would need to rely on his brothers and in-laws for help whenever they could manage it.

But he knew at last and for sure that his dream was going to come true: he would have his house.

8

MAN'S WORK

 W hen it came to working with his hands, my father knew no uncertainty, no self-doubt.

"Him, he knew everything," was the way my uncle Eddy put it years
later. "You couldn't tell him nothin'."

The cabin had bolstered Dad's confidence. It had been a trial run,
and it had worked out just fine. Built tight and strong, it had gotten us
snugly through the winter storms. Now, as my father looked ahead to
building a whole house, his confidence was running high.

I doubt that he had any illusions that the task ahead would be as easy
as building a one-room cabin. He may have been bull-headed, but he was
not stupid. Still, he had every reason to believe he was up to the job. After
all, lots of people with far less experience than he were building their
own houses. In those first years after the war, with hundreds of thousands
of veterans returning home and starting families, both housing and fi-
nancing were in short supply. For many people the do-it-yourself approach was the only solution. And like my father, they had plenty of
encouragement. Almost every issue of *Popular Mechanics* and of the
weekly Home section of the *Milwaukee Journal* carried inspiring stories
about young couples starting out on the great adventure.

One such story was about a man who built a house for a little more than six hundred dollars. "If you are not afraid of hard work," he told readers of *Popular Mechanics*, "if you can hit a nail on the head, keep to a straight line with a saw, and know how to use a square and level, and if you have the will to keep on the job until it is completed, such a house is yours."

My father fit the description to a T. He had all the requirements listed by the author of the article. In his hands, hammers and saws seemed to fit as naturally as if they were extensions of his anatomy. Unfortunately, my father also had an implacable, clenched-jawed determination to go it alone and never ask for advice from anyone. Especially not from people he knew. And most especially not from Eddy, the husband of my mother's sister, Pat. Ten years before, Eddy had built his own low-slung stone-and-timber masterpiece of a house, stirring my father's secret admiration and envy.

A short-legged strutting bantam of a man, Eddy loved to drink hard, play hard, and work hard. An electrician by trade, he was something of an obsessive genius when it came to building. He had mastered not only electricity but also woodworking, masonry, roofing, and plumbing. The beautifully finished cabinets in his and Pat's kitchen were his handiwork. So were the tennis court and the terrace and the stone barbecue pit with its wraparound stone benches.

By his own reckoning, Eddy was a master builder. So who better to offer advice to a neophyte? But my father would not ask. Eddy was too full of swagger and bluster, too eager to show off how smart he was, how well he did things. Besides, my father had other places to look for help. Books. He was comfortable with books. Books didn't talk back. Books didn't show off. And if one did, he could always shut it and pick up another one.

Certainly he had plenty to choose from. In the years after the war, as soon as the paper shortage eased up, a whole library of do-it-yourself manuals became available. One of the most popular was the *Amateur Builder's Handbook*. Another was *Your Dream Home: How to Build It for Less than $3,500*. Decades later, I found copies of both on my father's bookshelf, their pages yellowed and well-thumbed.

Say good-bye to crowded, substandard living quarters and sky-high rentals [read the jacket copy of *Your Dream Home*]. No longer need price tags of

77

$9,000 and $25,000 stand between you and the spacious, light, airy home — the sunshine and open fields — the good uncrowded schools and all the other advantages that spell health, happiness and success in life.

This amazing book shows how any family can build a home far more spacious, beautiful and comfortable than you ever dreamed possible — for little more than the cost of materials alone!

Full of the kind of confidence that would have gladdened the blurb-writer's heart, my father was all set to take the plunge. He began at the bottom, with the basement floor. After all, what could be so difficult about pouring a concrete floor? The instructions were right there in the *Amateur Builder's Handbook:*

A first requirement is that there be a fill placed under the floor. This fill should be of coarse gravel, crushed stone or screened cinders at least 6 in. thick over the entire area to be floored.

The concrete was to be poured on top of the gravel, then tamped down and smoothed out. Easy, nothing to it. At least, that's the way the book made it sound.

Years later, as I sat with a tape recorder in Pat and Eddy's Florida living room, Eddy recalled what happened once Dad got started: "He hired a bunch of guys from the VA hospital, see, and he ordered in a truckload o' concrete and brought in a case o' beer. And then he got those guys started on laying that floor."

Eddy sipped his afternoon highball and gave a smug laugh. "See, what they did was, they poured that concrete in there all at once instead of working it a section at a time the way you're s'posed to. And naturally parts of it started setting before they could get to work on it, to smooth it out, you know. 'Course, by this time the beer was going down real good, too.

"Well, I'll tell you, that stuff was setting and Walter realized it wasn't coming out right. So he calls me up in the afternoon. He's all in a panic and he tells me I gotta come over there right away 'cause he's got this problem on his hands.

"Well, hell, by the time I got there the stuff was setting. I watered her down and tried to level her off, you know, to get all the waves out of her.

78

But by that time there wasn't a whole lot I could do. We ended up chipping out channels in the concrete so at least there'd be some drainage down to the sump hole. See, he didn't have it graded properly for drainage, either. I'm telling you, he didn't stake it out or nothin'. See, what you have to do is put down these stakes —"

"Where are your stakes, Walter?" I could imagine Eddy asking him.

"What stakes?" says my father.

"What do you mean, what stakes? You gotta put down stakes, in a kind of grid, to the height and grade you want your floor. Then you pour the cement to the top of the stakes."

"Well, we didn't do it that way."

"I can see that."

Nowadays, most concrete work is done by machines. "Bull floats" are used to tamp down the wet concrete. Large rotary smoothers called power floats are used to smooth it out. But in 1949, my father and the vets he hired had only hand tools.

"See, first you'd go over the surface with your straight edge," Eddy explained to me as the tape recorder ran. "You take a good straight two-by-four, twelve or sixteen feet long, and you put a man at each end, and they tamp down the wet cement, then pull back on it to level it off, then tamp some more and pull some more.

"You keep on tampin' and pullin'. Tamp, pull. Tamp, pull. Then, when you know it's settled and you've got it pretty good and level, you go over it with your tamper. That's a heavy plate with, you know, a handle coming up out of the middle of it. And that plate is maybe two, two and a half feet square. You go up and back, up and back, until you got it all tamped. After that, you go over it with your hand trowel to smooth it off."

Eddy laughed and shook his head, enjoying his own story. "The thing is, before you do any of that, you gotta strike a level. Otherwise you're starting off bad to begin with. But your dad, he didn't do that. Oh, he had good ideas and all. But man, he knew everything. He wouldn't ask for advice if it killed him. Not him."

At six going on seven, I was unaware of any of this. All I knew was that work on the house had started again and that my father was in charge. He was the man who made great things happen, the master of the world.

Every day now, when Joyce and I stepped off the school bus, something new was going on at the building site. One afternoon, we found a pile of lumber stacked near the foundation. It was clean and smooth and yellow-white and sweet smelling. The next day, a mud-spattered pickup truck was parked in our driveway, along with a couple of cars that looked even older than ours. Over at the work site, three men in overalls, T-shirts, and heavy work shoes were busy hauling lumber from the pile, measuring it with steel tapes, then sawing it and setting it along the tops of the basement walls. My father was working alongside them.

Quickly I changed out of my school clothes and wolfed down some cookies and milk as I sat on the cabin steps. Then I inched my way over for a better look, being careful not to get in anyone's way so my father wouldn't chase me off.

What the men were doing was laying the beams along the tops of the basement walls and fastening them to the bolts that had been cemented there when the walls were being built.

"Sills," my father told me these timbers were called when I had a chance to ask him.

"Yeah, but what're they for?"

"Don't say 'yeah.'"

"Okay, but what're they for?"

"Just watch. You'll see."

I watched.

Once the sills were fastened down, other timbers were carried to the site, where they were measured, sawed, then jostled into position so that they spanned the top of the basement, from wall to wall. They were supported in the middle by a steel girder that ran crossways from one wall to the other, the girder in turn supported by a pair of steel columns that rested on concrete footings set into the basement floor.

After carefully measuring and spacing the new timbers so that they lay side by side and about a foot apart, the men stood them on edge, then nailed the ends to the sills.

"Joists," my father said these new beams were called. When all of them were in place, they made a kind of open roof over the basement.

By then I could see what the sills and joists were for. A pattern had emerged. What had once been only lines on my father's drawings had taken on substance and dimension. The flat, trellislike roof was not a roof at all, but the structure that would support the floor of our house.

When the workmen began laying down floorboards and nailing them to the joists beneath, my father was again working alongside them. Since he was on the night shift "down at the plant," as he said, he could spend every afternoon working on the house, and that was where Joyce and I usually found him when we got home from school: hunkered down on the floor, his hammer rising and falling, his T-shirt soaked with sweat, his ever-present fedora tipped back on his head. Sometimes he whistled to himself. Sometimes he sang:

> A *little bird told me we'd be happy*
> *And I believe that it's true.*

I wished I could be up there with him, banging away with a hammer. It looked like fun, and it looked important. Building, I could see, was not like doing homework or going to school. Building was real work. My father was making something you could touch and walk on, something that would be strong enough to hold us and our furniture — our whole house. Our whole world.

And I wanted to be part of it. I liked the easy way my father and the other men went about things. I admired the way they seemed to know just which board went where and were able to drive in a nail with just two or three quick blows. I also loved the racket they made, their hammer blows echoing against the woods at the back of our land.

Always, though, when I asked my father if I could help, the answer was no. "You'll be in the way," he'd say. Or: "It's not safe for you up here." There were too many gaps in the floor that I could fall through, too many loose boards to trip over, too many loose nails to step on.

"I'll be careful."

"No. Now you heard me. Go and play someplace else."

Then one day everything changed. It must have been a Saturday, because none of the other men had shown up. My father was working on the house by himself. I had heard his hammering even before I climbed down from my bunk. As soon as I was dressed and had breakfast, I wandered over to see what he was doing and if maybe this time I could help. I balanced my way along the plank that led from the ground up to the floor where he was working. I went quietly, fully expecting that the minute he saw me he would shoo me away. But he surprised me.

"Well, good morning, sleepy head," he said. "How'd you like to give me a hand?"

"Really?"

"Sure. Come on over here. Just watch your step."

Finally I was going to get a chance to be part of the great project. I skirted the yawning hole in the floor where the basement stairs would go and picked my way to where my father was kneeling, hammer in hand. A Hills Brothers coffee can of nails was spilled on the floorboards in front of him.

"Here," he said. "You can help me get these last floorboards nailed down."

While I watched he showed me how to get the nail started with a few taps and then to bang it in with a few good blows.

"What you do is hold the nail nice and straight. See the way I'm doing it? Then you tap it a few times to get it started. Just lightly. Tap, tap."

My father tapped the nail with his hammer until the tip was embedded in the wood and the nail stood by itself.

"See?" he said. "Now I can get my fingers out of the way."

I squatted beside him, watching intently. The only thing that mattered was that I learn to do it right and not disappoint him.

Already I had begun to learn that proof of his satisfaction was to be found not in encouraging words but in the absence of faultfinding. To my father's way of thinking, praise was as dangerous as a prescription drug. If it could be avoided, so much the better. If not, it must be administered in only the smallest of doses. Any more than a milligram or two, he seemed to feel, would lead to lethargy, indolence, a swelling of the head. Even then I sensed that not to disappoint him was in fact the best I could hope for.

My father raised his hammer to shoulder height. "Now I'm ready to drive the nail home," he said. The hammer came down. It hit the nail with a bang that made my ears ring. It hit again, bang, then a third time, bang. Each hit was square on. He did not miss, not once.

Three hits was all it took. The nail was gone, buried deep in the wood. The only part still showing was its flat head.

"See? It's easy," he said. "Now you try it."

He handed me the hammer. I almost needed two hands to hold it.

But if I used two hands, I would not be able to hold the nail in place. Shifting the hammer to my right hand, I held the nail with the thumb and forefinger of my left, then tapped it lightly, as he had shown me. But the nail would not stay standing the way it was supposed to. I tried hitting it harder and hit my fingers instead. The yelp I heard was my own.

"Not that way," my father said. "Do it the way I showed you. Just lightly. Tap-tap."

"I tried it that way. It doesn't work."

"You're giving up too easily. Come on. Try it again."

I did as he said. Tap-tap, tap-tap-tap. This time it worked. The nail stuck in the wood.

"That's the way. Now you can drive it home."

Holding the hammer in both hands, I gave it a mighty bash.

"Whoa. Take it easy. You don't have to kill it."

I eased up, but by now the nail was bent over sideways. I wiggled it out, threw it aside, and tried a new one. Tap-tap, tap-tap-tap. Surprise! The tip went in. The nail was standing upright. I hit it a good one. It bent again. Never mind. I clenched my teeth, growled, and kept on hitting it until I had mashed it flat into the wood.

My father was shaking his head and looking disgusted. "Now that's not going to do much good, is it?" he said.

"But it went in crooked."

"Sure it did. You weren't hitting it straight. You have to bring the head of the hammer straight down, so it meets the nail head flat on. Go ahead, try it again."

Ah ha! So here was something else to remember. Tap the nail lightly but not too lightly. Hit it hard but not too hard. Don't hit it crooked but straight on. Clearly there was a lot more to hammering nails than I had imagined.

But I was determined to get it right. As my father moved off to work on his section of the floor, I picked up another nail and tried again. And again. Soon the area where I was working was littered with bent nails, twisted nails, nails driven halfway in, then pounded flat on their sides. Yet little by little I began to get the hang of it. I even managed to get a few of them to go straight down through the floorboards.

"Lookit," I called to my father. "Come and see."

Scattered before me, amid the rubble of bent and twisted metal, I counted seven perfectly flat nail heads lying flush with the floorboards. Each one was a little gleaming badge of success.

My father came to inspect. Standing over me with the sun behind him, he looked down from his great height and uttered his solemn judgment. "Missed the joist," he said, then turned away.

Stunned, I looked at my work. Then I looked at the work that he and the other men had done. Sure enough, while all of their nails marched off across the floor in nice, neat, evenly spaced lines, each line marking the position of the joist beneath, my nails were strewn like grass seed. And not one of them was connected to anything below.

The worst part was, I had no way of hiding the evidence of my ineptitude. It was out in the open for everyone to see.

Everyone did, too. My sister made sure of that.

"You gotta see what my dumb brother did," she told Tim and Kathy the next time they came over to play.

With her pigtails bouncing against her back, Joyce marched up the plank walkway and led our friends straight to the scene of my embarrassment. But while she and Kathy had a good laugh, Tim did not crack a smile. "What's wrong with that?" he asked. "I think it's neat, getting to hammer things. I wish my dad would let me do stuff like that."

I liked Tim a lot.

"You're just jealous," I told my sister, my spirits buoyed.

She sneered. "Oh, really? And why should I be jealous?"

"Because you're a girl and girls don't get to build things."

"Just shows what you know. Mommy built the outhouse and she's a girl."

She had me there. I groped for a reply but couldn't come up with one.

"Anyway," she went on, "if I wanted to hammer I could. I just don't want to." She turned to Kathy. "Come on, I'll show you my new doll. My daddy got it for me for my birthday. You should see. Her dress is real taffeta and she's got beautiful hair, the kind that you can really comb." And with that, she flounced off, Kathy trailing behind.

"Dumb girls," I muttered.

"Yeah," said Tim.

Still, I must have touched a nerve, because it was a long time before she mentioned my nailing job again.

*   *   *

By now, the workmen had begun framing out the exterior walls. On the floor, at precisely marked intervals, they laid out parallel rows of two-by-fours — "studs," my father said these were called. Then they nailed the ends of the studs to crossbeams — sole plates and top plates. Openings were left for windows and doors, and these were framed double at the top and bottom for extra strength. As soon as a wall frame was completed, the men got together and pulled it upright. Carefully they jockeyed it into position along the outside edge of the floor, then nailed it down and braced it at the corners. One wall at a time, the house was being closed in.

I helped out whenever I could. Wary now of making any more laughable mistakes, I stuck to safe jobs. I stood by and handed my father the tools he asked for. I ran errands. I fetched water and cups of coffee. But as my father and the workmen proceeded with the framing, I dared to try the hammer again. To my great satisfaction I discovered that the more I did it, the better I got. I still bent nails now and then, still bashed my fingers once in a while. But more of my nails were going in straight and more of them were ending up in places where they would actually do some good. My father offered no praise, but since he had no criticisms either, I guessed I was getting the hang of it. Good work, it seemed, was nothing special and certainly nothing to crow about; it was just expected, and that, as my father liked to say, was all there was to it.

He seemed encouraged by my progress, however, because he was soon giving me lessons in how to handle a saw. Like hammering nails, sawing looked easy. For weeks I had been watching the carpenters as they cut joists, floorboards, and studs. For the big jobs they used electric saws: nasty things with circular blades that whirred and shrieked and could take off a finger or a hand in an instant. I had no intention of getting anywhere near one of those. But on smaller, more exacting jobs, the men used handsaws, which looked much less dangerous. With a handsaw, it appeared, all you had to do was pump the blade up and back across the wood and keep at it until the end of the board fell off.

But of course there was more to it than that. Whatever the job, there was always more to it.

Setting a scrap of lumber on the edge of a wooden milk crate, my father showed me how to brace the piece with my knee. Then, leaning over me from behind, he engulfed my saw hand in his huge fist. His breath was hot on my neck, and his sweaty warmth washed over me. I noticed for the first time that his fingers were thick and stubby, and that his hands had little black hairs growing out the backs of them. His embrace was as close to a hug as he ever gave, and I was torn between not wanting it to stop and feeling that I would suffocate if it went on any longer.

Leaning over me with his big hand on mine, he showed me how to start the cut by drawing the blade with light upward strokes.

"See?" he said. "Just lightly. Up and back."

Sure enough, a little cut began to appear on the edge of the wood. Next he showed me how to stroke the blade easily up and down, not forcing it but letting the saw itself do the work.

When he finally backed off and let me do it myself, things immediately began to go wrong. The board slewed away under my knee. I put more pressure on it and got it to stay put, but then my cut did not go straight. It was hard work and frustrating. But I didn't dare give up, not with my father so close, watching every move I made.

I ruined a lot of good scrap lumber that day and in the days that followed. But after a while I began to see a change. The wood did not wobble around so much. My cuts got straighter. One day, with my father helping with the measurements, I managed to cut four pieces of wood to roughly equal lengths. I nailed the pieces together, and when I was finished I stood back proudly to examine my creation: a box. Its sides weren't exactly even, and it had no top or bottom. But it definitely resembled a box.

My father seemed to agree. "Hmm," he said, and nodded exactly once.

Despite my first successes with hammers and saws, I knew I still had a long way to go before I'd be capable of building anything as grand as a house. But I was making a start.

These days, looking back, I realize that along the way I was also learning something besides an immediate, applicable skill. As I watched my father and the men who came to work on our house, I was acquiring an abiding admiration and respect for all those for whom the mysteries of tools and materials seemed to hold no mystery at all: men who cut boards without ragged ends, who drove nails without bending them, who built walls and roofs that were straight and strong. To me such men were as much heroes as the Lone Ranger or Hopalong Cassidy. That they also got dirty and sweaty, that "damns" and "hells" and even worse words rolled off their tongues with thrilling ease, only added to their stature in my eyes.

Working, such men had about them an air of competence that inspired in me envy and something approaching awe. There was nothing I wanted more than someday to be able to do the things they did and talk the way they did, and to do it all with the same cocky self-assurance. No matter what had to be hammered, sawed, cemented, or screwed in, no matter what had to be attached or laid down, fixed or finished, my father and the men who came to help him somehow seemed to know just what to do and how to do it. And if on occasion even the best of them made mistakes — missed a nail, or cut a board too short, or snipped a wire too long — it didn't faze them. They might swear a little, but somehow they knew which mistakes could be ignored and which ones needed fixing. They did not get stuck or give up, but simply did what had to be done and went on to the next job.

How did they manage it? I wondered. Was it just a matter of doing a thing so often that you could almost do it with your eyes closed?

Practice was certainly part of the secret. But knowing the right words also seemed essential — and not just the swear words. For as I was discovering, builders, like the priests in church, had a language all their own. A board was not just a board. It was a sill or a joist, a plate or a stud. If it lay at the bottom of a wall and had studs standing on it, it was a sole. If it spanned the top of a door or window, it was a lintel or a header. The name depended on the size of the board, where it was placed, and what it was being used for. Unless a man knew what to call things, unless he was fluent in the language of building, he would not know which board went where or what it was supposed to do.

Even nails had a special vocabulary, which varied according to the material being nailed (wood or masonry); the nature of the job (framing, flooring, siding, roofing, or trim); their size (from two penny on up to eight, ten, or even sixty penny); their type (common, finishing, or casing); and the material of which they were made (aluminum or galvanized steel).

The same was true of screws (which could be flathead, roundhead, or Phillips head) and bolts (machine, carriage, lag, or stove).

Hammers were not just hammers, they were claw hammers, tack hammers, and ball peen hammers, each of which came in many sizes.

Saws likewise came in multiple sizes and shapes. Ripsaws were for cutting a board lengthwise; crosscut saws were for cutting across the grain. There were backsaws for cutting molding; coping saws for cutting curves; compass saws for cutting curves and holes; hacksaws for cutting metal.

Of screwdrivers, too, there were a half-dozen types and sizes, as there were of pliers and wrenches; drills, braces, and bits; planes, chisels, and gouges.

Yet my father and the other men always seemed to know which tool to use for which job. And as if that weren't amazing enough, they also seemed to have a special language for the work itself, and this had mysteries of its own. They spoke of jimmying and bracing, routing and planing. Most of these words and the jobs they described seemed clear enough at first. But then it occurred to me that there was something odd about many of them. Planes and planing, for instance, had nothing to do with what we saw when my father packed us in the car on Sunday afternoons and drove us over to Mitchell Field to watch the airplanes take off and land. I was surprised, too, when I heard the carpenters speak of making something plumb when obviously the job they were doing had nothing at all to do with fruit. It was like what happened when my father spoke of driving a nail home. He clearly meant something very different from what he did with the car at the end of an afternoon outing.

Words, then, were not always so fixed and precise as they appeared to be. Their meanings did not stay put the way a board did when you nailed it down. The same words could have very different meanings. Words, it seemed, could be as slippery as oil, as elusive as the beads of mercury that rolled around in your hand after you accidentally broke open a thermometer. So knowing the words was only half the battle. Finding out what they really meant when people used them — that was the trick. But if you could manage it, you acquired a kind of power: the power to get things done. Real things. Things that mattered, like driving a car and making machines work and even building something as incredibly big and complicated as the house that was now taking shape in a place where before there had been nothing but an empty field.

9

GLORY

We were ghosts on the prowl, unsettled spirits come to haunt the living. We shrieked. We moaned. We cried unearthly cries. We drifted through walls.

For my sister and me it was a fine new game. We had made a wonderful discovery: in our new house we did not have to use doorways to go from room to room. We could walk right through the walls, like creatures from beyond the grave!

The game was only possible, though, because the interior walls were still only rows of studs. The whole house, in fact, was little more than a boxy framework of studs, headers, and joists: an airy wooden cage with smaller cages inside to signify rooms. It had no roof and no real walls. The wind blew through it. The sun shafted in through the crossbeams, painting the floor with zebra stripes. What better place to play at being prisoners? Or animals in the zoo? Or ghosts on the prowl?

Beauty had taught us the ghost game. It happened one Sunday afternoon in early June, when Aunt Marcella and Uncle Ray came to visit. With them came their children, Elaine and Edmund, who were at least four or five years older than my sister and me and so did not seem like children at all.

My father was happily showing off the work he had done since their last visit, leading everyone on what he referred to as "The Grand Tour."

"This will be the living room," he said, standing in the middle of the largest space. "That hole on the far wall, that's where the fireplace is going to go."

"Good planning," said Uncle Ray. "That'll make it easy for the smoke to get out."

"Tsk," said Aunt Marcella.

My mother giggled.

My father ignored the joke. "Through there," he continued, "will be the master bedroom. And through here . . ."

As he led the way from room to room, my father seemed taller than usual, his voice heartier, his chest puffed out beneath his baggy work shirt. I was strutting a little myself. I was proud of the new house that he was building for us, which, I was sure, was better than anything my cousins could imagine.

True, Elaine and Edmund had other advantages. Elaine could play "Moonlight Sonata" on the piano. Edmund was an Eagle Scout and got to wear a uniform with a yellow kerchief around his neck and a forest green sash across his chest, down which marched whole platoons of merit badges. Then, too, Elaine and Edmund had a father who read comic books and told silly jokes. My father was never silly. To him comic books were nothing but a waste of time. He never looked at one himself and barely tolerated them for us kids.

Still, I would not have traded places with my cousins for anything. Uncle Ray might be funny and easygoing, but was he building a house? He was not. Nor was any other father or uncle that I knew of. My father was the only one, and that made me feel a whole lot luckier than my poor deprived cousins, whose own home was a dingy upstairs apartment in a crowded neighborhood in the city and whose yard was the size of a postage stamp.

Nor did my cousins have a dog, let alone one as smart as ours.

"Hey, look at what Beauty's doing," Joyce said as my father was leading us from the front bedrooms to where the kitchen would be. While we well-behaved humans were dutifully following the prescribed route along the hall and through the various doorways, Beauty blithely ignored all such architectural niceties and was threading her dainty way in and out among the studs.

Well, if she could do it, why couldn't we? Which was how Joyce and I came to be ghosts: disembodied spirits, moaning and keening and cackling.

Unfortunately, our cousins were not at all interested in joining in. Worse, they acted as if they had no idea what we were doing. Elaine looked at us as if she thought we were crazy. Edmund simply walked away. Pretending to be ghosts was childish, it seemed. Big kids didn't do such things.

I wavered, my enthusiasm drooping in the face of my cousins' lofty disdain. But Joyce didn't seem to care what anyone thought. If anything, her groans and spooky noises only got louder and more insistent. Too bad for you, she seemed to say. This is our house and we can do what we want.

Her example was inspiring. My courage returned. Sometimes, I decided, my sister was okay.

No family visit could end without a photograph being taken, and today's visit was no different.

"Come on over here, where the light's better," my father told us. He had the little box Brownie in his hands.

Scenes like this happened on every special occasion, as well as on many that only became special because he thought to bring the camera. Cheerfully he herded us to the sunny side of the house: the back side, where the framed-out windows overlooked the still unfinished and un-roofed basement-level garage.

According to my father's plan, the flat roof of the garage would one day serve as a broad terrace running across the back of the house. When it was finished, you'd be able to step out the back door onto the sun-filled terrace, where you'd have a splendid view of a spreading lawn, a veg-etable garden, maybe some fruit trees, and the woods beyond. At least, that was the plan. For now, what you'd get if you stepped out the back door was a drop of eight or nine feet to the concrete floor of the garage.

To me it was a terrifying prospect. All I had to do was stand in that doorway and look down, and my knees would turn to jelly. I could see myself tripping over the edge, like some comic book character going over a cliff, arms and legs windmilling as I dropped through space, a vivid "yeeeoow" coming out of my mouth in ever-diminishing letters. In the end all anyone would see would be a puff of dust on the concrete floor below. Across the puff of dust a single word would be printed in capital letters, followed by at least two exclamation points: SPLAT!!

My mother, assigned the camera duties, took the Brownie to the far side of the garage, lined up the shot, and tripped the shutter. The picture she snapped that day shows most of us — uncle, aunt, cousins, my sister, and me — arranged safely behind the frame of the kitchen window. My father stands apart, framed in the back doorway, the peak of his painter's cap shading his eyes as he leans nonchalantly against the doorpost. Poised in that doorway to nowhere, on the very edge of disaster, he seems oblivious to any danger.

Examined now, all these years later, the photograph seems ripe with foreboding. Looking back I am able to see, God-like, so much of what lay ahead. But I have to remind myself that it is only hindsight that makes his pose so precarious, so freighted with symbolism. For on that sun-blessed afternoon, when not a cloud marred the late-spring sky, neither my father nor anyone else could have had any inkling of what the future held. On the contrary. Standing there on the brink, defying gravity, challenging fate, my father wears a look of utter satisfaction. He is in his glory, surrounded by the work of his hands: his house, his triumph.

During the days that followed, my father spent every afternoon perched on a scaffold, hammer in hand. The carpenter's apron he wore around his waist bulged with nails. And at his feet were stacks of rough lumber: the sheathing he was nailing to the frame of the house.

Sheathing, as I later learned, is used to brace the frame of the house, giving muscle to the skeleton of studs and crossbeams. It makes the outer walls airtight and provides a surface onto which the finished layer of siding can be nailed. Nowadays sheathing is usually made of plywood. But at that time, planking was more common. It was also cheaper than plywood.

Mostly my father worked alone. The job was fairly straightforward, and by doing it himself, he was able to save a good deal of money. He worked fast. He was using up vacation time, and every minute counted. The results were evident in just a few days. With the studs covered over, the house no longer looked like a giant bird cage. Now it had the squared-off, graceless shape of an overgrown shoe box: a still-roofless rectangle, with openings here and there for doors, windows, and chimney.

The work took its toll. My father spent so many hours swinging a hammer that he found it difficult to stop. Even in his sleep his right arm continued banging away, which made quite an impression on my mother as she lay beside him in their bed in the corner of the cabin. Only by shaking my father awake was Mom able to save herself from being pounded to the wall like one more piece of sheathing.

Once the frame was closed in, my father faced a job he could not manage on his own: raising the roof. A call went out to the builder as well as to every able-bodied brother and brother-in-law who could spare a few hours. Uncle Tad came. So did Uncle Ray and Uncle Norb, my aunt Bernadine's husband. So did Uncle Alray, a wiry, sharp-nosed man who was my aunt Laurie's husband.

That afternoon I watched as my father and the other men set to work measuring, sawing, and hammering sets of timbers into triangular patterns. At first I did not understand what they were doing. How could you make a roof by building triangles on the floor? But as soon as the first of the forms was lifted to the top of the house and set into place at one end, its purpose became clear. Suddenly, what had been a shoe box began to take on the contours of a real house. The bare outline of a peaked roof made all the difference.

After mounting rafters at each end of the house, the men used ropes and pulleys to hoist the ridgepole to the peak. Made of a series of timbers spliced together, the ridgepole was the longest board in the house. It took three men balanced on ladders and two others helping from below to ease the beam into the gap at the top of the rafters. Quickly they set a few more rafters into place to brace it, then leveled it and nailed it tight.

"Looking good," Uncle Tad said, climbing down from his ladder.

My father nodded. "Yes," he said. "Yes, it really is." And he looked as happy as I had ever seen him.

By the time the team of paid and volunteer carpenters had finished framing out the roof, sheathing it over with boards, and covering it with tar paper and shingles, full summer had arrived. The mud around the cabin had been baked hard by the sun. Robins chirped in the grass and tipped their heads, listening for worms. Redwings trilled on the fence posts.

The field across the road was ankle deep in alfalfa. My woods, which in winter had looked like a gauzy curtain drawn across the back of our property, all bare branches and gray light, now seemed as thick and green as velvet drapery.

My woods. I had earned the right to call them that.

Ever since the first day my father brought us to visit the site of our new home-to-be — the day we had our cowboy picnic of hot dogs and beans in the box-canyon excavation — I had felt drawn toward that mysterious world that began at the back of our property. On every other side of us the land lay open and broad. Fields spread to the horizon as far as I could see. Everything was visible: every lone tree and house and distant silo, every fence post, every cow. Nothing was concealed. There were no secrets, no fathomless shadows, nothing to dread.

The woods were different. The tree line marked the beginning of the unknown, the unseen. Where the woods began, there was no horizon to carry my eye far and beyond. I could see no farther than the first line of trees. Whatever else was to be found there was hidden behind a leaf-woven tapestry. There were secrets there, I was sure of it: exciting things, made all the more inviting for being hidden and unknown. But finding the secrets meant I would have to be much braver than I felt on that first day. I was still too small and too overwhelmed by the newness of everything around me to dare to venture far from the smoking cook fire of our Wild West camp.

Yet the haunting image of that curtain of trees stayed in my mind, turning up in my dreams, beckoning me each time we returned to the building site. Eventually I worked up my courage. One day early in that first summer, when I was wandering aimlessly through the acre of waist-high prairie grass that was our backyard, I found myself nearer to the tree line than I had ever been before. The woods, I saw, were guarded by an impenetrable tangle of shrubs and brambles. But beyond this prickly hedge I could see that the forest, far from forming a solid wall, was actually made up of a jumble of trunks, branches, and undergrowth, with trees beyond trees as far back as I could see. Then, somewhere in the middle distance, the trunks and branches blended together and became a shadowy blur.

A person could get lost in there, I realized as I stood peering past the brambles. The silence was oppressive. Nothing stirred — except my imagination. I pictured wild animals living in there: rattlesnakes, bears, cougars. Maybe Indians, too. Well, maybe not. As far as I knew there were no longer any Indians anywhere except in comic books and in the Lone Ranger movies my parents sometimes took us to see on Saturday afternoons. But I also knew that whatever or whoever was lurking there in the dimness and the silence could be watching me now, waiting for me to come closer, just a little closer. . . .

Suddenly I heard a rustling in the grass behind me. My heart leaped into my throat. I whirled around. Not five steps away stood — my sister!

"Scared you, didn't I?" she said, smirking.

"No, you didn't."

"Bet I did." She lifted her chin, giving me her most superior look. "Anyway, I can go wherever I want."

"Well, go someplace else." I didn't like her being able to sneak up on me.

"Maybe I will and maybe I won't. Besides, if I didn't scare you, why did you stop?"

"I didn't stop."

"I saw you. You were walking and then you stopped."

"I was just, uh, looking at the woods."

She turned her eyes toward the dark tangle of trees. She wound the end of one pigtail around her finger. Her voice fell to a whisper. "They're scary," she said.

I followed her gaze. The woods were full of shadows. Secretly I was relieved that she had come.

"There's nothing to be scared of," I said, bolstering my own courage. "Come on. Let's play explorers. I'll be Daniel Boone." I had learned all about Daniel Boone in one of the Little Golden Books that my mother read to me at bedtime.

"Who will I be?" Joyce asked.

I thought a moment. "How about Dale Evans?"

Dale was Roy Rogers's wife and a favorite of Joyce's. Besides, there weren't a lot of alternatives. Dale was the only frontier girl hero either of us had ever heard of other than Pocahontas. And *she* was an Indian.

That settled, we began working our way along the edge of the trees, looking for an opening through the shrubs and brambles. A crow called from a nearby branch. He was as black and shiny as a new car. He looked at us with one eye, then bent his legs, opened his wings, and flew away. We heard a rustling in the dry leaves and saw a squirrel hopping toward a tree. He stopped, sat up on his hind legs, and looked us over. Apparently he did not think we were worth worrying about, because he did not hurry away, but only hopped a few feet and went back to digging in the leaves.

At the far corner of our property, where the next-door neighbor's fence began, the woods ended abruptly, giving way to an open field. That's where I saw what we'd been looking for. "Hey, look," I said.

Running along the edge of the field was a narrow path. To the right it rose gently toward a distant house and barn. To the left it disappeared into the woods through an opening in the underbrush.

Joyce said, "We better go back."

But something had emboldened me. "Don't you want to see where it goes?"

"Well . . ."

"Come on," I said, and went ahead.

This was new for me. I was taking the lead, and when I thought about it later I decided I liked it. The amazing thing was that my sister didn't seem to mind a bit. Usually she could not tolerate my being first in anything. And usually I didn't disappoint her. Here in the woods, though, things seemed to be different for both of us.

The woods were not as dark from within as they'd looked from a distance. Sunlight filtered through the treetops, spotting the undergrowth and the darkest shadows with bright patches of light: shimmering greens, dazzling yellows and whites. It was like being in church, with the light coming in through stained-glass windows.

At first the path followed the edge of the woods. In damp places on the ground we saw the tracks of animals, though of what kind we did not know. We disturbed more squirrels. We passed trees with trunks so thick the two of us could not have reached our arms around them. Some trees were gnarled and bent, with low branches sprouting not far above our fingertips. Others were smooth barked and rose as straight as telephone poles, with the lowest branches well beyond reach.

As we walked, we saw amazing things. We came to a fallen tree that was alive with beetles and ants. "Eieww," said Joyce, wrinkling her nose. But I was fascinated. I bent closer and saw the bugs scrambling busily in and out of the dead wood, which was so rotten in places that it merged with the earth.

Off in the distance, we heard a hollow rat-a-tat-tat, like a carpenter with an incredibly fast hammer. When we got closer, we saw that the sound came from a woodpecker who was using his beak to dig a hole in the side of a dead tree. He had a red head, just like Woody in the comics, and was walking straight up the trunk as casually as if he were on level ground. How he managed it without falling off I could not tell. I was beginning to learn just how full of puzzles and surprises the woods could be.

Turning away from the sunny edge, the path continued deeper into the shadows. Here and there, it intersected other paths, each one offering its own invitation, its own promise of mystery. The path was like a story in a book. At every turn was a new page, and I wanted to go on turning the pages, to keep the story going.

How far we went I had no idea, but after a while I heard Joyce say, "Let's go back. Okay?" Her voice, I was pleased to hear, was just a little shaky.

"What's the matter, you afraid?" I asked.

"No, it's just —"

"Come on. Let's just see what's around that big tree over there."

"I think we should go back. We've been gone a long time. Mommy will wonder where we are."

"Aw . . ." Reluctantly I turned around, but only after promising myself that I would come back here again.

"Do you know the way?" Joyce asked as we started back.

For the second time that day I surprised myself. "Sure," I said, and knew with stunning certainty that I could lead us back with no trouble at all.

Sure enough, despite twists and turns and branching paths, I brought us out at exactly the place where we had started. Daniel Boone could not have done better. I didn't know how I knew the way, but I seemed to be guided by some instinct that until that day I had no idea I possessed.

I returned to the woods many times after that, sometimes with my sister or my friend Timmy but more often alone or with only Beauty for company. Confident of my newfound skill, I was never afraid of getting lost. Soon I knew all the paths — at least those close to home. I found a secret glade where two streams came together, and where, I was sure, no white man had ever set foot before. Not far beyond the glade, the woods were interrupted on one side by a farmer's field, and beyond that they went on again, farther than I could see and farther than I could go and still get home in time for supper.

The woods became my playground. Using castoff boards from the building site, Tim and I built a fort among some fallen trees, then took turns defending it from each other. For hours at a time the forest echoed with bloodcurdling Indian war whoops and explosions of gunfire. My Hopalong Cassidy revolver made only pathetic little clicks, and I longed for a cap gun that made real shooting sounds. But by puffing out my cheeks and gargling the spit at the back of my mouth, I was able to make a passable imitation of a gun going off.

"Kgsshh! Kgsshh! You're dead."

"No, I'm not. You missed me."

I fired again.

Tim screamed and fell.

I leaped up to make sure he was dead.

He wasn't. From where he lay curled up in the leaves, he got off a sneak shot at point-blank range.

I tumbled to the ground, mortally wounded.

Every trip to the woods and fields became an adventure, their secrets at once drawing me in and making me tremble with the thrilling anxiety of not knowing what might lie around the next tree, beyond the next windrow. A garter snake darting across my path could take my breath away in sheer surprise. The sight of a hawk wheeling silently overhead left me staring in awe and wondering what the world must look like from up there.

One afternoon, I found myself farther from home than I had ever ventured before. I was at least three fields away and tramping through high grass when I caught a whiff of something so foul, so sickeningly sweet that it made my eyes water. I took a few more steps. The smell grew stronger. I came around a stand of trees, and all at once the ground in front of me seemed to explode with a clatter of wings and huge black forms. I jumped back, my heart in my throat. The birds were enormous and ugly, and I realized all at once that what I was looking at were buzzards. Until now I had only ever heard the word in cowboy movies and radio shows. Yet suddenly I knew what buzzards were. They had scrawny red heads, vicious hooked beaks, and beady little eyes, and as they leaped up and away they looked like a dozen magician's cloaks flung into the air.

Where had they come from? I wondered. What were they doing here? Curiosity overcame my dread and revulsion at the incredible stink. Holding my nose, I took a cautious step forward, then another. Topping a small rise, I found myself staring into a shallow pit, and what I saw there made my stomach heave.

In the pit lay a stinking heap of flesh and fur. I recognized the vague shapes and color of deer, probably half a dozen of them, although it was hard to tell, so tangled were the body parts. I saw slashes of red. I saw white bones poking out. I saw ribs. Legs everywhere. Antlers. Skulls with empty eye sockets. Mutilated heads, fly covered and lying at twisted angles.

Was this what death looked like: not neat and tidy like the deaths of the bad guys in the movies, with just a little spot of blood here or there, eyes closed benignly? No, this was different. This was horrible. These mangled, smelly corpses were so incredibly foul that even as I turned away my stomach rose to my throat and I spewed my lunch out onto the grass.

What the corpses of those deer were doing there I never learned. Perhaps the deer had become a nuisance to the farmer who owned the land, foraging in his pastures or stealing his apples. Perhaps they were diseased or wounded and had been put out of their misery. But the sight and smell of their rotten flesh stayed with me for years, a nightmare vision of death, primal and unadorned, with no trappings of prayer or spirit or ritual to cloak its raw reality.

That evening, for supper, my mother served meat loaf. I couldn't eat a thing.

"What's wrong?" she asked. "Aren't you feeling well?"

"I'm just not hungry."

My father said: "You'll sit there until you finish, young man."

I sat there, but I couldn't finish. How could I tell them about the awful thing I had seen? I felt guilty, as if I had witnessed something I wasn't supposed to see and gone somewhere I wasn't supposed to have been.

I went to bed early. That night my dreams were full of terrible images. One was of an old man rising from under the ground with a set of antlers sticking out the top of his head and with half of his face caved in and bloody. I looked again and realized the face was familiar. But whose was it? Then he turned and I saw it was my grampa Froncek. I cried out and woke with a start, then lay awake staring at the ceiling over my bunk, afraid to close my eyes for fear he would be there again.

Grampa Froncek had died only a few months earlier. My sister and I had not been allowed to attend the funeral. "It's not for kids," my father had said. All he told us was that Grampa was dead and had "gone to heaven."

I was not unhappy about my grandfather's death. The few times I had seen him, I had always found him scary: a tall man with white hair and sour breath who seemed to be sullen and angry.

The night after the funeral, I heard my parents talking in low voices from their bed in the corner: "... a shame ... to be all alone like that ... that dingy room ..." At the time I had no idea what they were talking about. Only many years later did I hear the stories: how my grandfather had come to America from Poland to work in the iron foundries; how he had met his wife-to-be while singing in the church choir; how he had raised a family and prospered until he was brought low by the Depression, the country's and his own. In hushed tones I was told by an aunt and uncle of the drunken bully he had become, battling with his wife and oldest daughter until finally they drove him out of the house. He lived out the last twenty years of his life broken and alone, scraping together a pathetic existence as a janitor in a downtown apartment house.

One Sunday afternoon not long after the funeral, my father took us to visit the cemetery where Grampa was buried. We stood before a mound of bare earth. My father kneeled and bowed his head, then crossed himself and folded his hands in prayer. He looked very sad, so I bowed my head and tried to look sad, too.

And yet at the time I could not grasp what any of it really meant: to die, to close your eyes and not see or hear or even dream anything, and then to be laid in a hole in the ground and have the dirt piled on top of you and not be able to breathe! And what happened to you then? In school we were taught that you went to either heaven or hell — to a beautiful place of saints and angels or a horrible, painful place of ever-lasting fire. But I knew now what dying looked like. It was ugly and bloody, and it stank so bad it could make you sick. And I never wanted it to happen to me or my sister or my parents or Beauty or anybody else I knew.

Work on the house went quickly now.

With the help of a young apprentice carpenter, my father installed the windows and doors, fitting them snugly into their frames.

While they worked, a truckload of bricks was delivered, and a few days later two masons were busy in the basement on the foundation for the fireplace and chimney. Using levels and plumb lines to ensure that each row of bricks would be straight and true, they laid down row on row, building a massive tower that eventually reached to the main floor. Inside the tower were ceramic pipes: flues to carry smoke from the furnace up the chimney and ashes from the fireplace down to the basement. Reaching the main floor, the masons laid out a hearth and fireplace, fitting the bricks at complicated angles. Then they continued on, raising their tower toward the roof.

Observing them, I was amazed by their patience. I liked playing with blocks as much as any kid, but it was beyond me how anyone could spend days and days doing nothing but laying down one brick after another. If this was what grown-up work was like, I was pretty sure I did not want any part of it. And yet, when the masons were done, our house had a real fireplace and a tall chimney, just like the one shown in my father's drawings.

Electricians came, setting junction boxes for outlets, switches, and lights, then stringing cable through studs and ceiling joists until all the boxes were connected. It was like watching spiders at work. When the men were through, the whole house seemed spun together like a giant web. But it was a web that had power in every strand: power to light up the rooms at night, and to run my father's tools, and to keep his radio going while he worked.

From the house now drifted the cheerful sounds of Peggy Lee singing "It's a good day from morning till night," and a man with a milky-smooth voice crooning about how he was going to get someone on a slow boat to China. Now and then I heard my favorite: a spooky song about a cowboy who sees ghost riders in the sky. One of the riders calls the cowboy's name and gives him a stern warning:

If you want to save your soul from hell
a ridin' on our range,
then cowboy change your ways today
or with us you will ride,
a tryin' to catch the Devil's herd . . .
across these endless skies.

That summer, too, the radio brought the news that a jet airliner had been tested for the first time, opening up the possibility of commercial jet travel. What must it be like to fly in a plane, I wondered? And would I ever get to do it? Meanwhile, from Rome, where I knew the Holy Father lived, came word that the bones of Saint Peter were believed to have been found beneath the main altar in Saint Peter's Basilica.

"Imagine that," my mother said, so I knew it was somehow important.

In what the announcer solemnly referred to as "our nation's capital," the House Un-American Activities Committee was proposing to screen children's schoolbooks for "subversive material." I didn't know what that meant, but it sounded dangerous. So did a man with the sneaky, snake-like name of Alger Hiss, who was being accused of spying for the Communists — the same people who were going to come down from Alaska someday and torture us to make us stop being Catholic.

About such things my parents said nothing. In school I learned that in places like Communist Red Russia children were encouraged to turn their parents in to the police for saying things against the government. But my parents never uttered a word about the government that I ever heard.

No sooner had the electricians left than the carpenters began covering the inside walls and ceiling joists with thin strips of lathing. They were followed by a crew of men in white overalls, who covered the lathing with oatmeal-thick plaster. The ghosting days were over for my sister and me. No longer would we be able to walk through walls. The rooms had become real rooms at last: closed-in spaces that were filled for the moment with nothing but echoes.

102

Now, for the first time, I was able to see what my room was actually going to look like. It was the smallest in the house except for the bathroom. But it was mine, and that made it the best one of all: a palace, or better yet, a fort, just right for keeping out enemies. It needed only a door to make it perfect, and before long it had that, too.

The most fun came when a plumber set to work hooking up the pipes that would bring water to our bathroom and kitchen. A round, jowly man, he brought with him an incredible array of wrenches, odd lengths of pipe, and boxes of chrome fixtures that were so shiny I could see my face in them. But it was not the man's tools or the gleaming appliances that made him such fun to watch. It was his sagging trousers, which he wore without a belt or suspenders and which seemed forever on the verge of falling down around his ankles. Joyce and I particularly enjoyed bringing our friends to watch him when he was down on his hands and knees, with his head and shoulders jammed in under our kitchen sink. The view was hilarious, for above the waistband of his trousers we could plainly see the cleft of his broad, hairy backside.

"Come away from there," my mother demanded when she caught us pointing and struggling to suppress our giggles.

"What say?" came the plumber's voice from under the sink.

"Nothing. That's all right," Mom told him as she shooed us outside.

Then came a special day, when my father and a few of my uncles set to work laying the finished floor over the rough subfloor in the living room. What they did not know was that they were giving me a precious gift. For as I watched them laying down thin new strips of fir over the rough pine floorboards, I saw that if they kept going they would obliterate every trace of my first clumsy efforts with hammer and nails.

Sure enough, when they were through, not a single one of my bent or twisted nails was to be seen anywhere. I was safe. All evidence of my ineptitude had been concealed forever.

Not everything went smoothly all the time. Materials were not delivered when they were supposed to be. The plumber had to come back and fix a leaky pipe in the basement. There was a misunderstanding about which color the painters were supposed to have painted my parents' room, which ended up being light blue instead of pink, the way my mother had wanted it.

Then, in July, the weather turned bad. For days on end it rained and rained. All exterior work came to a halt. The ground was saturated, and when my father returned from work one day he found the garage entrance blocked by a mudslide. On the uphill side of the driveway, a concrete retaining wall that he had built to hold back the earth had caved in and would have to be rebuilt.

Concrete continued to be my father's worst nightmare. As with everything else he set his mind to, he believed that mastery would come if only he practiced enough. And if he could save some money in the process, so much the better. The retaining wall was one result. He was more circumspect when it came to laying the concrete roof of the garage, which would also serve as our back porch. For that tricky and potentially dangerous operation he hired professionals and swallowed the cost. But the broad cement steps that led from the porch to the backyard — that was another story. He tackled the project with a determination that was equal parts thrift and stubbornness.

But the concrete arts continued to elude him. Built on an inadequate foundation, the steps settled at an awkward angle, developed their own San Andreas Fault, and in the end had to be ripped out and done over again.

"He was okay, your dad," Uncle Eddy told me years later with an annoying touch of condescension. "But when it came to concrete he just didn't know his ass from his elbow."

Still, Dad had made the effort, and there were those who were mightily impressed. Among them was his oldest brother, Edward. So inspired was he by my father's accomplishment that he announced one day that he, too, was going to build a house.

"Are you crazy?" Uncle Tad remembered saying to him. "After all Walter's been through?"

But Edward eventually did what he said. When the stubbornness genes were being doled out, the Froncek family seems to have gotten more than its share.

By the end of the summer of 1949, the house was finished, at least enough so that my mother and father felt the moment had come when we could move in. Short of money and time, my father had not yet gotten around to putting the siding on the back wall. It was still covered in tar paper, which smelled like burnt cork and made your hands black when you touched it. As for the closed-in sun-room on the back porch, it hadn't even been started yet. And the yard around the house was still a sea of mud.

But after living in a cramped cabin for over a year, my parents were not about to delay moving any longer than they had to. Why should they? After all, the roof was on, the windows were in place, the walls were insulated and painted, and the floors were varnished. When you flipped a wall switch, the overhead light went on. When you turned a faucet, presto! water came out of the tap. A touch of the thermostat, and the furnace in the basement kicked in, sending warm air pumping through the house. When *this* winter came, there would be no more flashlight trips to the outhouse, and no more bathing in washtubs.

My father was enormously proud. He loved showing the place off whenever a sister or brother or in-law dropped by with their family to tramp through the still-empty rooms. Some saw only the flaws. Uncle Eddy pounced with relish on each place where the molding corners did not come together exactly right. Grampa Raniszewski wondered about the uneven floor in the basement and noticed that the back steps were crooked. Some, like Aunt Helen, widowed and bitter, were tight-lipped with envy. But most — among them Uncle Tad, Uncle Alray, Aunt Laurie — oohed and aahed in all the right places, causing my father to smile in a way that gave all of us pleasure.

I shared his pride. I was proud of him for planning the house and for knowing how to get it built. I was proud, too, of having been part of it. Even though I had not been allowed to help with all of the building jobs, I had seen each one of them happening. I knew firsthand how all the pieces went together. From now on I would never be able to look at our house — or any other for that matter — without seeing it as a living, breathing thing: how beneath its skin of plastered walls and siding lay a timber skeleton, arteries to carry water, and nervelike cables and junction boxes to carry power to light our lights and run our Hoover and toast our bread.

Yet pride is hardly an adequate way to describe what I felt. I could not have put it into words at the time, but what impressed me and stayed with me for years afterward was something more like awe: the sense of having participated in a great adventure.

10

MYSTERIES

"*In nomine patris . . .*"
Swish.
"*. . . et filii . . .*"
Swish.
"*. . . et spiritus sancti.*"
Swish.
With each flick of his silver wand, Father Beyer let loose a fine spray of water. Drops landed on the freshly painted walls and doorways, on my mother's new curtains, on the furniture, the rugs, the bedspreads.

I was amazed. If I had done such a thing, I would have gotten a good swat on my rear end. I looked up at my mother. "Mom," I whispered.

We were following Father Beyer from room to room, our palms pressed together, our fingertips pointed toward heaven.

"Come, Lord God, we humbly beg you," he intoned, "and fill this house with the serenity of your love, joy, and peace." He let fly another shower, this time hitting the mirror over my mother's dresser.

"Mom," I whispered again, tugging at the hem of her dress.

"Shush." She brushed my hand away.

I backed off. Apparently no one minded that Father Beyer was getting everything wet. I thought probably that proved just how holy the water was. It didn't look any different from regular water. It made the same spots and drips. But obviously it had special powers; otherwise, why would it come in a silver holder and be treated in such a special way?

As I followed close at my parents' heels, I wondered how the water got that way. For a moment I thought maybe I'd ask Sister George, who was my new teacher in second grade. But then I decided it was probably another one of those mysteries of the faith that Sister always spoke of when any of us kids asked too many questions — like, for instance, what it meant that Mary was a virgin, or how blood could be turned into wine and why anyone would want to drink it if it had blood in it.

"That, children, is a mystery of the faith," Sister would say. Or sometimes, if she was in a particularly bad mood, she'd reply, "If you're going to be a troublemaker, you can go and stand in the cloak room."

In either case, satisfactory answers were hard to come by.

One thing was certain: I was not about to ask Father Beyer. He was even scarier than Sister was. A big man with a big head, he had gray hair that was cropped close, like a soldier's. I had seen him many times at church and in school, where he was imposing enough. But close-up, here in our own house, he was positively terrifying. His voice was so deep it sounded as if he were speaking from inside a barrel, and his thin lips were set in a straight line that seemed never to deviate from the horizontal.

Back in the living room now, he swung around to face us. He raised his eyes to the ceiling. I looked up, too, but didn't see anything there. He prayed: "Sprinkle me, O Lord, with blessed water, and I shall be purified; wash me and I shall be whiter than snow."

He flicked the silver wand in our direction. Drops flew. A few fell on my cheek. They felt like tears. Now I, too, had been blessed. Now I was as holy as the water itself, and if I died in the next five minutes, before I had a chance to get into trouble, I would go straight to heaven.

"Shower your benediction upon all who dwell herein," Father Beyer prayed, "and may the peace and blessing of Almighty God rest upon this house and all who dwell in it. Amen."

"Amen," we answered, just as if we were in church.

The solemn prayers, the touch of the sacred water — everything was so mysterious and beautiful that I had no doubt whatever that God must have heard Father Beyer's prayers and from then on nothing bad would happen to us or to our new house. We were blessed. We were safe. Our lives would be filled with love and goodness and peace, and we would be completely happy for ever and ever.

I wonder now: Would all that followed — the disappointments, the seething anger — have been any less difficult if my expectations had not been raised to such heights? Or did that sweet childish belief make the rest easier to bear? I have no answer. Maybe it's just one more mystery of the faith. But at the time I had no questions, either. I was a sponge. I drank in everything that was poured out for me. I knew nothing of myth or metaphor or the power of ritual. To me, at seven, fantasy and reality were one and the same. God was as real as the gray stubble on Father Beyer's head; magic was as alive as the dancing drops of water that flew from his silver baton. Which was why, as I joined in the amen, I was so certain that our future in our new house would be utterly wonderful.

In the days that followed, my mother and father, too, seemed quietly content, as if something that needed to be done had been taken care of, settled at last. I doubt they took the ceremony quite as literally as I did, but neither was it a mere formality. Yes, it was their duty. Yes, it was what was expected of them as good Catholics moving into a new house. It was an obligation: to the Church, to their families, and not least to the edifice itself. "Unless the Lord build the house, they labor in vain who build it," says the psalm.

But in my parents' fervent "amen" there was also — I am sure of it — a yearning that went beyond ritual: a longing for reassurance, a hope of heavenly protection. They were out on a limb, my father especially. He had invested everything and more in this house: money, time, effort, pride. Building it was as much an act of faith in an uncertain future as bringing a new life into the world.

It had been built well, there was no doubt. The foundation was solid. The joints were tight. The walls were foursquare. And if the basement floor was a little wavy and the south front still needed siding, the roof at least was snug and secure. No water or drafts came in where they were not supposed to.

Yet my father of all people knew just how uncertain the future could be. The past was proof of that. He could not forget how, as a boy of seven, he had come close to dying of diphtheria. By that time two of his sisters were already dead — one in infancy, the other, Apolonia, at age seven, of tuberculosis. He himself pulled through only after spending two weeks in quarantine in the hospital, and only after his parents and his eight surviving brothers and sisters had prayed to his patron saints for his recovery. Then, when he was ten, his sister Violet, who was two years older than he, was stricken with leukemia and died a lingering death. At her funeral my father had walked behind her small casket and stood beside his grieving parents as she was lowered into the ground.

Standing there, at his sister's graveside, did my father weep? Did he think about how close he had come to being laid there? If so, he never talked about it. Some things you kept to yourself. Like grief, and fear, and love. But it was not the kind of thing you forgot.

The memory of death, depression, and war, and every day now the radio and newspapers shouting fears of a new war, nuclear war this time, more terrible than any that had gone before — there were more than enough reminders of just how precarious was the foundation upon which rested my father's new house. What comfort he must have found, then, in the priest's promise of God's blessing and protection, in the hope that it might just be true and please God, let it last, if only for a little while.

Not that you could have told any of this from the way my father and mother fluttered around Father Beyer once the blessings were done.

"Here, sit here," my father said, offering his own favorite chair. "Would you like something to drink? Would you like a beer? How about a highball?"

I watched Father Beyer returning his silver wand to its black case, nestling it in its bed of blue velvet, then snapping the case shut and tucking it away in his coat pocket. "Beer would be very fine," he said.

"One beer, coming right up. Alice, how about getting Father a beer."

"Of course, dear," my mother said in her sweetest voice and hurried into the kitchen.

Watching, I wondered what was happening. My mother and father seemed as jittery as Gramma's canary. I had never seen them this way before.

"So," Father Beyer said, settling into the seat of honor.

My father stayed standing. He seemed uncertain what to do next. Then, as if collecting himself, he turned abruptly and took a seat on the davenport. He gestured for Joyce and me to sit beside him.

"So," Father Beyer said again. He cleared his throat. "Very nice house you've built here."

"It, uh —" my father began, then he started again. "Thank you. It was a lot of work."

"I imagine so," said Father Beyer.

"It came out pretty good, though, I guess," my father went on, and he laughed abruptly, though what was funny I couldn't tell. "Of course, it's not done yet, so . . ."

"No," said Father Beyer.

"I still have to get the siding up on the back. And there's still no stairs to the basement. Anyone who opens that basement door better watch out. The first step is a doozy." He laughed again.

Father Beyer's straight mouth lifted faintly at the corners, but it was hardly a smile. "Did the work yourself, did you?"

"A lot of it. We all did. Even the kids here."

"Ah. Is that so?" Father Beyer raised an eyebrow. He seemed suddenly to notice that we were sitting before him, and he now turned his full attention upon us. In my mind, I pictured a wolf eyeing a pair of tender rabbits. "I imagine you children must be about ready for your First Communion, isn't that right?"

"Yes, Father," Joyce said brightly.

I looked at the floor. "Yes, Father," I whispered.

"I expect you both know your Apostles' Creed, then."

"Oh, yes, Father," Joyce replied without hesitation.

Uh-oh, I thought. He was going to test us. How does it go? I believe in God, the Father Almighty, and in . . . and in . . . My mind froze.

Fortunately, my mother returned just then with the beers and a dish of pretzels. She handed a glass and a bottle to Father Beyer and my father. Father Beyer poured his beer, then raised his glass in front of him. "To the new house," he said.

"To the new house," my father said.

Then I had it. "And-to-Jesus-Christ-His-only-son-our-Lord-who-was-buried-died-and-was-crustified," I blurted triumphantly.

Everyone's eyes turned toward me.

"What did you say?" asked my father.

Father Beyer glowered.

My ears burned. "The Creed," I said. "The 'Posles Creed."

Father Beyer nodded. He reached inside his black jacket. I don't know what I expected to see when he removed his hand. A catechism book? A ruler to swat me with? What he brought out was the longest, blackest cigar I had ever seen. He bit off an end, clamped his lips around it, then touched a match to it and puffed. Clouds of smoke enveloped his gray head. "I think," he said, puffing, then taking the cigar out and studying it carefully, "I think it needs a little work."

My father barked a laugh. "A little work! That's for sure. A little work is right. But he'll know it in time." He turned his grin on me. "Won't you, Tommy?"

I nodded earnestly. "Yes. Yes, I will."

"I'm sure he will," said Father Beyer, and for the first time he actually smiled.

That would have been the end of it, the last memory I had of that evening, except that what Father Beyer did next was so extraordinary it has stayed in my mind ever since. Taking a long draught of his cigar and tilting his head back, he made a circle with his thin lips, then sent a series of perfect little smoke rings rolling toward the ceiling. It was further proof — if any were needed — that magic had indeed been done in our house this night.

We had been in the house for little more than a week when Father Beyer came to spread blessings of water and smoke upon it and upon all who dwelled therein.

We had made the move on Labor Day weekend. From the cabin we had brought over the kitchen table and chairs, the pots, pans, and dishes, the clothes off the rack, the towels and bed linens from where they were stored in cartons beneath the bunk bed. From the basements and attics of aunts, uncles, and grandparents, my father retrieved our furniture, loaded it into the trailer, and hauled it to our new house.

"Where should I put it," I asked my father when he handed me a carton to carry in.

"Better ask the boss."

It was kind of a private joke of his, though what he meant by it I wasn't always sure. Sometimes he sounded annoyed or impatient when he said it, and other times there was a tenderness in his voice, almost as if he were calling her a nickname. Except that it never really made sense because we all knew perfectly well that he was the real boss. Grown-ups were funny that way, I thought. They could say things that seemed to mean one thing but really meant something else. Today, though, there was neither anger nor impatience in my father's voice. Today he was in a good mood. And so was my mother.

"Put it in Joyce's bedroom for now," she told me when I brought the box inside. She was busy laying shelf paper in the kitchen cupboards, and when I came in she'd been humming to herself. She wore pants and an old shirt, and her hair was covered with a scarf that was knotted in back, so it looked like a cap. She almost looked like a boy instead of a mom, I thought. But she also looked happy, and that made her look pretty, too. "And take that other box to your room," she added.

I looked around. The "other box" could have been any one of a dozen. But I chose the nearest one and carried it away.

By now there were boxes everywhere, in every room, along with end tables, chairs, lamps, dressers, rolled-up rugs, a piano bench, framed pictures propped against the walls, bundles of curtain rods, a sewing machine, a hassock, a coffee table. There were also headboards and slats from various beds, including Joyce's and mine, which matched and which we hadn't seen in more than a year.

The sight of the beds made me happier than anything. From now on, my sister and I would no longer be sharing the rickety bunk bed. We would have beds of our own, in rooms of our own.

"Watch your fingers," my father said later that first day, as I helped him knock together the pieces of my bed.

It was a moment I had been anticipating ever since that long-ago afternoon when he had first sketched the outlines of our rooms on the dirt floor of the excavation. My room might be the smallest, but it could have been a broom closet for all I cared. What really mattered was that it was mine and that it had a door I could close whenever I liked.

In years to come I would occupy many splendid rooms. I would doze on eiderdown in a stately country house in Oxfordshire. I would savor the view of Copenhagen harbor from the windows of an elegant duplex suite. I would lounge with my wife beneath the vaulted ceilings of an ancient stone inn in Safed, where our private terrace overlooked the Jordan Valley. In a room high above the Bosporus I would stand gazing out upon the domes and minarets of the Blue Mosque.

112

I relished them all. Yet none would ever give me the pleasure I felt the first time I found myself alone in that small, plain, square room with its single bed and its single window, which looked out only on our muddy front yard and the shabby little cabin where my parents, my sister, and I had spent so many cramped months with no privacy. The romance of pioneer living had long since lost its charm, even for me. But this only heightened the pleasure I now felt as my father finished assembling my bed, and my mother finished making it up. And then finally everyone was gone. And I went over to the door. And pushed it shut. And I was alone at last.

According to my father's drawings the room was barely ten feet square. But to me it was a palace, an ivory tower. Or rather a cowpoke's bunkhouse, for that was the way it eventually took shape once the decoratin' began, thank ya kindly, ma'am. The curtains my mother made for the window were printed with pictures of cowboys riding bucking broncos. The bedspread she found was woven with a pattern of lariats and fences. The base of the lamp on my bedside table was an imitation horseshoe, painted red.

The only thing that didn't fit the Wild West motif was the glow-in-the-dark figure of Jesus, which hung over my bed and was nailed to the cross with miniature versions of the spikes the Romans used. I knew that Jesus had probably never been on a horse or handled a six-shooter. But he and my cowboy heroes were somehow mixed together in my mind. It was as if they were all part of the same story: a heroic and gory drama of dust and blood, of goodness overcoming evil.

Of course, it didn't seem fair that Jesus had to die for good to triumph. In the cowboy stories it was always the bad guys who died, never the good ones. Still, it was really something that he went through all that pain and suffering and then died, just so my sins would be taken away. What I couldn't understand, and what I often pondered as I knelt to say my prayers and gazed up at the figure glowing on the wall, was why, if he could perform miracles for everybody else, he couldn't perform just one little one for himself and get himself down from there before it was too late. But then, I knew that was just the kind of question I wasn't supposed to ask. And if I did, I had a pretty good idea what kind of answer I'd get.

It was too bad, though, I'd think as I lay beneath the ghostly green

113

image and listened to the sound of the crickets outside my open window and to the low, distant whistle of a night train. It was too bad that Jesus didn't have a gun. It was for sure that he would have drawn it faster and shot straighter than any Roman. And as I closed my eyes and drifted off to sleep, all the images would get tumbled together: Romans in cowboy boots, cowpunchers in togas, the distant train whistle, and Jesus jumping down from the cross with his six-guns blazing, then leaping onto the back of a waiting horse and tearing out of town with a hearty "Hi-oh, Silver!"

In the evenings that first week, after my father got home from work, he helped my mother arrange the furniture. With a meekness that did not seem at all like him, he would follow her instructions as she told him where she thought the davenport and easy chair should go, then move them when she changed her mind, then move them back again the next evening, grumbling only a little as he did so. I had no idea what all the fuss was about. To me, one spot seemed as good as another. Yet when the furniture was finally arranged to her liking, it looked exactly right, as if no other combination were possible.

For my mother, rooms and furniture had a certain enigmatic logic. A piece that looked right in one spot, if shifted to another, suddenly looked awkward and out of balance. And my mother could tell the difference. She had an artist's eye and a quiet persistence that would not let her — or anyone else — rest until things were arranged to her liking.

My father found the whole process maddening. "It looks fine," he'd insist when he found her, arms folded, nibbling on the knuckles of one hand as she studied the latest layout of the room.

"I don't know," she'd muse. "Maybe if that chair were over there —"

"Believe me, it's fine where it is."

"Let's just try it," she'd say.

Quietly, like water on rock, she'd wear him down. And in the end, he'd usually give in: move the chair one more time, or shift the picture two inches to the left. I didn't realize it until many years later, but he wasn't the only one who called the shots. She was just quieter about it.

Everything was new. Everything we did was done for the first time: the first meal cooked on the new stove and eaten in the new kitchen; the first grace, led by my father, head bowed, his strong hands making a pointed roof under his chin:

"Blessed art thou, Christ, our Lord, for these thy gifts, which we are about to receive from thy bounty. Amen."

"Amen," we said, then dug into our meat loaf, mashed potatoes, and green beans.

That first week, too — perhaps that first day — came my first bath in the new tub. No longer did we have to go traipsing off to Gramma's house on Saturdays. No longer were we the poor relations without even a bathtub to our name. We had our own tub at last, and as I sat in it for the first time and watched the water pouring out of its mirror-bright spigot, it occurred to me with a shiver of awe that I knew just where that water was coming from.

It was coming from straight up out of the ground behind our house, exactly where an old farmer with a dowsing stick had told my father he'd find it. Somewhere down there in the darkness, far below the holes dug by the snakes and gophers, deeper even than the foundation of our house, ran a rushing river. Or maybe it was a quiet lake. It was hard to tell because no one had ever seen it and no one ever would. But the well driller's pipe had dipped into it, the pump had brought it to our house, the water heater in the basement had heated it, and now here it was, rushing in upon me, covering my legs, my belly, my chest, cradling me, lifting me like a wiener in a kettle as it rose toward the top of the tub.

No, I didn't let the tub overflow and the water spill onto the floor. I turned off the faucet before that could happen. But I wondered: Would the water just go on forever if I let it — the underground river gushing up and filling the house, then running out into the yard, carrying me and everything else with it? For one moment I had a hint in the back of my mind, a half-formed notion that there were places and things that I knew nothing about but that could affect my life in powerful, unknowable ways.

But the thought slipped away before it could take shape, and soon I was absorbed in launching my ships. The back brush became a Communist Red Russian destroyer; the American battleship was a bar of Ivory soap — "Ninety-nine and forty-four-one-hundredths percent pure! It floats!" There were splashes. Cannonades.

"You going to be in there all night?" The voice at the door was my father's.

What a good idea, I thought. But I did not dare talk back, not to him, so what I said was, "Coming," as if I'd been planning it all along.

That night, though, I went to bed feeling oddly uneasy. I had sensed something, glimpsed something, however vaguely, that was strange and unsettling.

As soon as a hint of autumn chill touched the air, my father laid the first fire in the fireplace. He set twigs and branches in the grate, arranging them carefully in just a certain way, small pieces on the bottom, then larger pieces on top, the whole thing set in a little square, like a miniature log cabin.

"See?" he said. "If you do it right, the air can circulate and the fire will burn evenly." He was always eager to teach. He seemed to know the right way to do just about anything, and he knew it better than anybody else — better, certainly, than his dolt of a son, which often seemed to be the main lesson of his teaching.

"Watch," he'd tell me if my attention drifted. "You might learn something." Or, if I tried to do a job myself: "That's not the way. What did I tell you? Won't you *ever* learn?"

When the fire was blazing nicely, my mother brought in a bag of marshmallows, which we roasted on the ends of green twigs. Joyce cried out in alarm when hers caught fire, but those were the kind I liked best. They burned a startling blue on the edges, and when you blew them out they were crispy charcoal on the outside, soft and mushy on the inside. I gobbled the sweet, sticky things by the fistful.

"That's enough," my mother warned. "You'll make yourself sick."

But I didn't stop, and, sure enough, I soon felt bloated and queasy.

"I told you," my mother chided, while my sister looked on smugly.

My father shook his head. "Telling doesn't do any good with him. He needs a good wallop. That's all he understands." He called me "he" as if I wasn't even in the room. He might have been talking about the dog.

And a sick dog I was, too. Why were they always right? I wondered. When would *I* get a chance to be right for a change?

*　　　　*　　　　*

There was no first Thanksgiving dinner that year; we went to Gramma's and Grampa's instead, along with lots of other aunts and uncles and cousins. But a few weeks later we were getting ready for our first Christmas in the new house.

Donning boots and overcoats, my sister and I went with my father to the Christmas tree lot that had sprung up by the highway, where we helped him pick through the rows of trees that stood beneath strings of bare lightbulbs. Our breath came in clouds, and we stamped our boots in the snow to keep warm as my father examined first one tree, then another. Finding a likely prospect, he turned it this way and that, but then discarded it and moved on down the row.

"Here's a good one," I called, trying to be helpful.

"This one's nicer," Joyce insisted.

But my father shook his head and pointed out the flaws of our candidates. One was too scraggly, another too short, another . . . "Hmm. That one's possible. Hang on to it." But he kept looking.

What he had in mind I couldn't tell. All the trees looked pretty much the same to me. But after a while he found one that met his exacting specifications, and I could see that indeed it did look different from the others: not too thin, not too tall, not too short, but nice and full, nice and even. And since he had waited until two days before Christmas, he got it for half price, as he proudly announced to my mother when we brought it home.

"It was marked three dollars. Can you imagine? But I got him down to a buck and a half."

The tree went up in front of the picture window, and that night we decorated it. Decorating, too, had its right way and wrong way. The big ornaments went on the bottom, the smaller ones toward the top, and each one had to hang free and not touch any branches. The tinsel also had to go on just right, hanging loose, not bunched in clumps. But the effort paid off. When we were done, the tree sparkled beautifully, the tinsel and ornaments catching the reflections of the colored lights and giving the whole room an enchanted look. A fire crackled in the fireplace, and while my father softly played the piano we all sang "Silent Night" and felt peaceful and warm.

"Remember last year," Joyce asked, "when we were in the cabin?"

"And how deep the snow got?" my father said.

"And remember how we had to go outside to go to the bathroom?" I added.

Already our year in the cabin was becoming the stuff of legend.

Meanwhile, there had been another "first" that I knew nothing about at the time, but whose consequences became apparent several months later. Even then, many years were to pass before memory and curiosity pulled me back to those days and made me realize what must have happened, and when: how, after a year of no privacy whatsoever, my mother and father were at last able to close their bedroom door behind them and be alone together.

As self-absorbed as any seven-year-old, I never imagined that my parents might be even more eager than I for a few moments alone, and what they might do once they had it. Nor did I have any inkling of cause and effect when, months later, I gradually became aware that my mother was beginning to bulge in places where I had never seen her bulge before. When I asked her about it, she astounded me with her reply.

"You're going to be a big brother," she said.

"I am?"

"Mommy's going to have a baby."

Suddenly I understood. "Ohhhh!" I said. I had watched Beauty deliver a litter of puppies the previous winter, so I had a pretty good idea of how it worked. Still, to imagine my mother in the same situation was a wonder of a whole other magnitude.

I liked the idea of being a big brother. It meant I would no longer be the youngest in the family, or the smallest or the slowest. As great news this ranked right up there with being told I was getting a pony, which was my fondest desire of all. The only hitch was that for me to be a big brother there'd have to be a baby in the house, and I wasn't sure I liked that idea one bit. All the babies I had ever seen were either boring or maddening. Either they lay around doing nothing, to be oohed and aahed over by every female in sight, or they cried all the time. Either way, I couldn't imagine that one would be much fun as a playmate. And I was right.

The new arrival appeared in early June, almost nine months to the day after we'd moved into the new house. The creature that now entered

Dad, the proud young father and builder, takes center stage in the kitchen of the finished house, summer 1950. At left, Mom holds infant Michael. Joyce and I stay in the background.

Background, my father's reworking of his original two-story plan.

Background, my father's drawing of the site plan.

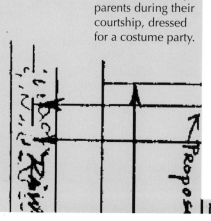

"Sweethearts." My parents during their courtship, dressed for a costume party.

My mother's smile belies her dread. The cabin, 12 feet by 16 feet, was where we would live for more than a year while the house was being built.

My father hangs the cabin door while Joyce and I watch. The house in the background belonged to our next-door neighbors.

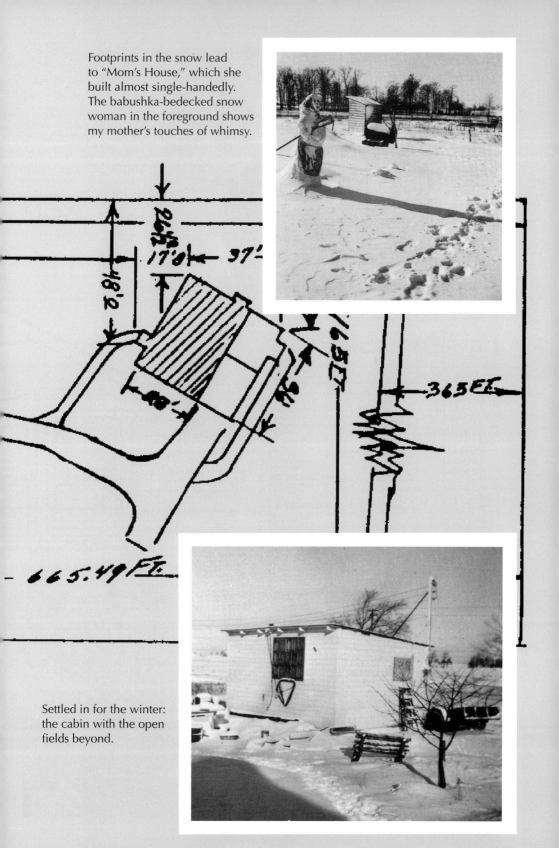

Footprints in the snow lead to "Mom's House," which she built almost single-handedly. The babushka-bedecked snow woman in the foreground shows my mother's touches of whimsy.

Settled in for the winter: the cabin with the open fields beyond.

Background, my father's drawing of the front elevation.

Beauty's winter litter shows little family resemblance to her breed. That's me on the left, with my mother and sister. Behind us is the snow-draped foundation of the house.

The foundation waits for the spring thaw, when building can begin in earnest.

A fresh load of lumber lies waiting to be used. The small house in the distance served as a toolshed. It was later Joyce's and my playhouse.

Mud time. Uncle Tad (left) and Uncle Ray (center) help Dad tackle the mud problem, spreading stones on the driveway. At right is my cousin Ed, Ray's son.

My father poses in the back-door frame during a visit from Uncle Ray and his family. That's me, perched on the sill.

Background, a sectional view, with a detail of the fireplace wall.

Hired workmen lay the concrete floor of the garage.

EAST WALL of LIVING ROOM.

1 course of 5" BLOCK.

Pump Room

Dressed for Sunday Mass. Me, my sister, and my mother—and Beauty, of course—at the retaining wall that later collapsed and had to be rebuilt.

A crew of masons tops off the chimney while Joyce and I pose in the foreground.

Sunday again, but Dad's already changed into his work clothes.

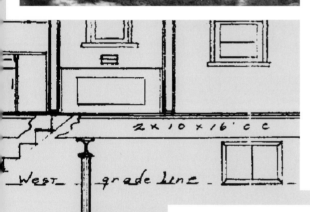

Home at last, December 1950. The curtains are on the windows, the car is in the drive, and all's right with the world.

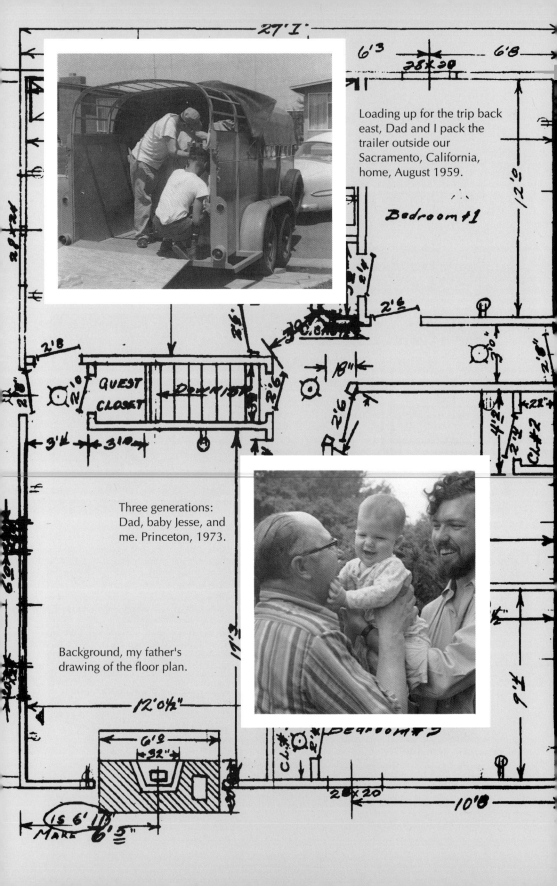

Loading up for the trip back east, Dad and I pack the trailer outside our Sacramento, California, home, August 1959.

Three generations: Dad, baby Jesse, and me. Princeton, 1973.

Background, my father's drawing of the floor plan.

our lives was so incredibly tiny that it looked like one of my sister's dolls. But it was far more trouble than any doll could ever be. It squirmed. It bawled. It spit up. It had to be fed and changed at all hours of the day and night. What amazed me most was that something so small could take over so completely. A robber bursting through the door of a bank with both guns drawn and shouting "Hands up!" could not have done a better job of grabbing everyone's attention. Whatever my mother might be doing at any particular moment — making me oatmeal for breakfast or sewing a button on my shirt or making me feel better about a bad day in school — all it took was a wail from the newcomer to send her running.

Even when the baby didn't make a peep, it somehow managed to make its presence felt: "Be quiet or you'll wake the baby." "Don't do that, you'll upset the baby."

Michael John was the name my parents gave it, but from what I had learned in school about dictators, I thought a better choice would have been Stalin — Joe for short. And yet, even though he wasn't quite as fun as one of Beauty's puppies, I had to admit that the little tyrant, with his squinched-up face and miniature fingers and toes, had moments of being adorable. He'd be looking up at you very seriously from his crib and get this silly expression on his face that made you think he was smiling. And just then he'd fart a big one or burp or throw up. He was a hoot.

As promised, though, the best thing about him was the newly elevated status that he brought me. As the big brother, I now had a degree of freedom I had not known before. I could come and go pretty much as I pleased, without first asking permission. I also had new responsibilities. I was counted on. Sometimes it was just a matter of watching the stove while my mother changed a diaper, or of feeding Beauty in the morning before I went to school. But I also got to beat the rugs, which I liked because of the noise I could make, great whacks like gunshots if I hit them just right with the beater, while the dust flew like gunsmoke. If my mother needed a loaf of bread or a jug of milk from the store up the road, I got to hike there by myself, with real money in my pocket, and return triumphant, the brave hunter bringing home the provisions.

My mother was very proud. She had the new baby to show off and the new house as well. No longer did she have to be ashamed in front of her family for the way she lived. Her house was as good as anyone's — better, because her Walter had built it. And now she was a mother again, as well, still not too old, still a woman having done what only a woman can do, and this pleased her no end, especially when it came to showing off little Michael to my father's family, who, she felt, always looked down their noses at her because she had only two kids and they all had at least three.

My father, too, was enormously pleased with the way things had worked out. He was thirty-two years old, a father again, and the owner of a house he had built himself.

> *To market, to market, to buy a fat pig,*
> *Home again, home again, jiggety-jig.*

The old nursery rhyme, which he invariably recited whenever we pulled into our driveway after a day trip to a park or to visit relatives, sounded sweeter than ever on his lips now that the house was the one he had dreamed of for so long. True, the place wasn't quite finished, but it was livable. The dream was all but accomplished, and everyone — his brothers, his sisters, his mother, his in-laws — could see what he had done, and they had no choice but to be impressed and give him the respect that was his due.

Had he known what lay ahead, would he have savored his triumph any less? Or would it have tasted all the sweeter because it was destined to be short-lived? There's no way to tell. But the fact was that that summer and fall of 1950, my father was truly happy. I could tell by the way he laughed and the way he would sit at the piano and sing, his head thrown back, his stubby fingers scampering over the keyboard like demented sausages. And when my mother put the baby in Joyce's lap and joined my father on the piano bench, the music they sang together told the story better than any words alone could have done:

> *Sweethearts make love their very own,*
> *Sweethearts can live on love alone.*

I loved hearing them, because it meant they were happy.

For me, too, it seemed the happiest of times. My world was new and opening before me. I had a best friend, Timmy. At school, I was no longer the new kid. I still worried about bullies and didn't much like my new teacher, Sister Andrew Jerome, but at least I was on familiar ground. I knew my way around, I had a pal or two to play with at recess. And when I got home, I had my woods and fields to go adventuring in, with the world's best dog at my side. I was Columbus, discovering new continents every day. I was Kit Carson, scout and pathfinder. I was Adam, wandering blissfully in my own sun-filled Garden of Eden. And I had no reason to think that it would not go on forever.

PART II

Ah, but a man's reach should exceed his grasp,
Or what's a heaven for?

— Robert Browning

11

WATCHING

When I came into the kitchen the next morning, my father's drawings lay where I'd left them the night before, on the table, folded inside the manila envelope. But the envelope had been pushed aside to make room for the breakfast things: boxes of cereal, bottles of vitamin pills, jars of jam, instant coffee, a pitcher of orange juice, a carton of milk. On the stove the kettle simmered, giving off a low, meditative whistle.

"Morning," I said, taking a seat at the table. The milk carton, I saw, was adorned with a grainy photograph of a small boy. MISSING, said the headline in capital letters. Below was an 800 number to call with information.

"Good morning, dear," my mother said without looking up. Dressed in a pink bathrobe and pink moccasins — color coordinated even at breakfast — she was busy at the counter opening a can of food for the overstuffed orange cat that pranced around her ankles in a prediabetic frenzy. "Did you sleep well?"

"Mmm. Fine."

I was not yet sufficiently awake to be chatty or cheerful. My head was still clouded with images from the night before: a priest blowing smoke rings; my father at the piano, singing; my mother, decades younger, sitting by a window, humming to the baby she held in her arms; myself as a kid, scouting a path along the edge of the woods. Missing. All of it. Gone forever. And no 800 number to call it back.

It was hard to imagine that once it had all been so real: the whole world opening before me, everything fresh and new and full of magic and sunlight. Now nothing of that world remained except wisps of dream and memory, a handful of drawings in a manila envelope, and a few photographs — arbitrary moments caught with the press of a button and held fast while everything else continued moving, changing, disappearing. The photos and the drawings were like potsherds from a vanished civilization, trivial artifacts that were now more real and alive than the world they had come from. They were all that survived — they and the people we had since become.

"Hmm?" I said, becoming aware that my mother was speaking to me. "Sorry. I wasn't listening."

"I said I hope the bed was all right."

"Oh. Yes. It was fine. Very comfortable."

I used the lid of the coffee jar to measure out an approximate serving of instant.

"Use a spoon, why don't you?"

I tipped the coffee into a mug. "This works just as well."

"But you can't tell how much you've got."

"Too much precision is bad for the soul."

She clicked her tongue. "You sound like your father."

I laughed. "God forbid." I added water from the kettle. "Anyway," I said, warming to the subject, "I always thought of him as extremely precise. What about all those incredible tools he used at work — the micrometer that measured thousandths of an inch? The beautiful chrome pencils with the incredibly fine points? And you saw the lettering he did on those drawings. The words looked like they were printed by machine."

My mother shrugged. "That was different. That was work."

"Yes, but it was there. It was part of him."

"Only a part," she said, conceding nothing.

It was an odd reversal of roles for us. For once I was the one defending him. But the truth was that however impossible it became for me to get along with the man himself, I never stopped admiring him for all that he was able to do with his capable hands. The exquisite grace of the lines

126

he drew, his ability to fix anything from broken plumbing to a clogged carburetor — these things never ceased to evoke my awe and admiration. And of course there was the house, always the house, which for me would forever remain his greatest triumph.

Yet as I stirred my coffee, I knew that my mother was right. Granted, she may have exaggerated the disorder of his life, which contrasted so sharply with her own meticulous will for order and propriety. Even so, there was no escaping the fact that life had been far more chaotic and unpredictable in the days when my father was in charge. That it also happened to be far more interesting was, as far as my mother was concerned, beside the point. True, even she conceded now and then that, with my father, things were never dull. But at such times it was clear from her tone that given her druthers, she would have preferred a little less excitement and a little more stability.

"Thank you for showing me these," I said, tapping the manila envelope with its treasure trove of drawings. "It's great that he saved them. All the other stuff, too. It's amazing. He even saved the lumberyard receipts."

Clearly these scraps of paper must have been as important to him as they were now to me. Otherwise, why would he have hung on to them all this time, carrying them from one house to next, year after year? They were more than souvenirs. They were the last vestige of his glory days.

"You may as well have them," my mother said.

"Don't you want them?"

She shook her head. "He's not going to be looking at them again. And I don't need reminders."

We were back on touchy ground. I would have to tread carefully. I sipped my coffee. After a minute I said, "What happened anyway? What went wrong?"

"What do you mean? When?"

"Rawson Avenue. Why did we leave? I never understood that."

"You're not the only one," she answered ruefully. She opened the loaf of bread. "Would you like some toast?"

She was stalling. But I said, "Sure."

She slipped two slices into the toaster and pushed the lever down. Then she brought her mug to the table and sat. She added milk and sugar to her coffee and stirred them in. Her face, without makeup, was a pale mask.

"Would you rather not talk about it?" I asked.

She shrugged, resigned. "No, it's all right. It's just —" She took a deep breath. "It was just so hard, leaving that place. I didn't want to. But I couldn't change his mind. You know what he was like. Once he made a decision, that was that."

I nodded. I knew.

"I think —" She stopped. "No, I shouldn't say it."

But I could see she wanted to. "What?" I prompted.

She hesitated, then continued. "It's an awful thing to say, but when he said we had to leave, I actually hated him. I'm sorry, but it's true. For the first time in my life. I really hated him."

The room was silent except for the quiet ticking of the toaster on the counter. When it popped neither of us made a move.

I had never heard her admit such a thing before. I remembered all too well my own times of hatred — hatred bred of fear and rage and fruitless yearning for even the slightest hint of his approval, let alone love. But my mother had never been anything but loyal. Never once until now had I heard her say anything against him; always she pleaded for understanding, for peace between us, for forgiveness. Now here she was, forgiving nothing, excusing nothing. It was breathtaking.

And yet I was not entirely surprised. I remembered well enough hearing their raised voices as I came in from playing or as I lay in bed at night, and I remembered hearing her crying afterward. I realized now that at least some of the arguments must have been about selling the house and moving away. But at the time, all I knew was that he was yelling at her and making her cry. And I remembered vowing that someday I would get back at him, someday I would make him sorry that he ever caused her so much unhappiness. And I remembered, too, beginning to be afraid.

"You better clean up now," my mother called from the kitchen. "Daddy will be home soon."

I said nothing. I was too busy. High in the mountain pass an ambush was under way. A stagecoach carrying passengers and a gold shipment was being attacked by Indians. War cries pierced the air. Arrows flew.

128

Thhup! One hit the stage driver, who fell from his seat. The man riding shotgun fired back. Kgssh! Kgssh! Two Indians fell. But now the stage was out of control. The horses were racing down the mountain road in panic. The guard fought to grab the reins. The Indians kept coming.

The stage was just about to reach the safety of the fort in the valley when my mother called again.

"Come on now," she said.

I heard the clatter of plates being set on the kitchen table and the sizzling sound of the fish she was frying. It was Friday, so we were having fish. It was a rule. The Church said so.

"In a minute," I said. The gunfire sputtered on. Kgssh. Kgssh.

"Not in a minute. Do it now. And don't make so much noise. You'll wake the baby."

I gave up. The stagecoach rolled over. Everyone was killed.

"I can't do anything," I muttered to no one in particular.

In my gloom I gave one last look at the mighty land that was about to be destroyed. The mountains were sofa cushions with blankets spread over them. The hills on the far side of the valley were made from blocks pushed under the rug. The valley itself was an endless broadloom prairie. Horses grazed there, and when I lay on my stomach for a cowboy's eye view, the plain seemed to go on for miles before running into the stubby legs of my father's easy chair.

The fort, which stood in the middle of the plain, was made of Lincoln Logs. There was a watchtower on one corner and a ledge that ran around the inside, where cowboys could stand and fight off rustlers and Indians.

The cowboys themselves were plastic and came in an array of colors and positions. Some stood tall, with pistols drawn, or with coiled lariats in their hands. Others crouched and pointed rifles. None of them was more than a few inches high, but I didn't care. My cowboys could still do all the things real cowboys could: round up cattle and break horses, ride fast and shoot straight.

To survive, I knew, a cowboy had to be quick and he had to be smart. The frontier was a dangerous place. There were enemies everywhere: bears and snakes, Indians on the warpath, holdup men. Get careless and you got hurt.

"Don't make me ask you again." My mother was standing in the doorway, wiping her hands on a towel. She was almost pleading. "You know Daddy won't like it if your things are spread all over. Now come on. He'll be here any minute."

"Oh, all right," I said, and got busy. I did it for her sake as much as my own. I had seen how she cringed when he shouted and slammed doors. And I did not want to be the cause of it happening again.

When was it that my wide-eyed awe of him began to shift to wariness and fear? When was it that I first began hearing the warning voice in my head? Be careful, said the voice. Don't get Daddy upset. Stay out of his way. Watch out. Watch out for Daddy.

Probably there was no single moment. Probably it happened little by little over months or years, an accretion of small moments, gestures, words, the raising of a threatening voice or, what was even more frightening, the ominous, distant silence. But each incident left its mark, its small wound, and together these accumulated like the drips of calcium-laden water in underground caverns, each drip leaving its minute deposit on my heart until together the deposits accumulated into rock-hard formations.

This much I know: the change began in that house. It was there that something shifted for my father, so that afterward nothing was ever the same again.

He was always busy now. We saw him hardly at all. His days were devoured by his job at the power plant, where he was back on the day shift. His evenings were spent either downtown, where he was taking classes at the county vocational school, or hunched over stacks of books at a card table set up in the corner of his and my mother's bedroom.

As an eight- or nine-year-old I could not imagine why anyone would want to go to school if they did not have to — especially a grown-up. Grown-ups, I'd always thought, never had to do anything they didn't want to do.

"Why does he have to?" I asked my mother.

"It's not that he has to," she explained. She had just finished feeding Michael his milk from a bottle. She had him on her shoulder and was patting his back to make him burp. "He wants to learn more," she told me. "He wants to be able to get a better job. And to do that he has to study."

"Oh," I said, as if I understood. But I was still puzzled. What could be better or more important than keeping the power plant running and making sure that all the houses and factories and stores in the city kept getting electricity? It didn't make sense, which only added to my budding conviction that I would never in a million years comprehend the adult world.

The fact was, I knew nothing of what drove my father in those years. It certainly never occurred to me that he might have his own longings, his own dreams and frustrations. Not he, who knew and did everything that needed knowing or doing, who provided everything and decided everything that was important in our lives. As a child, I simply could not imagine that he might have problems that had nothing to do with me.

What I did notice was that my father was having trouble getting out of the house in time in the morning. At breakfast on workdays, while Joyce and I spooned our cornflakes and my mother fed Michael his pablum and apple juice, my father would drag himself into the kitchen looking haggard and bleary-eyed from another late night of poring over his schoolbooks and homework assignments. Smelling of sleep and shaving cream, he'd dawdle over breakfast, munching his toast and sipping his coffee while my mother, growing increasingly agitated, would try to get him to move faster.

"Mr. Stoltz won't like it if you're late again," she'd warn. Mr. Stoltz was my father's boss. Whenever my mother spoke his name, she did so with the same deference that she usually reserved for priests and nuns.

"Well, that's just too bad about old Stoltz," my father replied grandly, leaning back in his chair. "I'm going to have another piece of toast. And come to think of it, I'll have an egg, too. No, make that two eggs."

"But Walter . . ."

"And another cup of coffee."

Watching, I couldn't help but be impressed. No one, not even Mom, was going to get him to move one bit faster than he wanted to, and no boss was going to intimidate him. Not my Dad. In our house he was the only boss that mattered.

Not until many years later did I learn what happened after he finished his leisurely breakfast, pulled on his jacket, picked up his lunch pail, and ambled out to the car. Pulling out of the driveway, he would wait until he was out of sight of the house. Then he would jam the accelerator to the floorboards and keep it there as he raced to make up for lost time.

My mother only learned the truth by accident. One afternoon when she was putting his laundry away in his dresser, she discovered a handful of traffic tickets at the bottom of one of the drawers. They were hidden like guilty secrets inside the folds of his flannel pajamas. There were at least a dozen of them, and when she examined them she saw that every one was a citation for speeding. The police along his route to the power plant must have been getting to know him quite well.

Telling me about it in later times, my mother had to laugh. But she also remembered how humiliated she was when he had to go to court and settle his fines, and how angry she was to see all that money thrown away for nothing.

Still, that was a trifle compared to what my father faced every morning when he finally got to work: an irate supervisor, another dreary day of mindlessly minding row on row of gauges and dials and checking the color of the smoke that came spewing out of the chimneys. It was not the kind of life he had ever imagined for himself, and he must have often wondered how it had all turned out so miserably. What had happened to the studious young man who was so determined to pull himself up and make something of himself? What had become of the swashbuckling operetta pirate prince?

But my father was not about to settle for things as they were. He was determined to change his life while he still could, to find something better. That was what kept him to his grueling schedule of work and study, work and study. Never mind that it was giving him headaches and turning his stomach into a gurgling pool of acid, giving him gas and making him belch. Never mind that by the time the weekend rolled around he was too exhausted and cranky to do much more than sleep. Those night-school courses were his passport to something better, and he'd be damned if he was going to give them up.

As for finishing the house, well, that would just have to wait. Since my father lacked both time and money to go forward with his plan to build an enclosed porch over the garage, the tar-papered back wall remained an eyesore for months after we moved in.

Nor was he getting around to installing the inside steps to the basement. A rickety ladder remained the only way down, and this was what my mother had to use on wash days and to clean up after Beauty, who my father kept locked in the basement overnight and who he never seemed to have time to let out in the morning before he hurried off to work. My mother used the ladder even when she was pregnant with Michael. Her sole alternative was to go around the long way, through the garage. Meantime, only a high latch on the basement door — and stern warnings — prevented one of us kids from tumbling to disaster.

The yard was still a mess, too. The outhouse had been broken up and the hole filled in, but out front, the old cabin still stood, a shabby reminder of our pioneer days. Likewise, the ground immediately surrounding the house remained a wasteland of mud and discarded building materials: rusty pipes, old boards, unused bricks and chimney tiles, half-used piles of sand, leftover concrete blocks. Not that I minded any of this; the piles of dirt and the forests of tall weeds made great places through which to drive my toy trucks and stage battles with my plastic cowboys and Indians. My mother, however, did not share my enthusiasm for the mess, and she found ways of letting my father know that she was not happy with it.

"I'll get to it on the weekend," he'd promise her when she dropped broad hints about one or another of the jobs that needed doing.

When the weekend came, however, it was about all she could do to get him up on Sunday morning for church. Much of the rest of the time he was invisible behind the bedroom door.

Those were the days of tiptoeing and whispering. All of us learned to step and speak quietly so as not to disturb him while he was studying or napping. His silence and his snores alike filled the house, creeping into our lives, controlling our every move. The wonderful new house, which had seemed so roomy and luxurious when we first moved into it, now seemed oppressively small and even more confining than the cabin had been.

To disturb my father was to incur a fearful anger. Anything might set him off: a door that I'd accidentally let slam, toys left on the living room floor, Joyce's and my voices raised too loud, the sound of our shoes on the hardwood floor.

"Pipe down, damn it," he'd bellow from behind the closed bedroom door. Or the door would fly open and he would come out shouting: "If you can't play quietly, get the hell out of the house." Or: "How many times do you have to be told? Once more and you get hit. Do you hear me? I'm not going to say it again."

The smallest thing could set him off. One winter evening, when Gramma Raniszewski was visiting and could watch the baby, Dad took the rest of us to a movie. On the way, Joyce and I got to squabbling in the backseat. Dad, fed up, turned around to yell at us and ended up driving off the road and into a snowbank. He had to walk to a nearby farmhouse to get the farmer to pull us out with a tractor. By the time we were out of the ditch, Dad was so disgusted that he decided there'd be no movie that night and maybe not ever. The silence in the car as we drove home was complete.

Not even the baby was immune from his short temper. "Can't you shut him up?" my father's voice would boom if Michael dared to cry at the wrong moment.

My mother did her best to head off trouble. She did not want Dad getting upset any more than we did. There were times, though, when she found that Dad's impatience came in handy. I'm not sure how much she was aware of what she was doing. But at the end of a long day, with two rambunctious children underfoot and a third needing attention in his crib, it was not uncommon for her to invoke Dad's anger as a last resort when she ran out of ways to keep Joyce and me in line.

"Daddy's not going to like it when he hears about this," she'd say, wearily pushing a lock of hair off her forehead with the back of her hand. "Then you'll be sorry."

Usually that was all we had to hear. We knew then that she'd reached the end of her tether and that for her sake as well as ours we'd better shape up.

This happened so often that eventually the mere threat came to stand for the thing itself. And while I doubt that either of my parents intended it, in the end I began to feel the same trembling and fear about my father that the children of Israel must have felt about God in heaven when the prophets of old threatened to call down his wrath upon their sinful heads.

Meantime, my mother had begun to worry that my father was driving himself too hard. She saw his impatience and frustration, his chronic fatigue. She began to dread that his being late for work might cost him his job.

She worried, too, that he might be making himself sick. But when she suggested that he see a doctor, he resisted. What was the point?

There was nothing wrong with him. What was she talking about? All he needed was a few good nights of sleep. What he could not tell her — what he had trouble admitting even to himself — was how frightened he was of doctors and of illness. It had been that way ever since childhood, when he watched his sister die of illness and had himself nearly succumbed to diphtheria. Seeing a doctor was the last thing he wanted. What if the doctor actually found something? What then?

But even he had to admit that the fatigue was not going away. Nor were the headaches, the dizziness, the stomach pains. At some point he finally gave in and went for a checkup.

At the time, of course, I knew little about any of this. I may have known that he went to see a doctor, but I was certainly not told what the results of that visit might have been. I did notice, though, that various bottles of pills now appeared alongside my father's plate at the breakfast table and at supper. And that he began to drink milk with his meals as well as coffee. And that when he came home from work and wanted his usual beer or two to relax, my mother tried to discourage him, telling him that it wasn't good for him. Which made him grumpy, as so many things now seemed to do.

At about this same time, he and my mother began using words that I had never heard before. Serious-sounding words like hypertension. Short, nasty words like ulcer and diet. Most fascinating of all were their references to high blood pressure. What this meant was not at all clear to me. But I knew one thing for sure: it must be very dangerous. When my mother's pressure cooker once built up too much steam, the top had blown off and the kitchen ceiling had been spattered red with tomato sauce. Would my father explode the same way? I wondered: the top of his head gone, his brains blasted into the air? Ka-blooey!

Afraid of sparking a fatal explosion, afraid of his anger, I learned to read the danger signs. I became as sensitive to his moods as the grass was to the wind. I learned to sense trouble in the downturn of his lip and in the lift of his eyebrow. I began to live in dread of his temper and his sarcasm. Unable either to please him or to stand up to him, I grew cautious and tongue-tied. Afraid of saying the wrong thing, I learned to placate, to make jokes, to pretend that nothing I said or did was meant to be taken seriously. Most of all, I learned to stay out of his way.

Every chance I got, I escaped to the woods. In the woods, there was no one I could displease, no one whose expectations I could disappoint, no one watching my every move, then rushing to tell me what I was doing wrong and wondering when was I ever going to learn to do it right, for crying out loud. I could be myself there. Or rather, I could be someone better than I secretly believed myself to be: someone stronger, bolder, more self-reliant, dependent on no one, afraid of no one.

In the woods, it did not matter if I made a mistake — if I took a wrong trail, say, and had to backtrack. Often it was just such mistakes that led me to places and things that I would otherwise never have seen: a badger's hole at the base of a tree; an enchanted spot where two streams came together, the water sounding like children's voices as it gurgled and trickled in and out of the sunlight. Or were those real voices that I heard? Sometimes it was hard to tell. Spooked, I'd stand stock-still in a shadow and wait, only my eyes moving, my ears cocked. But no, there was no one. I was alone, unobserved in my secret place.

Sometimes, when I went tramping by myself, without Beauty tagging along, I saw wild animals: deer and snakes and even, once, a red fox loping along the path on the far side of a field. Beauty was good company, but I never saw as many animals when she was with me.

My favorite spot was a big, comfortable old oak that stood sentinel on the edge of the woods, its broad and sturdy branches shading the verge of a farmer's field. A fence post was close enough to the trunk that I could climb up on it, grab the lowest branch, and pull myself up. The next branches were easier to reach, and I used them to climb higher, until the branches got too small and frail for me to go farther without the risk of one of them snapping under my weight. I'd sit there, as snug as any squirrel, with the sky only a few feet over my head and the world far below. Crows flew by. A jay alighted on a branch not far from mine, then, surprised to see me perched in his domain, rasped out an angry cry and jumped up and away.

An airplane buzzed overhead. As close as I was to the sky, he was closer, and I wondered again what the world looked like from up there and promised myself that someday I'd find out. I'd go up in a plane, too, and learn where planes went when they flew beyond the farthest fields.

I could see the plane, but he could not see me in my leafy roost. Nor did anyone on the ground know that I was there. Not the skunk sniffing around in the bushes below, nor Joyce, when she came looking for me, nor the strange man who one day came along the path at the edge of the woods.

Stopping beneath the next tree, the man glanced around, then opened his fly and took out his wiener. I held my breath, afraid he might look up and see me. I thought he was probably going to pee, but instead he seemed to be doing something else. From where I sat I could not get a good look at what he was doing, but he appeared to be spitting in his hand, then stroking himself.

It was embarrassing, but I couldn't pull my eyes away. I even thought of shifting my position so I could get a better look. But I was afraid to move. Meantime, I could feel my own wiener stiffening in my pants. I wished the man would stop and go away. But he only kept on stroking himself. Then, as I watched, he gave a shudder and seemed to sag, exhausted.

For another minute or so he stood there, as if catching his breath. Then he zipped his pants up and slowly walked on, disappearing around the stand of trees that separated the nearer field from the farther one.

Sitting up there in the tree, I felt my emotions lurch between excitement, resentment, and fear. This intruder brought into my private domain something so bewildering and strange that I wasn't sure I wanted to understand it. One puzzle was solved, though. Until now I had never been able to figure out just what the catechism book meant when it talked of "sins of impurity." I thought maybe it had something to do with not washing your hands before supper or dropping your food on the floor but eating it anyway. But after the strange man I knew better. I had no doubt whatever that what I had just witnessed was an impure act. And that I probably had committed an impure act by watching it and not closing my eyes. Would I have to report it the next time I went to confession? I wondered. And, if I didn't, would I be committing another sin?

The one thing I did know was that I was going to be even more vigilant from now on when I went exploring alone. I did not ever want to stumble on that man when I was by myself. Who knew what he might do next? Or what he might have done to me had he known I was watching him.

I became even more wary once Beauty disappeared.

My sister and I were at school the day she vanished. When we got off the school bus, she was not waiting to greet us at the end of the driveway.

Puzzled, I looked toward the house, expecting to see her running toward us. I whistled and called for her as we walked up the driveway, but she was nowhere to be seen. I began to have an awful feeling. Something was wrong. I looked at Joyce. We started to run.

My mother was in the kitchen when we burst in the door. "Where's Beauty?" I asked her. "Why isn't she here?"

"Is she all right?" asked Joyce .

"I'm sorry," my mother said. "She's gone. The Humane Society came for her."

I couldn't believe what I was hearing. "You mean they took her away?"

My mother nodded. "They had to. She's been sick, you knew that. And Daddy and I decided —" She shrugged. "I'm sorry. We had no choice."

I was too stunned to speak.

Joyce had started to cry. "Was it the whaddya-call-it?" she managed to ask.

My mother, too, had tears in her eyes. "The mange. Yes. Other things, too."

I should have seen it coming. For the last few weeks, Beauty had been acting funny. Not eating. Scratching herself like crazy. Her hair had been falling out in clumps. When I'd call her to go out and play, instead of bounding eagerly to her feet she'd barely lift her head from her paws. If I tried to coax her, she'd curl her lip at me and growl. But I thought she was just tired or cranky. I'd had no idea she was really sick, so sick they'd send her away. It felt like I'd been punched in the stomach.

My mother sat down in a kitchen chair and tried to explain. "What she had is highly contagious. She could have spread it to us, too."

Joyce was bawling hard now, choking on her tears. "Can we go visit her?"

My mother shook her head. "I'm sorry."

Mange, my vet has told me, can be treated nowadays if caught early enough. Back then there was no cure. Usually the only thing to do was to put the animal out of its misery.

My mother reached out a hand toward me. "I'm sorry, Tommy," she said again. "I wish —"

But I pulled away. "No," I cried. "NO!"

I ran out of the kitchen and out the back door, tears pouring down my cheeks. I ran down the back steps, and kept on running, not knowing where I was headed, wanting only to get as far away as I could from the terrible news. I raced across the backyard toward the woods. Behind me I heard my mother calling, but I did not stop.

My Beauty. Gone. Taken away just like that, without my even having a chance to say good-bye. How could they? How could my own mother and father do such a thing?

Inside I felt a tearing that was unlike any ache I had ever experienced. At the time I could not have said what it was. All I knew was that a terrible weight had descended on me, a suffocating weight that was also a kind of emptiness. It seemed to be pulling me down even as I ran, making my feet heavy and slow.

Although I did not yet recognize it, the feeling was one that I came to know all too well. It was the pain of irredeemable loss. Before long it was to become such a frequent part of my life that, whenever I saw it coming, I would greet it like the old familiar it was. "Oh, hello," I'd say numbly, "it's you again." And I'd resign myself, because there was nothing to do but accept it and get used to its heartbreak.

I ran until I could not run any longer. Slowing to a walk, I wiped my wet cheeks on my sleeve and trudged on. I was not crying now but raging in fury. It wasn't fair. They shouldn't have taken Beauty away. A doctor could have made her well. Wasn't that what doctors were for?

Following the edge of the woods, I did not stop to climb my favorite tree but kept to the path as it beelined along a wheat field, then cut through the narrow stand of trees that marked the boundary between one field and the next. On the far side I came to what had been a field of corn but was now stubble, dry and broken. As I tramped onward in the bright autumn sunlight, I knew there would be another path running along the edge of the next field and another one after that. I had explored enough to know that every field had a path running somewhere along its edge, and now I was going to follow them all. I did not care where they led or how far they went.

Coming out from the shadows of a line of trees, I saw a rabbit crouched on the path ahead.

"Go get 'em, girl," I whispered, knowing that if Beauty had been there with me she would have been after that bunny like a shot.

But Beauty was not there. Beauty would never chase rabbits again. She would never run ahead as I walked, her nose up, her eyes bright and ready for adventure. I would never feel her head under my hand when I reached out to pet her, or feel her furry back pressed against my side as I lay in a grassy field and looked up at the passing clouds.

Suddenly my eyes filled with tears again.

"Damn it," I said, but felt no better for swearing.

I tramped along the edge of a field of soybeans, then another of alfalfa. I was now farther from home than I had ever been before. Would I see the strange man again? I wondered. Would he see me? Could I hide in time or run fast enough to get away from him? But I saw no one. I was alone.

At the far side of the alfalfa field I picked up another path, following it through the next line of trees. Stepping into the cool shade, I was surprised to catch a glint of sharp light ahead, as if someone were shining a mirror through the foliage. But there was no one there. Instead, what I saw before me when I came out into the sun was what seemed like a piece of sky that had fallen to earth: a pond, which lay in the middle of the grassy field, mirroring the blue overhead.

Drawn to it irresistibly, I stood on the bank, gazing at the still water. So perfectly did it reflect the blue depths of the sky that for a moment I lost all sense of what was sky and what was pond. I had the dizzying feeling that, if I were to fall forward, I would go tumbling into space, falling and tumbling forever and ever.

My knees turned rubbery. Quickly I sat down on the bank, afraid of the water's strange pull.

My sudden movement startled a bullfrog. He leaped from the grassy shore, and his tiny splash was like a stone tossed through a window. Instantly the still patch of sky was shattered by ripples that transformed it safely into water again. I was relieved, as if an unbearable tension had been broken, and I could breathe once more.

One kick, two, and the frog was gone, vanished into the depths.

What if I had fallen in? I wondered. I did not know how to swim, so probably I would have drowned. And since no one but me knew about the pond, or knew that I was there, it might be weeks before anyone found my body.

How awful that would be! How terribly sad! I imagined my parents watching, grief stricken, as my poor sodden corpse was pulled from the water and laid on the grass at their feet. Then they would feel about me the way I felt about Beauty, and they'd be sorry. I imagined my mother cradling my poor wet head in her lap and crying her eyes out. My father, filled with remorse for all the injustices he had inflicted upon me, would take my limp, cold hand in his and beg my forgiveness. But it would be too late. I'd be dead. And they'd have to live with grief and regret for the rest of their lives.

There'd be a funeral, of course. Everyone would come to Saint Stephen's to see me lying in my coffin in my white communion suit. All my aunts and uncles and cousins would be there, and my grandparents and all the kids from school, even the ones who didn't like me while I was alive. I'd have a pretty satin pillow under my head, and I'd lie there with streams of colored light pouring down on me from the beautiful stained-glass windows. There'd be candles and incense, and everyone would cry.

And then, to my astonishment, I'd discover that there had been a mistake. I could feel myself breathing. I wasn't dead after all. I could move my toes and my fingers. Surprised, I would open my eyes and find myself staring up at the church ceiling far above. I'd smell incense. I'd hear muffled sobs and murmured prayers. Puzzled, I'd sit up and look around.

There'd be gasps of amazement. Father Beyer would be staring at me with his mouth open.

"I don't believe it!" someone would say.

"It's a miracle!" someone else would chime in.

"He's alive!"

"Well, for heaven's sake."

And while I sat there beaming, everyone would break out into cheers and laughter. My mother would hug me and give me a big kiss. My father would put his hand on my shoulder. "Glad to have you back, son," he'd say, and shake my hand. Then there'd be a commotion at the back of the church. The crowd would part, and down the aisle would come Beauty, her head high, her beautiful golden coat showing not a trace of mange. And she'd come right up to the front, and I'd climb down from the coffin and put my arms around her, and we'd be together again and we would all be happy.

Across the pond, the bullfrog reappeared. He was squatting on his haunches on the muddy bank just below the grassy overhang. "Ba-gum," he said.

"Ba-gum yourself," I answered, annoyed at having my beautiful reverie intruded on by reality.

But he was right. I had been sitting in his backyard long enough. The sun was low, and I was getting hungry. I got to my feet and started home.

Whether anyone missed me when I got there, whether my mother hugged me and told me how worried she had been, whether she said again how sorry she was about Beauty, or whether she was too busy with my brother to even notice I'd been gone, all these years later I can only guess. Any and all are possibilities.

What did stay with me from that autumn afternoon was the first, wrenching pain of loss . . . the dizzying beauty of a shard of sky lying in a grassy field . . . and a sudden, startling vision of just how easily that breathless eternity could be shattered by a thing as harmless as a frog.

Little did I know.

12

IF KINGS CAN DIE

*T*hat was the year the king died. I heard the news flash over the radio: "Britons mourn . . . a reluctant monarch . . . led his country through the dark days of war . . ." From the announcer's solemn tone I could tell that an event of enormous significance had taken place. People everywhere were paying attention.

Until that moment I did not know that there was a real king. I thought a king was just another character in a fairy tale, a make-believe someone who lived in a palace and did make-believe things, like have parades and order people's heads cut off. But now it turned out there really was a king — except he was dead, and everyone in the world was "shocked and saddened." Those were the words that the man on the radio kept using. All the people in England were shocked and saddened. So were all the people in India and Burma and Australia and Canada. Even our president, Mr. Truman, was reported to be "shocked and saddened."

I found it all oddly disturbing. Something had been broken that wasn't supposed to break. A king, especially a real one, was supposed to be different. A king was not supposed to die. What would happen now? And how come they were saying his daughter would be queen? Why couldn't there be another king?

Then all at once it struck me that, since I was the only one in the house who was listening to the radio, I was probably the only one who knew anything about what had happened. I left my marbles and my blocks and hurried to tell my mother.

I found her in the kitchen, peeling potatoes over the sink.

"Mom, guess what. The king is dead!"

"Well, imagine that," she said. She did not turn around. She did not miss a stroke with the potato peeler.

I couldn't believe it. She did not seem at all shocked or saddened. I tried again. "I mean, he was the king, you know. Of England."

"Mmm. I know. It must be sad for the queen. Have you finished your homework yet?"

"No, but — I mean, I thought —"

"Well, you better get to it. And since you're here, take this out to the compost."

She handed me a Hills Brothers coffee can. It was brimming with garbage: eggshells, coffee grounds, and soggy potato skins.

I did as I was told. But as I tramped out to the compost heap by the garden, I kept wondering how it could be that my mother did not care at all about something that everyone else in the world thought so important.

For the rest of the afternoon I kept one ear glued to the radio and tried to decipher the meaning of what was said. The dead king had come to the throne after his brother's abdication, whatever that meant, and he had only reluctantly taken up the royal scepter and crown. But why should he be reluctant? Who wouldn't want to be king? The whole business was mystifying.

Yet in our house that evening not a word was spoken about the great event. Over supper, my father seethed and grumbled as usual about his miserable job and his boss, who was apparently the most ignorant and thoughtless man who had ever walked the face of the earth. My mother listened patiently as usual, while Joyce and I kept quiet and watched for the silent glare or the pointed fork that meant that my father wanted the butter or the peas or some other dish that was beyond his reach. Then we hurried to pass it over, anxious that he not be kept waiting.

We breathed more easily once my father had eaten his fill and finished his beer. He sat back in his chair, calmer now, cooling his steaming coffee with cold water from a glass. Only then did my mother tell him about the wash machine, how it was making funny noises again and would he please take a look at it when he got a chance because she was afraid it was about to go for good.

My father crumpled up his napkin and threw it down on the table. "Damn it, what next?" he snapped. Then he picked up his coffee cup and headed for the basement stairs.

"I didn't mean you had to do it right now," my mother called after him.

"Yeah, yeah," came my father's voice from down below.

Clearly my parents had other things on their minds than the death of a king, which I realize now must have seemed to them as remote and inconsequential as the once-upon-a-time operettas that they used to sing but sang no longer. For me, though, the wide world continued to intrude and intrigue, teasing its way into my imagination over the radio and through the pages of *Life* and *National Geographic*.

We did not get the glossy picture magazines at our house. They were too expensive. But Uncle Leonard, who was a bachelor and could afford such things, had subscriptions to both. He had them sent to Gramma Froncek's house, which was where he stayed when he was on leave from one of his postings. A sergeant in the marines, he guarded embassies in places like Turkey, Japan, and the Philippines. When he wasn't home, the magazines piled up on the bookshelves in Busha's sun-room, which was where I buried myself during the long, boring, cabbage-smelling Sunday afternoon visits while the grown-ups droned on and on in the next room.

Those luxurious stacks of picture-crammed magazines absorbed me for hours. In their pages I saw battle scenes from Korea, where our troops were fighting in mud and snow to hold back the invading Red armies. I saw Paris streets, where kids my age wore shorts and berets. I saw camel caravans in the Sahara. I saw jungle villages, where dark-skinned native girls walked around in broad daylight with their breasts uncovered. (I knew perfectly well I was committing an impure act by staring at them, but stare I did — and memorized the issue cover so I could find it again next time.) I saw photographs of angry crowds in Berlin (the Reds again) and pictures of houses swept away by floods on the Mississippi and by hurricanes in Florida. And if I was lucky, and searched long enough — stories featuring palm trees were always the most likely places — I could usually find still more pictures of dark-skinned native girls with their naked breasts standing up neat and smooth. Did white girls' breasts look the same? I wondered. Did my sister's?

Slouched on the daybed on Busha's sun porch, I saw glimpses of the wide world that existed beyond the ordinary one I lived in every day. Exciting events happened there. Important people did things that got talked and written about and photographed.

Such people and events began to seem even more important when they started turning up on the screen of the brand new Philco television that my father brought into our house that summer. The set came in a beautifully polished rose-colored cabinet, and once the knob was turned and the tiny screen fizzed and flickered to life, and once my father had reached around back to straighten the jagged lines that scrolled up the screen, and once he had aimed the rabbit-ear antenna in the right direction, it was as if we had our own private magic window through which to peer out at the rest of the world, like submariners gazing through a periscope.

Of course, I watched all the kid's programs, especially *Howdy Doody* and *Kukla, Fran, and Ollie*. But my favorites were the cowboy shows. Instead of just listening to Gene Autry and Roy Rogers and Hopalong Cassidy, I could see them riding and singing and shooting their way across real Wild Western landscapes. I had seen such things in the movies, of course, but now they were right there in our house, part of our life.

In the evenings, all of us gathered around to watch Ed Sullivan and Burns and Allen and Milton Berle, who, despite being a grown-up, wore goofy costumes and did such silly things that even my father laughed out loud — great hearty explosions of delight that I loved to hear because it meant that for those few moments he was not angry or unhappy or disappointed.

But television brought a world not just of actors and comedians. It also showed me real people, real stories, real events. I saw the coronation parade of the new queen. I saw the launching of a brand new ocean liner and pictures of train wrecks. That summer, too, I saw lots of men making speeches.

Since it was an election year, the speeches were mostly about who was going to be the next president of the United States. I liked Ike. Although my parents said little about it, I got the impression that they preferred Governor Stevenson. But to me, General Eisenhower just *looked* like he should be president. He seemed strong and grandfatherly, and anyway he had been a great hero in World War II. So Ike was who I voted for when we fifth-graders held our class election that fall. And when all the votes were counted, I was happy to discover that I was on the winning side.

By that year, too, our own United States senator, Joseph McCarthy, was appearing regularly on television. The senator impressed me, because he was the first person I knew from Wisconsin to be on TV. However, I didn't like him. He was balding, dark, and scowling, and I knew a bully when I saw one. But he was our very own senator, and he kept talking about the same things that the nuns at Saint Stephen's had been warning us about for years: the dangers we faced from godless communism. Only now the Communists weren't on the other side of the world, waiting to send their armies and their new atomic bomb against us. The senator was saying that the Reds were already among us, in the government, in our towns, in our schools, even in the movies. There were Communists everywhere, giving away our secrets and waiting for the day when they could take over our country and make us all slaves and force us kids to turn our mothers and fathers over to the police if they said anything against the government.

The world was becoming scarier and more complicated every day. Nothing seemed to stay the same. Kings died. Armies fought. Earthquakes and floods killed thousands. Communist spies were everywhere, and the Russians could blow us up any time they wanted to if our leaders weren't careful to stay ahead of them in what everybody on radio and television called the arms race.

And yet in other ways, nothing seemed to change at all. I still had homework to do every night. I still went to school and ran around at recess and got on the school bus at the end of the day and came home to find my mother waiting in the kitchen with a glass of milk and a dish of windmill cookies. Life at home stayed very different from the life I heard about on the radio or saw on television or in the magazines.

Not that things didn't happen to us. My brother coming along and Beauty being taken away had certainly interrupted the even course of my life. But my room, our house, my fields and woods — these all remained the same. My father came home from work at the same time every day. We had supper at the same time and went to ten o'clock Mass on Sundays and visited with the relatives on weekends and holidays. And I took it for granted that our lives would just keep going on the same way as always.

I suppose that's why when the big change came it was such a shock.

It was a weekend in the fall when I heard the news. I remember the sunlight slanting low across the yard and the air being tinged with the smell of dry grass and burning leaves. In the field across the road I heard the drone of a tractor: a farmer plowing under the last cornstalks.

I was out in the yard at the time, building the boat that I planned to sail on my secret pond. I knew just how I wanted my boat to look: graceful and sleek, like those I saw when my father took us to Lake Michigan for a Sunday afternoon picnic and a swim. The lake was so big that you couldn't see the other side, but only water and sky, and here and there a creature of both: a sailboat sliding on a breeze.

I wanted to build a boat like one of those. It would be big enough for me to sit in, and it would have a point in front and a red stripe down the side and a sail that would billow in the wind as I glided over the pond. So far, though, my boat did not look anything like the one I saw in my mind's eye.

Materials were part of the problem. I was using scrap lumber — leftovers from the cabin, which my father had finally torn down — and none of the boards really matched. But I had managed to cut the two long sides to almost exactly the same length, and I was pleased with the way they narrowed a little toward the front. But somehow the shape of the thing reminded me less of a boat than of something else, I couldn't think what.

Part of the problem, too, was that I hadn't yet figured out how to make a point for the front. Even if I could figure a way to bend or cut a couple of boards into a pointy shape, I did not have the slightest idea how I would attach them to the rest of the boat. Nor did I know what to do about the cracks that gaped between the boards. Some were so wide that I could see grass poking through the bottom and daylight coming in through the sides. Unless I could close them up, my boat would fill with water the minute I tried to launch it.

While I puzzled over these problems, I kept working on the parts I knew, or thought I knew. At the moment this meant devising a way to rig the mast. I had found a length of two-by-two that made a good mast, so now I was trying to attach the crossbar — an old broom handle — that would hold the sail.

Kneeling on the grass as I worked, I hammered a three-inch eight-penny finishing nail partway in the top of the mast, leaving most of the shank sticking out. This part I now hammered sideways until it bent over the middle of the broom handle. It worked, kind of, but clearly one nail wasn't going to be enough to make the broom handle stay put and not wobble. I was just starting on another when my sister came butting in.

"Somebody die?" she asked.

I sat back on my heels. "No. Why?"

"You're making a coffin, right?"

A light went on. So *that* was what my oblong box reminded me of. "Yeah," I said. "It's for you."

"Ha, ha, very funny."

"Good. I'm glad."

She pouted. "No, really, what are you making?"

"If you can't see it, I'm not going to tell you."

"It's a toy box."

"No."

"A planter."

"No."

"A bathtub."

I wondered: If I took a good swing at her with the mast, would it hurt her so much that I'd get into trouble? "It's a boat," I said through clenched teeth.

She looked at the boat thoughtfully before delivering her judgment. "It needs a point in front."

"No, it doesn't." I was not about to let her tell me how to build my boat.

"Does, too. All boats have points. Otherwise how can you tell the front from the back?"

"Because the seat's in the back, that's how."

She considered this and shrugged. "Anyway," she went on, "where do you think you're going to float it? There's no water around here."

"I know a place. There's a pond."

All at once she was interested. She hated it when I knew things she didn't. "There is? Where?"

I waved vaguely toward the distant fields. "Off over there."

"Will you show me?"

My first impulse was to say no. Until now I had not shared the secret of my pond with anyone. But I realized that transporting the boat there would be a lot easier with someone's help.

"Okay," I said. "I'll show you later."

She was not happy having to wait, but she had no choice. She hung around for a while, watching me work, then got bored and drifted away. Vaguely I may have heard the screen door slam behind her as she went back into the house. But by then I was deep into my work once more.

I hammered two more nails partway in, abutting the broomstick, then bent them around it. After that, I nailed the bottom of the mast to the front of the boat. Next came the sail, an old bedsheet that my mother had dug out of the rag bag. I hunted around in the basement until I found some twine, and this I used to tie the top two corners of the sheet to the ends of the broomstick. But the sail caused a new problem. No matter what I did, its weight kept pulling the mast over sideways.

Ropes. That's what I needed: ropes to hold the mast in place. I'd string them from the top of the mast, then nail the ends to the sides of the boat. Didn't all sailboats have ropes on them? Now I knew why.

I was just starting for the house when I heard the screen door slam again. I looked up to see my sister running down the back steps.

"Guess what," she called, bursting with excitement. This time she knew something I didn't know.

"What?" I asked, pretending indifference.

"Guess."

"I give up."

"We're moving."

I was all attention. "What are you talking about?"

"It's true. I just heard them talking. Daddy was telling Mommy. We're selling the house. We're moving someplace else."

In the pit of my stomach I felt a weight like a stone. If I had been dropped into the pond just then I would have sunk straight to the bottom. I sat down on the seat of my boat. "Did he say when?"

"Soon, it sounds like."

"Did he say where we're going to live?"

"Well . . . no."

"What about school? Where will we go to school?"

Joyce was looking less pleased with herself. "I don't know," she said. Obviously she had been so excited about hearing the news that she'd neglected to get the whole story. "He didn't say anything about that. Just that we're moving."

The thought filled me with dread.

We had now lived in the same place for four years — one year in the cabin and three in the house. I was no longer the new kid at Saint Stephen's. I knew my way around. I knew who the bullies were and how to stay out of their way. I had friends. I was no longer the last one to get picked for teams. In the new place I would have to start all over. I would be a stranger again.

Joyce sat down at my side. Her glow of triumph had faded. She now looked as dejected as I felt. "I don't want to move," she said at last.

"Me neither."

"I like it here."

"Me too."

First a baby brother, then Beauty gone, now this. I could see why people said that bad things happened in threes. It seemed so unfair. But clearly what I thought or felt didn't matter. Nobody asked and nobody wanted to know.

Suddenly nothing seemed to matter: not getting the mast to stand up straight, or filling the cracks between the boards, or whether the boat had a point in front. It didn't even matter whether I built a boat at all.

Joyce put her arm around my shoulders. "There's one good thing."

"What?"

"Even when we move, we'll still be together."

13

MOVING DAY

"*I*'ve got a good one," my father said.

He liked jokes and riddles. He would hear them at work, and if he was in a good mood, he would try them on us.

"Where was Moses when the lights went out?" he asked over supper one night.

"I don't know," Joyce said.

I shrugged.

"In the dark, of course." He grinned, showing uneven teeth.

I was puzzled. Wouldn't anyone be in the dark when the lights went out? What did Moses have to do with it? But I laughed anyway, anxious as ever to please him.

He looked at me. "You don't get it, do you?" he asked.

I shook my head miserably. How did he know? I wondered. He always seemed to know.

The fact was, when it came to understanding anything about my father, I was in the same place as Moses when the lights were on the fritz.

I doubt that it even occurred to him to tell us why we had to leave our home. He had made the decision, and as far as he was concerned that was all any of us needed to know. End of story. Case closed. To raise questions meant to challenge his authority. And I, for one, was not about to do anything so foolish. Not at age ten.

As usual it was my mother who tried to make sense of what was happening. In our family drama she was both narrator and interpreter. She commented on the action but did not seem to affect it in any way — at least not that I could tell.

At times I would hear her voice raised. It would come from somewhere off in the wings, behind closed doors, and I was always astonished by the volume and intensity of those brief outbursts. But what the arguments were about I seldom knew. All I saw was what happened once the curtain went up and the drama began to unfold, with my father at center stage and my mother standing modestly to one side, ready to explain but scrupulous to avoid upstaging the leading man.

She always spoke her lines quietly, unobtrusively, as befit the once-upon-a-time chorus girl who never in her life imagined stepping forward to assume the lead. Nevertheless, her role was crucial. Without her, we would have had no clue about the reasons for the changes being wrought in our lives by the star performer.

It was my mother who told us about his new job: how he was leaving the power plant to take up a position as a teacher in a vocational school.

"It's why he has been going to classes at night," she explained later that evening, as she cleaned up the kitchen and Joyce and I did the supper dishes. "He was learning how to be a teacher. Do you see?"

"I guess so," Joyce said, her hands in the dishwater.

"What's a cational school?" I wanted to know.

My mother brought the last of the kettles over from the stove. "Vocational. It's where boys go to learn how to do jobs. Daddy will be teaching them about . . ." She paused, not too sure of the next part. "Well, I guess about how to run different kinds of machinery. Things like that."

"But why do we have to move?" I asked. "Why can't we live here and Daddy can drive to work the way he always has?"

"The school is too far away. It would take him forever to get there."

Clearly there was no hope; nothing we could say would change things.

My mother did her best to soften the blow: "You'll see," she said. "It'll be okay. You'll make new friends in no time."

"I don't want new friends. I like the ones I have."

"I know. But —" She seemed stumped again. "Sometimes things happen, that's all." She tried pleading for understanding: "This means a lot to your father. It's what he wants to do."

Looking back, I wonder: Was she beginning to have her own doubts? Did she remember having used almost exactly the same words a few years before, when the time came to tell us about another move, another uprooting? Building his own house had meant a lot to him. That, too, had been something he wanted to do, wanted it so badly that he was willing to put his family through a whole year of living like Dust Bowl refugees in a cramped one-room shack, while the sisters and brothers and in-laws shook their heads and clucked their tongues and whispered about us behind our backs. This had been followed by more months of living in a half-finished house, with no stairs to the basement and the back wall covered with tar paper like some hillbilly shanty.

But she made no apologies to anyone. Far from it. What he was doing made her proud, made her straighten her back and hold her head high. Who else in the family was attempting such a thing? Who else dared to dream the way he did, then carried through the way he did and managed to make the dream come true? He was no stick-in-the-mud like the rest of them. Not Walter. Not a chance.

Yet here he was, ready to give it all up in pursuit of a new glimmering hope. And this time she had to work hard to put a good face on it, because this time she hated what was happening, hated the thought of leaving the place, which she had come to love as much as she had ever loved any place in her life. Because it was no one else's, only theirs alone, made the way they wanted it to be.

Of course, my father had his reasons. I just never knew what they were. Only now was I beginning to find out: now, all these years later, while I sat across the kitchen table from my mother and sipped morning coffee and leafed through my father's drawings while the man himself was wasting away in a nursing home across town.

The distance to the new job was the simple answer, the part we kids could be expected to understand. But it wasn't the real story. All you had to do was look at a map to see that the vocational school was not all that much farther from home than the power plant had been.

"I think he just got overwhelmed, is all," my mother said now, staring into her empty cup.

The unfinished house and the sprawling property apparently got to be too much for him, especially since the new job was taking so much of his time and concentration.

I was thinking back, putting the pieces together. "Wasn't that also about the time that his blood pressure started acting up?"

"Yes. There was that, too."

She looked incredibly sad just then, and for a moment I regretted having stirred up the memories. But I wanted to know. The reasons had been a mystery to me for years.

It was odd, though. Now that I knew them — now that the past had been dragged kicking and screaming into the present — I realized that all the reasons in the world didn't matter worth a damn. They were not going to heal the hurt or bring back what had been lost.

Mom looked off somewhere over my shoulder. "I remember wondering what his reasons would be next time? When would it end? When would he ever be satisfied?"

But she had told no one of her doubts, neither us nor her sisters, not even her mother, who was still her closest confidante. She would never *ever* undermine my father or betray him. Not to them or to us or to anyone.

As for me, as a child, no amount of explaining, no reasons, nor words of comfort, would have made the least bit of difference in the misery or bewilderment I felt. After all, it wasn't just any house we were going to be leaving behind. It was the house I had first seen my father sketch on the ground with a stick one cold March afternoon. It was the house I had watched grow from foundation to frame to rooftop and chimney. In the living-room floor there were nails that I had banged in with my own hammer.

What I could not understand was how my father could do it. Barely three years had passed since Father Beyer came to bestow his blessings of holy water and cigar smoke upon our new home. Now, suddenly, it was as if none of it mattered: not the nights my father spent poring over his drawings as he struggled to adjust his plans to reality; not the weeks and months of building; not the pleasure of finally moving in; not the pride we all felt in showing the place to aunts and uncles and cousins. It was as if none of it counted for anything.

Why, the house wasn't even finished! True, there were now real steps to the basement and the tar-papered back wall had finally been sided over. But the sun porch that my father had planned to build over the garage had not even been started, and aside from a narrow swath of mowed lawn close to the house, most of the yard was still given over to mud and wild prairie grass. And although my father had put in a few fruit trees, they were still young and spindly and hadn't given us a single apple or pear.

Yet my father was now going to leave behind everything he had started. It was incomprehensible to me.

What my father himself must have felt I could imagine even less then than I can now. Was he sorry to be leaving his triumph behind, forever unfinished, forever a promise? I would never know.

Every chance I had now, I ran to the woods. I was a squirrel, storing up the last days before everything changed. Perched in the fort that I had built in my oak tree on the edge of the woods, I gazed across the autumn fields with their fringes of red and gold and promised myself that I would remember every detail: the wind combing the dry grass; a hawk soaring and circling, wings outstretched against the clouds; a chipmunk rummaging in the flame-red leaves on the ground below, picking its head up as the hawk's shadow passed over him, then giving a squeak and darting under a log. Even then I was convinced that the world would never seem as big and beautiful as it did here, where the sky-arched fields seemed to go on forever and where the woods still held secrets I would now never discover.

Savoring the moment in all of its sad, autumn-scented beauty, I was not about to admit to myself that I also felt a small tremor of excitement at the prospect of moving. But it was true. Something new and surprising was about to happen. A new house awaited. There would be new places to explore, new discoveries to be made, and somewhere inside, not far beneath the buttons of my shirt, I felt a slight stirring of anticipation, like the first hint of a breeze that sends a shiver through the still air and sets the leaves dancing on the tips of the trees.

It was there. I felt it. But I suppressed it. For now, all I knew or cared about was that the new place would not be anything like the one that had become so familiar, the one that was home in a way that no other place had ever been before or would ever be again.

On moving day there were boxes everywhere. Each had a label scrawled on the side in black grease pencil: KITCHEN. FRONT BEDROOM. BATH. JOYCE'S CLOTHES. LINENS. TOM'S. MICHAEL'S.

My father backed the trailer up to the front door. Eager to help, I carried a carton of clothes out to the front stoop.

"Just put it down on the grass," my father said, brushing past me. "Big things first."

As with everything else, there seemed to be a right way and a wrong way to load trailers.

"Where do you want the dishes?" my mother asked. She was in the kitchen wrapping the last of the glasses and cups in newspaper and packing them in boxes.

"Hold your horses," my father said. "I can only do one thing at a time."

He had hired one of his students to help. "Easy now," he said as the two of them jockeyed the refrigerator onto a dolly.

"Lift your end a little," the young man said. "That's good."

"All set now?" my father asked. "Okay. Upsa daisy."

My father was different with this young stranger than he was with me. It was the way he had been with the men who helped him build the house. Few words passed between them, yet each seemed to know what the other meant and what was expected. They were two men together, self-assured, calm, trusting, and I couldn't wait for the time when I'd be grown up and my father would be that way with me. I didn't yet know that my age had little to do with it: that between us were already growing prickly hedgerows of hopes and expectations, of hurts and disappointments, that would make me forever wary and him invariably impatient and annoyed.

"What can I do?" I asked my mother.

"You and Joyce can roll up the rugs," she said.

That done, we were given lamps and boxes and small pictures to carry out to the grass, where they sat until my father could decide what he wanted to do with them.

He and the young man were busy in the trailer, fitting our dressers

157

and pieces of our beds into different odd-shaped niches. The davenport came next, then a file cabinet, then the top of the kitchen table, its legs removed. This my father slid neatly behind the dressers.

"Bring that box over," my father told me. "No, not that one. The other one." He shook his head. "Kid never stops daydreaming," he said to the young stranger.

My ears burned as if he'd just swatted them. I handed the box up to the young man without looking at him and told myself to pay better attention.

My father nestled the box into a corner. Then he spent more time arranging and rearranging the pieces, making sure everything was tight and nothing got scratched or nicked. Like a bird fussing over a nest, he tried one piece here, then moved it there, then moved it back again. I couldn't see what difference any of it made. But when he was finished everything fit tightly. Nothing wiggled, and there was no wasted space.

"That's about it," he said, closing the trailer gate. "We'll get the rest on the next trip." He opened the car door. "Want to come along?"

I shook my head. One ear-burning for the day was enough. But I wanted badly for him to ask again. If he did I would go.

He only shrugged. "Suit yourself," he said, and got in. The young man climbed in on the passenger side, and they drove off together, leaving me feeling both disappointed and relieved.

I went up the steps and into the house. My sister was busy in the kitchen helping my mother scrub out the empty cupboards.

I wandered through the rooms and listened to the echoes.

Empty rooms. I see them in my dreams. Hear them. Smell them. There are light shadows on the walls where pictures used to hang. The windows are bare. They have shades but no curtains. Footsteps echo on wooden floors. There are cardboard cartons stacked in the corners, their flaps folded shut. They may be waiting to be carried out to the trailer, or maybe they have just arrived and are waiting to be unpacked. In my dream it's impossible to tell.

I smell fresh paint and old carpets.

Amid the echoes I hear whispers, voices weighed down with sadness and regret. Something has ended. But other voices are alive with excitement. Something new is about to begin. Some things now will never hap-

pen, but other things have become possible. The good times are over.
The best times are just ahead.

Our new house, a redbrick bungalow, sat in the middle of a city block,
with the street only a few feet from our front door and the neighboring
houses shouldering close on either side. There was a dinky little yard out
back, with a chain-link fence around it like a dog pen. When I walked to
the end of our block, all I could see in any direction were more streets and
more houses. There were no fields or woods or creeks anywhere in sight.
The sky, which had once seemed so endlessly high and wide, now
pressed close overhead, just above the housetops. The only time I was
able to glimpse the horizon was when I rode my bike to the busy avenue
where the buses ran. I'd squint up the length of the avenue, past the
stoplights and the stores and the filling stations and out to the end, where
the pavement narrowed to a pinpoint and disappeared in the west.

Out there somewhere was open prairie: endless miles of grass, with
cattle ranches and horses and a sky as big as an ocean. There were mountains, too, if I could ever get to them. I wondered how long it would take
me to bicycle there. For now, though, I was stuck where I was. My world
had shrunk, and I felt as if I had shrunk along with it.

To make matters worse, I was now sharing a room with my brother.
At the old house his crib had been in Joyce's room, which seemed only
right since she was the one who liked to play with dolls. But now that he
was an energetic two-year-old, he was put in with me.

"Boys should be together," my mother explained.

There was no escaping him, and I had no one but myself to blame.
Without fully understanding the consequences, I had foolishly helped
him learn to walk, urging him on, holding out my hands to him, cheering
when he toddled across the room and into my arms. Now I was paying
the price. As far as he was concerned, the sole purpose of this new accomplishment was to enable him to follow me around. Wherever I went
in the house or out in the yard, Michael was right behind me. He stuck to
me like lint. He drew in my comic books with crayons and knocked over
the airplane model I was building on my desk. He borrowed my cowboy
hat, then sat on it. When I took it back, he threw a tantrum.

"Tommy," my mother called from the kitchen, "what are you doing
to your brother?"

"Nothing."

"It doesn't sound like nothing. Stop it. Right now."

"But he started it."

"You heard me."

School might well have provided a refuge. Although it was only a few blocks away, it was still distant enough that my brother couldn't follow me there. But school presented another kind of trouble. Because I was starting at Blessed Sacrament in the middle of the school year, I felt as if I had just arrived from another planet.

Making my way down the corridors through noisy mobs of strangers, I was sure I must have green skin, purple antennae on top of my head, and ears made out of red balloons. Every earthling in the place was looking at me, or so I imagined. My knees turned to water. My stomach twisted into knots. That I somehow managed to reach my classroom without throwing up was a triumph of self-control.

But worse was yet to come. Stepping through the door and into the classroom, I found myself once again facing a roomful of unknown faces. Memories of my first day at Saint Stephen's came flooding back. I shoved my hands into my pockets to keep them from trembling. I was vaguely aware of Sister Jean Marie speaking my name as she introduced me to the class. When she pointed me toward an empty seat, I was afraid for a moment that my legs would not move. But somehow they carried me to my place.

I was relieved when the bell rang and class began. At least everyone would now be paying attention to Sister and not to me. I would not have minded sitting there all day. But then came recess. On the playground, friends clustered together, their backs to me, while I stood to one side and became intensely interested in making martian patterns in the gravel with the toe of one martian shoe.

It wasn't long before I became aware of another pair of feet standing toe-to-toe with mine. I looked up. I was staring into the face of a boy with a brush haircut, a sharply pointed nose, and a sneer. I recognized him as one of the kids from my class. Behind him stood three other boys, all of whom were eyeballing me.

"Where you from, kid?" asked the boy with the sneer.

I swallowed hard. "Um, I just moved here."

"Um, no kidding? Um, why do you think I asked you? Um?"

160

His friends laughed.

I glanced around to see whether there was any help nearby. Sister Jean Marie was the closest, and she was all the way on the other side of the playground, watching the girls. I was on my own. "Look, I don't want to fight," I said. "Okay?"

"Hey, whoa. Take it easy. Who said anything about fighting? I'm just being friendly. Right, guys?"

"Yeah," said a boy who had a chin like a bulldog's. "Jerry's a very friendly guy."

I didn't believe him for a minute. I could smell a bully a mile away. I could smell one even better when he was practically standing on my shoes. "Do you like riddles?" I asked.

Where the question came from I had no idea, but its effect was gratifying. Jerry looked baffled by the change of direction.

"What are you talking about?" he said.

"Where was Moses when the lights went out?"

"What?"

"It's a riddle."

"Yeah, Jer, it's a riddle," said the boy with the bulldog chin.

"I know it's a riddle. All right, so where was Moses when the lights went out?"

"In the dark, of course."

Jerry's friends laughed.

Jerry looked puzzled. "I don't get it."

I didn't gloat. "That's okay. I didn't get it the first time either. Wanna see my fast draw?" I put my hand on my hip as though I were going for a pistol, but I didn't move it from there. "Wanna see it again?"

Jerry tipped his head to one side, the way Beauty used to do when she heard the teakettle whistle. He wasn't exactly smiling but he wasn't glowering either. He didn't seem to know what to do.

I was on a roll. "When is a door not a door?"

But Jerry had had enough. Instead of attempting an answer, he just shook his head. "The kid's nutty as a fruitcake," he told his friends, jabbing a thumb in my direction. And he walked away, his buddies trailing behind.

"When it's ajar," I called after them. "Get it? A jar?"

But they did not look back.

161

I was relieved. I may have come off looking like an idiot, but at least I didn't end up getting socked in the eye. It was a useful strategy and one I would resort to more times than I cared to think about. I always felt rotten afterward and hated myself for not having the guts to stand up and fight. I knew that neither Roy Rogers nor Sergeant Preston of the Yukon would have allowed himself to be pushed around the way I did. But I swallowed my pride and made a joke and usually got away without a scratch. It was, after all, the way I was learning to get along at home, where standing up to my father was out of the question and being a joker was the best way to avoid trouble.

The only problem was that sometimes the joker got out of hand. I seemed to have in me a foolhardy imp that kept wanting to poke out and stir things up at exactly the wrong times — like the day Sister Jean Marie asked me in class where my homework was.

"In my left breast pocket, ma'am," I answered solemnly.

I don't know where I had picked up the phrase; probably I had heard it in one of the British war movies that sometimes ran on afternoon television. But I liked the way it dressed a dirty word in respectable clothing.

To my fellow fifth graders, it was as if I had stood on my desk and waved one of Uncle Leonard's *National Geographic* pictures of a naked aborigine. Snickers and giggles erupted everywhere.

Beneath her wimple, Sister's face turned red. "Young man, you will go and stand in the cloakroom."

"What did I say?" I protested, pretending astonishment.

More snickers and giggles.

"Quiet!" shouted Sister, her gaze sweeping the room. She glared at me. "You are an impudent young man, and your impudence has just earned you extra homework and a note to your mother. Now go."

"Yes, ma'am," I said, trying to sound contrite. But my classmates weren't fooled. As I trudged to the back of the room, I was met with grins and winks. One boy gave me a secret thumbs-up. I felt like a hero and I loved it.

My mother, however, was not pleased.

"Why must you always be getting into trouble?" she said after she had read Sister's note. She sounded weary and very sad.

Fortunately my mother did not show Sister's note to my father. I sensed that she dreaded his reaction as much as I did. But she could not prevent him from seeing my next report card. As bad as the grades were, Sister's comments were worse. Shows poor deportment and disrespect, she wrote. Needs discipline.

"What's the matter with you?" my father growled. "When are you going to shape up?"

I hung my head. I was silent.

"You think school is for goofing off, is that it?" He grabbed my arm and shook me. "Look at me when I'm talking to you. Your sister doesn't get comments like this. Why can't you behave the way she does? Is that too much to expect?"

I shook my head, biting back tears. I was determined not to let him see me cry. And I succeeded. That was my victory. Not until I was safely alone in my room, and rubbing the sore place on my backside where he had swatted me, did the tears come free.

Although I couldn't have articulated it at the time, I was in a dilemma. I had discovered that my popularity with my classmates seemed to increase in direct proportion to the number of times I got sent to the cloakroom or the principal's office. On the other hand, I learned that I could win the approval of Sister Jean Marie if I behaved myself, raised my hand in class, and offered now and then to stay after school to clean the erasers and empty the pencil sharpener. But I had to be careful not to get carried away, or otherwise I'd get to be known as a goody-goody by the other kids.

It was tricky, this business of trying to get along with everybody, trying to please everybody: my father, my teacher, the other kids. Sometimes I felt like a chameleon on a tightrope, balancing when I could, disappearing if I had to. I kept having stomachaches. At night, in my dreams, I was forever being chased by shadowy figures, dark cars, and prowling animals, and I could never make my legs move quickly enough.

Somehow I managed, though. Sister sent fewer notes to my parents, and while I was still worried about my next report card, when it finally appeared it showed "improved deportment." I was relieved. My father was sure to be pleased.

He was, too, in his way.

"Can't you do any better than that?" he asked.

I was stunned. I thought I had done better. But since his question was not followed by angry shouts and swats on my behind, I figured I was getting off easy.

"I guess so," I said.

"What's that supposed to mean? Will you or won't you?"

"I will."

"See that you do."

Though I could get no further with him, I was having better luck with some of the kids in my class. A few of them started including me in their ball games during recess, and one of them, a boy named Greg, invited me to play at his house after school. He and another boy, Bobby, took me around and showed me all the good places in the neighborhood: the culverts under the highway, the vacant lots, an abandoned house where an old man had once hung himself from the rafters in the attic — or so they said.

The best time was when we refought the battle of Iwo Jima at a nearby building site. I was in the thick of it and happy to be fighting as a GI instead of a Jap. Charging up and down the dirt mountains that surrounded the excavation, I fired my homemade rifle, lobbed dirt-ball grenades, died with screams of agony, then sprang up to fight again. By the time I got home that afternoon, I was scraped, bloody, and supremely happy.

I decided that I liked the new neighborhood and my new friends. Greg and Bobby and I continued to hang around together all that summer. I was getting my feet under me at last.

Then we moved again.

At home, pictures came down off the walls, books disappeared into boxes, rugs were rolled up. Cardboard cartons began piling up in every room and were soon being filled with pots and pans, dishes, glassware, clothes, shoes, linens, lamps.

Friendships were packed away, too. I said good-bye to Greg and Bobby and promised to write them from our new home, which this time was to be not just in a new neighborhood or a new city but in a whole new state.

My friends were in awe and so was I. I was about to move on to a new life. While their lives remained the same, mine was about to change dramatically. I was off on an adventure, and by itself that would separate us.

It would make my life unusual and therefore more interesting than theirs.

Later, when I was alone, it struck me that at the last house, too, I had promised to write to my friends. I had never written a word, and now I could not even picture what my old pals had looked like. I wondered if they had forgotten me, too, and if the same thing would happen with Greg and Bobby. Unlike the pots and pans, the clothes and linens, friendships, once they were packed away, did not get reopened. Only our family stayed the same: Dad, Mom, Joyce, me, and Michael. The rest of the world came and went. And once it was gone — once we left it — it vanished forever.

"Daddy has to go where the work is."

Again it fell to my mother to explain to my sister and me the reason for this latest upheaval.

What had happened to my father's dream of being a teacher? Had he been disappointed? Had he failed somehow? Had he discovered that teaching did not pay well enough for him to support us? Or was it that he had simply grown restless and decided to change course, to pursue a new dream? My mother did not say. Such things were not discussed with children. All we knew was that my father had a better job lined up. After teaching for a year, after following the dream that he had worked toward for so long, he was going to start over in a new profession. He was going into sales.

Sales! That was where the money was, and the promise and the excitement, or so it must have seemed to my father in the middle of the 1950s. He could see it in the ads in the newspapers and the magazines. He could see it in television commercials and the shiny billboards that sprouted like wildflowers along the highways, tempting, inviting, luring the viewer to buy, buy, buy. Newer and better products were appearing every day: new soaps got clothes cleaner and brighter; frozen foods tasted better than fresh; toothpaste with fluoride made cavities a thing of the past; Wonder bread built strong bodies twelve ways.

Anything was possible. Optimism was everywhere, starting at the top with the confident grin of the new president, Mr. Eisenhower, whose inauguration I'd watched on television, having been allowed by my mother to stay home from school for the historic occasion. Sister Jean Marie was not nearly so civic-minded. When the reason for my absence came out — thanks to my bragging about it to one of my classmates — both my mother and I were called into the principal's office, to her embarrassment as well as my own.

America was booming. Millions of automobiles were now being sold every year — more than ever in history. More houses were being built, more refrigerators sold, more frozen food packaged. Television showed us a world where father knew best (except in the kitchen); where Lassie always came home; where good families — like Ozzie and Harriet's and the Cleavers — always stuck together, whatever their comic differences, and where everything came out all right in the end.

The only real cloud on this sunny horizon was shaped like a mushroom. Although the Korean war was over, the threat of nuclear war with the Soviet Union was still very much alive. *Life* carried features on civil defense procedures and showed pictures of the hardy soldiers who manned the snowbound radar stations of the Distant Early Warning system, the DEW line, which would alert the country to incoming Soviet bombers or missiles. *Mechanics Illustrated* published plans for bomb shelters that you could build in your own basement, and included charts of how much food and water the average family should store away in order to survive below ground until the danger of radiation exposure had passed. In school, we had air-raid drills as often as fire drills. When the siren sounded, our teachers led us out into the hall where, we were told, we'd be safe from flying glass in the event of an atomic attack.

Yet even the fear of nuclear annihilation did little to dampen the go-ahead spirit of the day. The American bandwagon was on the roll, and my father, enthralled at the spectacle, dropped everything to go running after it.

Sales ought to have been a good fit for my father. He enjoyed people, and he knew everything there was to know about machine tools, which was what he'd be selling. Did it matter to him that the new job was in Detroit? Did he care that his pursuit of this latest enthusiasm meant uprooting his family again? If he had any such reservations, we never heard about them. In any case, they were not strong enough to change his mind. The move was on.

One day, just after the end of the school term, I looked out the front window to see my father backing up a U-Haul to the front door. The boxes, the beds, the sofa and chairs, the kitchen table, the ironing board — everything went into the trailer. The next morning we were on our way.

We left before dawn, and I immediately fell asleep in the backseat. When next I opened my eyes, a cherry-colored sun was rising out of Lake Michigan. We were heading south along Lakeshore Drive in Chicago, a place I had never been before. The road ran through a beautiful park. Sometimes I caught a glimpse of the lake; other times I saw fountains shaped like wedding cakes and marinas full of pretty white sailboats. It all seemed glorious and new.

Before the day was out we had crossed Illinois, Indiana, and Michigan. That made three new states in one day, and this pleased me enormously because it meant we were becoming adventurers! We were seeing the world!

Our new house was in the northern suburbs of Detroit. It was a large, handsome brick affair with a big yard. We were only renting it until my father could decide where he wanted to live, but its impression of grandeur and solidity seemed in keeping with my father's new profession and his high expectations.

One evening soon after we moved in, my father called us all into the kitchen. Supper was done, the table had been cleared, and now, in the middle of it, sat a small white box.

"What is it?" Joyce asked.

"Have a look," my father said. "Are everybody's hands clean?"

After making sure that they were, he carefully removed the lid. With his stubby fingers he reached delicately into the box and drew forth five small cards. He passed the cards around with the reverence of a priest placing the sacred host upon the tongues of his communicants.

"Ooh," said Joyce.

"It's very nice," said my mother. She leaned toward Michael, who was only three and did not yet read. "See," she said, "it's Daddy's name. It says 'Walter T. Froncek, Sales Representative.' "

The words were printed in shiny raised letters. And beside my father's name was that of the company he now represented: Do-All.

In retrospect, I cannot imagine any name suiting my father better. Men could shake hands on such a name. It was honest and forthright. It evoked all the unequivocal confidence of the era. The fact that my father was associated with such a prestigious-sounding company confirmed what I already knew: that he really could do everything — handle machinery, repair cars and plumbing, design and build houses, teach. And now he was going to be what he called a sales rep. He would even have his own "territory" — a word that in my mind called up images of white-hatted marshals with gunbelts hanging from their hips.

I did not yet know about the things he could not do, like finding contentment. And staying put instead of running. But I was beginning to learn.

My father now spent much of the week on the road, traveling to the factories and machine shops of southeastern Michigan and northern Ohio. The trunk of his car was crammed with sample cases, catalogs, and order forms. His wallet bulged so with notes and business cards that only by wrapping it with rubber bands was he able to fold it shut.

He was always busy, always in a hurry, always going someplace or meeting someone. On weekends he made time to take us on vacation trips: to Greenfield Village; to a beach on the shores of Lake Saint Claire; across to Canada (our first foreign country!) and on to Niagara Falls, where we took an elevator down to a tunnel behind the falls and stood in yellow slickers behind the thundering wall of water. Mostly, though, we saw little of him.

Not that my sister and I really noticed. We were too busy getting used to the new neighborhood, the new school, the new friends who were not quite friends because we had only just met them and because I, for one, could not shake the gnawing suspicion that this sojourn, too, was going to be short-lived. In which case, why should I bother trying to make friends, since the chances were I was only going to have to say good-bye again?

14

ANY PLACE BUT HERE

"*I* don't know what happened," my mother told me years later, when I came looking for explanations. "He told me he quit, but maybe he was fired." She shrugged. "Who knows what the real story was? He always had some story."

I shifted uneasily in my chair. This was not what I wanted to hear. Not from her.

Our morning coffee hour was edging toward noon. Since sitting down to breakfast, we had not moved from her kitchen table except to get more hot water from the kettle on the stove. I felt weighed down by the past and by too much Nescafe. I wanted to leave this table, with its litter of toast crumbs and memories, and walk out the front door and into the light of the present day. But my mother had never before spoken so openly about those years, and I was afraid that if I stopped her now, she would never want to start again.

"He was paid on commission," she was saying. "But he didn't bring in enough sales, so he didn't get paid very much." She shook her head. "I guess he just wasn't cut out to be a salesman."

"I'm surprised," I said. "He always enjoyed being around people so much."

"Oh, that part he loved. Absolutely. He could talk to anybody. It was the paperwork he had no patience for. All the follow-up — writing up orders, making sure they got filled — he just hated all that. When he was home and had time to do it, he'd put it off and put it off." She sighed. "And then of course he wasn't very good at drumming up new customers, either. He didn't have the — tsk, what's the word? You know what I mean."

"The hustle."

"The hustle. Right. He just wasn't any good at that at all. He had such a hard time bringing himself to pick up the phone and make those calls. I'd try to push him, but it didn't help. It just made him angry. I was interfering."

I squirmed in my chair. The litany of his failures and her disappointments was getting depressing. Besides, my body was beginning to make demands. A quart or so of coffee was rising to flood stage. Excusing myself, I headed for the bathroom.

The interruption was a relief in more ways than one. My mother was getting close to the heart of things, which was exactly where I'd thought I wanted to be when I began dredging up the past. Yet as we edged toward what mattered most, I found myself flinching and wanting to turn away. She was talking of things that I wasn't sure any son ever wants to know about his father. To speak of him with such brutal honesty and even, yes, with disgust, for that was what I heard behind her words, seemed not just distasteful but disloyal. And the surprise was that I minded.

When I was a kid, and later, well into my teens, I had been able to tell my mother everything. She had been my closest confidante. In the seething war between my father and me, she had been my advocate. More than once she had even been my protector, like the time when I was fourteen or fifteen and managed to provoke him to such fury that he came after me with blood in his eyes and a leather belt in his hand.

I no longer remember what I had done to spark his rage, but in those days I had an unerring instinct for raising his hackles. Instead of doing everything I could to avoid trouble, I seemed to go out of my way to rile him up. It didn't take much.

Loud music could do it. Cranking the volume on Elvis or on Bill Haley and His Comets was surefire. Best of all was my recording of the *1812* Overture. High school music appreciation classes had stirred my interest in the classics, and the more pyrotechnic the better. That my father

170

happened to be taking a nap at the moment the cannons went off somehow escaped my attention.

"Turn that damn thing down!" I'd hear from the next room. Of course, I'd jump to do as he said, but the damage had been done.

Dragging my feet and sulking when he asked me to sweep the basement or take out the garbage were also winning tactics. So was making wisecracks about the polka music he liked to listen to in the car, on the way to church.

"All right," he'd growl, "that's enough."

"What did I do?" I'd protest.

Most of the blowups were over in a flash. I'd get off with a tongue lashing and a single swat from the back of his hand. But watch out if the demon in me acted up at the wrong time, or went a little too far.

Whatever it was that set him off on that day, his anger flared immediately to fury. He bellowed like a maddened bull. His face got red right up to the top of his receding hairline. He whipped off his belt and made a grab at me. I dodged away, tore out of the room, and went racing down the basement steps, stumbling, catching myself, plunging on with my father right behind me. At first I managed to stay out of reach, keeping the furnace between us. But he cornered me by the coal bin. Grabbing my arm, he threw me against the wooden wall. Later I saw that my head had just missed the point of a protruding nail. For now, though, all I could do was cower, covering my head with my arms as the first blows fell.

The leather stung, but I did not cry out. I refused to give him the satisfaction. I clamped my jaws together, and when tears came, I fought to hold them back. The whole time I did not make a sound.

My resistance only fueled his fury. In our unspoken battle of wills, I was winning. He yelled louder and hit harder, and God knows what would have happened if my mother hadn't reached him in time. "Don't hit him, Walter," she was shouting. "Don't hit him." She was behind him then, clawing at the arm that was swinging the belt. Finally she managed to get a grip and, holding on, made him stop.

He staggered back, blowing hard. In that moment I crawled to my feet and slipped away and raced up the stairs to my room, where I locked myself in and stood, shoulder to the door, heart racing, back and arms burning where the leather had landed.

Not until then did the tears flow, and my body begin to shake. There was blood on the front of my shirt, and I realized that in my effort to keep silent I must have bitten through my lip. But even that pain was small compared to what I felt inside. For the first time I had seen the full depth of my father's fury, and it was terrifying.

It was also utterly bewildering. Why should he be so angry at me? I had done something he didn't like, no doubt about it. But whatever it was, it couldn't have been that bad! Only after many years passed did I begin to have an inkling of how little my father's pent-up rage and frustration had anything to do with me.

I did not know how long I had been in my room, trying to catch my breath, before there was a knock at my door.

"Go away," I said.

My mother's voice came from the other side. "Are you all right?"

"I'm fine," I said, but my voice cracked, giving me away.

"Can I come in?"

I wiped my eyes, took some deep breaths, then opened the door. She came in.

"Oh, no," she groaned when she saw my shirt.

"It's just from my lip. It's okay."

"I'll get some peroxide."

"It's okay. It stopped. Never mind." I threw myself on my bed and stared out the window. My room, which I shared with Michael, was upstairs, under the eaves of our small Cape Cod–style house. It had a slanted ceiling, and the window overlooked our backyard, where an hour before, my mother had hung the laundry on the clothesline. As always, the wash was carefully arranged by size, color, and function: underwear together, towels together, and all precisely clipped to the line at the top corners.

"I don't understand why he hates me so much," I said.

She sat down on my desk chair. "He doesn't hate you. He's just — upset. He's got a lot on his mind."

"Well, I hate him."

"Don't. Don't say that about your father."

"How can you stay with him when he's like that? How can you stand it?"

"He's not feeling well, is all. He'll get over it."

He was feeling so poorly, in fact, that when he finished with me, he

172

had taken to his bed, with the shades drawn and a hot washcloth over his eyes. Now and then my mother went in to change the washcloth and to make sure he took his pills.

That afternoon I watched her comings and goings with resentment. How could she be so tender toward him after the way he treated me? Yet even then, part of me grasped the strength of the bond between them. Although I trusted that her sympathy toward me was complete and wholehearted, I knew that her loyalty to him was impregnable.

I liked to imagine that in the war between my father and me, I was her favorite, and that some sort of subversive alliance existed between us. Our long talks seemed to confirm it. So did her pride in my achievements: the funny poems and stories that I managed to get published in the high school paper, the prizes I won for public speaking, the parts I got in the school plays.

Yet for all the pride and support she gave me, never once in all those years did my mother utter a word of criticism against my father. If she had, I would have savored every syllable. I would have wallowed in vengeful delight.

But that had changed. As I stood there in Mom's bathroom, I realized to my surprise that I felt affronted by her recital of his failures and defeats, as well as by her disparaging tone. He always had some story, she had practically sneered, and I resented her for it. Perversely, I found myself wanting to come to the defense of the man I used to regard with never anything less than wariness and often with enmity.

Or was it myself I wanted to defend? For the first time I began to wonder if the truth really was what I desired from this visit. I realized that what I had been hoping for more than anything was a chance to make some sense out of the craziness, to find some rational justification for the seeming randomness and misdirection of our lives during the years I was growing up. But that was not at all what was happening.

I zipped my fly. Turning to wash, I was taken aback by what I saw in the medicine cabinet mirror. The face was familiar enough: wrinkles around the eyes, temples going gray, hairline creeping up and back. But just over that man's shoulder and not very far off in the distance was another image. It was of a fresh-faced boy of seven or eight. Curly haired and blue-eyed, he was squatting on a bright new yellow-pine floor, hammer in hand, watching intently while his father showed him how to start

173

a nail — tap-tap, tap-tap-tap — then how to drive it home, keeping it straight and true. In the boy's eyes, the father was a hero right up there with Roy, Gene, and Hoppy. He was wise and confident. He knew everything and could do everything.

Funny, but despite all that had happened since, the child's awe and belief in his father was still alive in some small corner of myself. Just as that child had once clung to the notion of Santa Claus long after he suspected the truth, part of me still harbored the foolish hope that I might yet discover that the seeming chaos of my father's life was in fact the working out of a magnificent plan. Somehow I had convinced myself that if only I peered deeply and diligently enough into the past, I would find the lodestar, the single guiding light, the grand unifying theory that had led him on and on, here and there, around and around. Surely, I thought, he must have had a vision of his personal promised land, like the one that had driven his parents and so many others to make their way to the New World.

Instead, I was learning that that hope of mine was nothing but romantic nonsense. There was no plan, no grand scheme. My father had simply been making up his life — and ours — as he went along. All the moves and uprootings and dislocations were in reality nothing more than random missteps, false starts, compulsive flights from failure. Or from the fear of failure.

My father stuck with Do-All until the school year was over for Joyce and me. Then he rented another U-Haul and moved us back to Wisconsin. Our new house was a lakeside bungalow, which came complete with a boathouse (but no boat) and an ice-fishing shack that could be towed out to the middle of the lake during winter. I loved it. I walked to school through woods and fields, and that year I even belonged to a gang and got into a few fights. But we stayed for only a year before my father decided the place was too far out in the country and moved us closer to town: to a tract house in the suburbs, on a street where all the houses looked alike. After that came other houses, other jobs, other schools.

The unpleasant truth was that once my father walked away from the house on Rawson Avenue — the one into which he had poured so much of his energy and hopes and creativity — nothing ever seemed to go right for him again, or to last for very long.

174

If there was any pattern to my father's comings and goings in those later years, it was a pattern of restlessness and discontent. Jobs followed one another in quick succession. Sometimes there were layoffs; sometimes he quit or was fired. If a job remained steady for too long, it was a good bet that he'd find some reason to end it. He'd realize that the boss was a blowhard or a fool, or that the work was not what he had expected, or that he was not getting paid enough, or that the commute was too long. He could always come up with something. It was only a matter of time.

Then, too, our latest house usually turned out to have some problem or other, some built-in flaw that made it unlivable after a year or two. Some houses were too small, others too big. Some were too far out in the country, others too close to town.

Inevitably the rest of us found ourselves being dragged along in the churning wake of my father's discontents. At the start of each new school year, my sister and I — and soon little Michael as well — found ourselves walking down the long corridors of yet another new school and facing yet another roomful of strangers. We did it time and again, and it never got any easier.

Not until many years later did I realize just how deeply I had been affected by the repeated shock of all those new beginnings. I was an adult by then, with a small child of my own. I had not thought about first days of school in a very long time. But then came a day in late summer when my wife and I decided to prepare our son for kindergarten by taking him to visit his new school. I was not expecting anything in particular to happen, certainly not to me. But as we approached the building's front door, I suddenly felt as if I were wading through water up to my waist. I could hardly get my legs to carry me forward. The blood drained from my head, and I was having trouble breathing. I felt as if I were going to pass out. I reached for my wife's hand.

"What's wrong?" she asked. "You look as white as a sheet."

I forced my legs to move. "I'm fine." I did not want to alarm my son, who, gripping my hand tightly, was certainly feeling his own kind of terror. "I just felt a little . . . dizzy," I said. "I'm okay. Let's go."

Somehow my legs carried me inside, where all the familiar smells came rushing back: a piquant combination of disinfectant, floor wax, cleaning compound, and chalk dust. And still I was having trouble catching my breath.

This is ridiculous, I thought. I'm a grown man. I'm not the one who's starting school. And yet, as we walked down the long, empty corridor, with its banks of lockers, I felt as if I were suffocating. I had been thrown back twenty-five years, and were it not for my son, I would have turned and fled. But I took deep breaths and somehow I managed to keep going.

Nothing like it had ever happened to me before. But it did not happen again either. In the years ahead, as I endured successive parent-teacher conferences and classroom visits, I became immunized at last to the experience. Eventually I was able to walk through the front doors of my son's grade school, then middle school, then high school, with hardly a qualm. Still, I never forgot that first day, or what a vivid reminder it had been of those innumerable times when I was the child facing the doors of yet another hell.

In those days, in fact, new beginnings were so frequent that my sister and brother and I began to take it for granted that wherever we were at the moment, we were not likely to be in the same place next year. And since we knew that any friendships we made were likely to be short-lived, friendships became dispensable. We always said we'd write, but we never did. Once we moved, friends were gone without a trace. What was the point of writing when we knew we'd never see them again?

Moving became a habit, and since there was nothing any of us could do to change it, we convinced ourselves that moving might just be a virtue. We began to pride ourselves on our adaptability. Laughing (sometimes ruefully), we compared ourselves favorably to those other noble wanderers, the Gypsies.

"Tramp, tramp, tramp, the boys are marching," my father would sing as we drove on to yet another house. My mother, grasping at straws to ease the transition, was fond of reminding us that we were, after all, the descendants of immigrants: "Where do you think we'd be now if Gramma and Grampa had decided to stay back in Poland?" she'd ask.

We began to take perverse pride in our talent for efficient packing.

"Ah, ha!" My father would chortle with glee when, loading a trailer, he found he was able to jam yet one more item in before closing the door.

Watching him, I learned that heavy items like sofas and refrigerators were best centered over the wheels of the trailer; that ironing boards fit perfectly under sofas; that bureaus were best lifted and carried from a room only after the drawers had been tied or taped shut; that tabletops could be protected from nicks and scratches if they were covered with blankets; and that mirrors and large framed pictures could be saved from damage by wedging them in between the mattresses that had been stood on end along the inside walls of the trailer.

"We should hire ourselves out to give lessons for U-Haul." One or another of us was sure to say it as my father swung the trailer doors closed on yet another perfectly packed load.

Unloading at the new house, we sometimes found ourselves carrying cartons that had not been unpacked since the last move, or even the one before. Mostly these were the ones identified by scrawls in black crayon as PHOTO ALBUMS or GOOD SILVER or CRYSTAL BOWL or TAX RECORDS. But it was certain that at least a few of them contained unused curtains and drapes.

We counted on Mom's curtains and drapes the way the weatherman counts on that Pennsylvania groundhog to tell when spring will arrive. When the curtains went up, we knew we were home.

The minute we stepped through the front door of a new house, Mom would be at the windows with a tape measure and pencil, getting the dimensions. Then, with single-minded determination, she'd get down on her knees and start rummaging through the curtain boxes, hunting for the sets that would fit our new reality. Never mind that the stove was not yet hooked up or that the beds were still lying in pieces on the bedroom floors. Those were jobs for other people. The only thing on Mom's mind was getting the curtains unpacked and hung in their proper places.

At the time, it seemed to me just a funny thing she did. A little surprising, maybe, but not very important, especially when I was so busy helping Dad haul boxes and furniture into the house and then from room to room. Only much later did I realize that getting the curtains up was Mom's way of making our strange new surroundings familiar, of sewing at least some small thread of continuity into the chaotic fabric of our peripatetic lives.

It was also her way of keeping prying eyes at bay. Mom was a private person. She did not intend to give the neighbors any opportunity to see how we lived or whisper about what we owned or didn't own. "What will people think?" "What will people say?" These were questions she asked so often that it might have been a refrain written especially for her by Sigmund Romberg or Victor Herbert. What she thought we had to be ashamed of I could not imagine, but I guessed there must be something.

177

Otherwise, why would she be so worried that someone might be watching, judging, whispering?

So anxious was she to avoid those presumed attentions from the neighbors that, if it was up to her, we might never have moved anywhere except under cover of darkness. The next best thing was to get the curtains up as quickly as possible. And she was never at a loss when it came to finding just the right ones. In the course of our numerous changes of address she had acquired enough different styles and sizes to fit just about any window known to the history of western domestic architecture: double hung, casement, jalousie, square, round, half-round, or oblong. Some curtains Mom had sewed herself. Others she had bought. But none did she ever throw away. She kept them all, because she never knew which ones she might need in the next place, and because I think she realized early in her marriage to my father that there would always be a next place, and a next place, and a next.

So there she'd be, on her knees amid the lamps and the unarranged furniture and the rolled-up rugs, digging through the curtain boxes. Around her on the floor would be heaps of fabric: ruffled and pleated, striped and flowered, plain and valanced. There were long curtains for bedrooms and short ones for bathrooms. There were café curtains for kitchens and floor-length drapes for picture windows of assorted lengths and widths. There was even a set of formal, silken, taupe-colored drapes, which she kept in hopes that we might one day again have a dining room, like the one in Detroit.

When finally she had the curtains she needed, out would come the ironing board and the iron, and by the end of a day or two, presto! The windows were decorated, and the strange new place looked familiar, as if maybe we really belonged there and were not just camping out.

It was Dad who called the shots on when we'd move and where. It was usually he who picked out the houses where we lived. But always it was my mother's curtains that made those houses home — or at least, as much like home as we would ever get.

The fact was that, by the time I reached high school, we had moved so often that each new house and neighborhood felt not like home at all but like just one more stop along the road to somewhere else.

It was odd, though: after a while I managed to convince myself that I was actually looking forward to each new move. After all, starting over did have its advantages. Did the bully down the block turn my walk to school into a nightmare? Was my teacher a tyrant? Did I have no close friend I could count on? Was I always among the last kids picked when it came time to choose up sides for baseball? Never mind. None of it mattered because in a few weeks, or a few months, or next year we would be moving away. Then all my problems would disappear. I would flourish and bloom, the way my mother's stunted houseplants bloomed as soon as she trimmed their roots and transplanted them to bigger pots.

I came to believe — as I suspect my father believed — that any place was better than here and any time was better than now.

It was an illusion, of course, but a seductive one. Many years were to pass before I began to understand that every time we packed up and transported our furniture and lamps and books to some new place, we also carried with us all of our history and all of who we were. Careful packers, we arrived at each new place with every bit of our personal baggage intact. We could no more leave our past behind than my father could leave behind the massive drill press and the solid steel lathe that he had picked up somewhere and that he insisted forever afterward on moving from house to house on the off chance that someday he might find a use for them.

Meantime, I had to admit that our frequent relocations did bring into our lives an element of excitement and drama that no other kids I knew seemed to enjoy. Mixed up with my feelings of fear and dread of the unpredictable future, there was a kind of thrill in not knowing where we would end up or how it would all come about.

Among ourselves we joked that if we were ever to have such a thing as a family crest, it would definitely include among its symbols a hand dolly, stacked cartons rampant, a roll of twine, and another of tape. Our family motto, printed upon one of the swags from Mom's curtain collection, would be the slogan that was emblazoned on the sides of every U-Haul truck and trailer in America: Adventures in Moving.

The motto fit remarkably well, for none of our moves was ever entirely predictable or free of astonishments. And one in particular was so extraordinary that in years to come all of us would remember it as our Great Family Saga.

15

ORANGES

*T*he box appeared on our doorstep in the middle of a winter gale. It was the kind of storm that the weatherman called a Manitoba clipper. The wind howling down on us from the Canadian Arctic rattled the storm windows and sliced under the front door. My mother had to jam a rug against the sill to keep out the draft.

In our backyard, snow lay two feet deep on the flat. Out front, between the sidewalk and the curb, the plows and my own shoveling had heaped the stuff into a range of little Grand Tetons that were nearly up to my shoulders, which meant they had to be at least five feet high. Looking out the window, I could see plumes of snow being whipped off the peaks by the bitter wind. It was then that I saw the UPS man pull up and stop his truck in front of our house. When he got out, he was carrying a large box in both of his mittened hands.

The man was so well bundled up — hat pulled low, earflaps tied down, scarf wrapped over his mouth and chin — that when my mother opened the door for him, all we could see of his face as we crowded around were his eyes and the bridge of his nose.

He handed me the heavy carton, then pulled off a mitten and dug around in his pocket for a pencil. Finding one, he held it out to my mother, along with a receipt pad. From behind the scarf came a muffled voice. "Sign here, ma'am," it said.

My mother signed, then quickly closed the door and jammed the rug back against the sill.

In the kitchen, I hefted the box onto the table and got a knife from the drawer.

"Who's it from?" Michael asked, his eyes bright with excitement.

"From Daddy," Joyce said, reading the label.

"But what is it?"

"A box of coal," I told my brother. He was eight and fun to tease.

His shoulders slumped. "Why would he send us that?"

"Because he knows we're almost out and he didn't want us to freeze to death. Okay? Satisfied?"

"Cut it out," Joyce said. "Just open the box."

With a flourish I ran the knife under the binding straps. These days, with my father gone, I was the man of the house, and I reveled in every bit of my newfound authority. It was I who had chosen the Christmas tree this year. It was I who had decorated the front of the house with colored lights and a handmade wreath. And it was I who opened any interesting packages that arrived on our doorstep. I was sixteen and in charge, and the best part was that my father was not around to belittle everything I did or pounce on every word out of my mouth.

The box was really two boxes, one nested upside down over the other to form a lid. Slowly I pulled the covering box free.

"Tah dah!" I said.

"Oh, my," my mother said.

"Oh, boy," Michael said.

We stared in wonder. Inside the box, glowing like so many little sunbursts, were dozens of oranges: ripe and plump and fresh. Some of them still had their stems and leaves attached, which proved that they really did grow on trees! On that snow-blown winter day, no pirate's treasure could have looked more bountiful. Nor were these any ordinary store-bought oranges. We could tell the difference as soon as we sliced open a few and took our first bites.

"Mmm-mmh," said my mother, and none of us disagreed.

These were the sweetest, juiciest oranges we had ever tasted. But what made them really special was what they represented, which was nothing less than a golden vision of the bright, warm, sun-filled future that lay just ahead for us. Laughing giddily as the juice ran down our chins, we realized for the first time that what we had long been anticipating was actually going to happen. California really did exist. As soon as my mother could sell our house, we'd be going there to join Dad, who had been working in Sacramento for the last few months. From now on there'd be no more Manitoba clippers for us: no more snow to be shoveled, no ice to be chipped, no stoking the furnace at six in the morning while my breath hung in gossamer wreaths around my head.

God had sent Noah a dove; my father had sent us oranges as a savory foretaste of the wonderful new life that would soon be ours.

We moved to California because of the Russians.

In October 1957, the Soviet Union had launched an intercontinental ballistic missile and sent the first man-made satellite into orbit around the earth. They called it Sputnik, which meant "fellow traveler," and all of the authorities in the American government and the press agreed that it was a great triumph for the Russians. For weeks afterward, Sputnik was the single biggest item in the news.

I was fascinated and read everything I could about it. Mr. Schweiner, my high school science teacher, filled a bulletin board with newspaper clippings and photographs from magazines. Arching over the display was a paper cutout of the satellite, a silver ball with half a dozen antennae sticking out. Streamers of blue construction paper marked its path across the heavens, except it wasn't called a path, it was called a trajectory — a new word in my vocabulary, and one I enjoyed using at every opportunity because it showed how knowledgeable I was.

Visions of space travel filled my head. I followed all of the news stories. With my allowance I bought and assembled model rocket ships. At night I would lie on our garage roof and gaze at the full moon through my father's binoculars and try to guess its trajectory. I found a map of the moon's surface in *National Geographic* and used it to pick out the Sea of Tranquillity, the Ocean of Storms, and the Bay of Rainbows.

But in the wake of Sputnik I also couldn't help wondering whether I would ever live beyond high school, let alone go to the moon. Because from what I saw in the newspapers and heard over the radio and television, the fact that the Russians had launched a satellite meant it was only a matter of time before they would also begin launching nuclear-tipped missiles against the United States. And when they did, not even the fastest fighter planes or the best antiaircraft weapons would be able to stop them.

Suddenly no place in America was safe. What we had to fear now was nothing so quaint as an overland invasion through Alaska or a bomber attack over the Pole. At any time, an angry or deranged Soviet premier would be able to send swarms of ICBMs raining down on us at the push of a button. Then, in mere minutes, we would all be burned as crisp as toast. Even so lofty an authority as Secretary of State John Foster Dulles was scared. An article he published in *Life* was called "Arguing the Case for Being Panicky."

America's only hope of survival lay in catching up with the Russians, and then passing them. That was what everyone was saying on television and in the newspapers and in the halls of Congress. The pressure was on. Within weeks after the launching of Sputnik, whole Potomacs of money began pouring into programs for missile and satellite research and development. The "space race" was on in earnest.

In January 1958, only a few months after the Russian success, the United States launched its own satellite. Mr. Schweiner's bulletin board now carried displays comparing the American and Russian orbiters, complete with statistics about the heights, speeds, and weights attained by the two systems.

But this was only the beginning. The push was for more and bigger rockets, more and bigger satellites. Around the country, aerospace companies rushed to hire every physicist, chemist, mathematician, and engineer they could find. Draftsmen were needed, too, and this was where my father came in.

My father had never stopped educating himself in his trade. By the time I was in high school, he had become a fully qualified mechanical draftsman. At the machine tool companies where he worked, it was his job to take the ideas of engineers and inventors and transform them into working drawings: precisely detailed renderings of machine parts and tools, complete with materials specifications and exact dimensions.

My father had moved up. Having started out on the shop floor as an apprentice tool-and-die man, he worked now in clean, quiet, well-lit rooms, amid ranks of drafting tables, surrounded by colleagues in white shirts and ties. Instead of drill presses, wrenches, files, and lathes, he worked now with slide rules, T squares, and shiny chrome drafting tools: protractors, compasses, calipers, and mechanical pencils that never needed sharpening. With these delicate instruments poised in his pudgy fingers, my father drew exquisitely fine lines on large sheets of fine paper. Converted into blueprints, his drawings became the guides that the machinists down on the factory floor used to manufacture the dies and molds that would in turn be used to fashion particular parts or tools.

Mechanical drafting was a highly adaptable craft. It did not matter whether the piece my father drew was going to be made out of steel, iron, tungsten, or plastic, or whether it was going to be used in a tractor, a can opener, or a satellite that would be sent hurtling into orbit around the earth. The same drafting skills applied. So when companies in places like Texas and California began tooling up to beat the Russians in the space race, my father was quick to answer their newspaper ads. The money and benefits were better than anything he had ever been offered anywhere else. And most companies were even willing to foot the bill for moving expenses. How could a man resist? All it took was a willingness to uproot home and family. Which of course was no problem where my father was concerned.

"California, here I come!" That was the song we heard Dad singing around the house in the fall of 1958. Then he was gone, and it was our turn to sing, as we waited for the day when we would be able to join him.

California! The name itself breathed seduction, its mellifluous syllables bearing the scent of oranges, the promise of sunshine, the whisper of dreams.

I could tell California was going to be different from the minute we stepped off the California Zephyr in Sacramento. Instead of midwestern wood or red brick, the station was pink stucco, with Spanish arches and a red-tiled roof. Out front, the sidewalks were lined with palm and eucalyptus trees, and brilliant red flowers bloomed amid emerald lawns. The place looked like a movie set.

Our new neighborhood had the same effect. Instead of high-peaked Cape Cods, all the houses were low-slung, sprawling affairs with wide overhangs for shade and carports instead of garages. There were orange

184

groves right down the street, the boulevards were lined with palm trees and cactus. If the morning breeze was right, it was possible to catch the scent not only of the exotic flowers and shrubs that grew everywhere around us, but also of the blonde next door who wore the most amazing halter tops and short shorts that my seventeen-year-old eyes had ever beheld outside the pages of Uncle Len's *Esquire* magazine.

It was an extraordinary summer. On weekends my father took us to explore our new world. In San Francisco we visited Fisherman's Wharf and Chinatown, where a kind old Chinese waiter showed us how to use chopsticks and where another man kept refilling my water glass faster than I could empty it.

Driving to Los Angeles over the July 4th weekend, we visited Disneyland and swam in the ocean for the first time. In the evening we strolled the crowded sidewalks along Hollywood Boulevard, and passed the famous Brown Derby night club, gathering place of the stars. Stopping in front of Grauman's Chinese Theater, my parents gawked at the names and handprints of Hollywood celebrities who had been immortalized in sidewalk cement.

"Hey, look! Here's Marilyn Monroe!"

"Oh, and here's Clark Gable!"

They pointed and laughed at each new discovery.

I inched away, embarrassed, hands stuffed into my pockets, and tried to look as if I didn't know these country bumpkins. (Dad was wearing a plaid shirt and a baseball cap, for God's sake!) But secretly I was as starstruck as everyone else, thrilled to be standing where all those famous stars had pressed their hands or feet or other parts of their anatomy into Mr. Grauman's sidewalk. And when I stumbled on the handprint and signature of Gary Cooper, who had succeeded Roy Rogers and Gene Autry in my book of saints, I couldn't help stopping to stare. But I moved on quickly. I was sure that Coop would never have been caught dead gawking on Hollywood Boulevard.

On another weekend jaunt, my father drove us into the Sierra Nevada, where I stood for the first time amid real mountains. These were no make-believe backyard dirt piles, but rugged, forest-covered peaks, cut by steep valleys and rushing rivers. I inhaled the pine-scented air at our picnic stop. I watched a chipmunk dart under a log, saw a hawk — or maybe it was an eagle! — wheeling on an updraft. And I relished the feel of the rocky slopes beneath my feet and longed to get off on my own and go tramping among those magnificent peaks.

San Francisco, Los Angeles, the ocean, the mountains, the sunshine — I loved it all and would gladly have stayed forever. But my father had other ideas. Stay put? Get along? Settle down? Not him.

I did not know the problems at the time — never knew until years later that it was a secret government program he was working on. But you didn't have to be clairvoyant to tell that he was under tremendous pressure. Long hours of overtime, frequent security checks, incessant demands for speed and precision — it was more than my father could bear. And the summertime climate of the San Joaquin Valley didn't help. What was a paradise in winter was hell in July. For weeks at a time afternoon temperatures topped one hundred and ten degrees. And as the thermometer went, so went my father's blood pressure. More often than not he came home tired, distracted, edgy.

In retrospect, I suspect he was also more than a little homesick. California was just too foreign, too different. The way people behaved, the way they dressed — that woman next door was only the nearest offender — made him wonder if he hadn't brought his family to Sodom. Besides, he missed the support of his brothers and sisters, who might have helped him through what was becoming an increasingly stressful time.

One weekend afternoon in early August, he called us together around the kitchen table to tell us that he was thinking of moving back to Wisconsin. He asked us how we felt about it. It was a solemn moment. Never before had he consulted us or asked our opinion. Things must indeed have been serious. I did not know what to say. I liked California and wanted to stay. But somehow I doubted that was what he wanted to hear. I finessed. "When would we go?" I asked.

"As soon as possible. In two weeks at the latest. That way we can get settled before you kids start school."

"Will we ride on the train again?" Michael asked eagerly.

No, Michael. Not the train. Trains and moving vans were fine when the company was paying the bills. But that only happened when people were moving to the promised land. Once you turned your back on Eden you were on your own.

Which is why our family album contains a snapshot of a car and trailer stranded in the Nevada desert in midsummer. From the look of it, the photo was taken close to noon. The sun is high. The desiccated tussocks of sagebrush cast no shadows upon the dull expanse of sand. In this empty wasteland, only two man-made objects are visible: our 1953 Chevy sedan and the oversized, overloaded, and unbalanced U-Haul that is attached to it. So far away are they that they look like toys in a sandbox.

You can tell the trailer is overloaded and unbalanced from the way its front end and the car's rear end pitch downward, toward the hitch. The car's snout is pointed toward the sky, and its hood gapes open like a mouth gasping for air. The tiny, T-shirted figure standing in front of the car is obviously my father. He is turned toward the steaming engine compartment, and from the slump of his shoulders and the downward tilt of his head he looks utterly desolate. Right about then he must have been wondering how or whether he would ever manage to get us the rest of the way across the country, back to the green hills of Wisconsin. Was he also thinking about all the steps and missteps that had brought him to this point in his life? The notation under the photograph reads "40 to 60 miles east of Winnemucca." It may as well say "Despair."

Since leaving Sacramento we had endured at least three other radiator blowouts. Two of them had happened the day before, while we were headed up the western slope of the Sierra. One had happened that morning, just east of Reno. By now they were almost routine. Yet none of them had happened in the desert at noon, miles from any town or gas station. What if Dad couldn't get the car started again? What if we ran out of water?

Those were the thoughts that ran through my head while my father got out and opened the hood and waited for the radiator to cool off enough to unscrew the cap and add more water.

Seized by the drama of the moment, I left the shelter of the car and went tramping out into the blazing sun to immortalize the scene with a photograph. Having reveled since childhood in tales of frontier heroics and tragedy, I had no trouble imagining some ill-fated pioneer perishing in a place like this. Historical plaques along the way had been drumming it into our heads that the highway we were on followed closely the old immigrant route. So it stood to reason that some of those dead guys may even have keeled over not far from that very spot.

Looking back at the car and trailer, I could picture us all gasping our last, our tongues swollen in our mouths, our brains baked to madness. I could picture our bleached bones lying beside our pathetic trailerload of worldly goods. Never mind that we had broken down on the edge of a major highway and would certainly be rescued if bad came to worse. Drama was drama, and from the way I shot the photograph it's impossible to tell that there's even a road nearby, much less any passing cars or trucks. After all, why spoil a perfectly good adventure story with boring reality?

Still, although our trip back to Wisconsin was not nearly as perilous as my photograph made it seem, it was difficult enough. Withered by August heat, unable to travel more than thirty-five miles an hour because of the enormous weight we were pulling, we had dragged that trailer up the western slope of the Sierra, then slid down the other side, praying the whole time that the brakes would hold and that the trailer would not push us off the road and send us plummeting to the bottom of some rocky canyon. Even now, when I catch a whiff of a burning transmission or see steam rising from a car radiator or hear the long, tooth-grinding screech of brakes from a truck on a downhill run, my mind goes back to that torturous journey east from Eden.

Crossing the Nevada desert, we passed through places with names that sounded as harsh as the landscape: Sparks, Winnemucca, Elko. When the heat rose to unbearable levels and brought us to a stop there in the desert, all we could do was wait for the radiator to cool and hope that there was enough water left in the water bags that Dad had strapped to the fenders.

Cooled at last, we pushed on to the next arid wilderness, Utah's Great Salt Desert, which my father wisely chose to cross by night since a daylight passage really could have meant disaster. As we rolled for hours across those immense salt flats, the earth glowed an eerie blue in the moonlight, like snow on a winter night. The salt in the air parched our lips and made our eyes dry and our skin feel sticky.

Arriving on the far side, we made a pit stop at a gas station, then slept huddled in the car until the sky began to brighten over the Wasatch Mountains — a glorious sunrise, the horizon going from inky black to pale gray to pink and orange.

We paused to have breakfast and see the sights of Salt Lake City, then started up and over the Wasatch. More radiator blowouts. A flat tire.

188

But we made it to Wyoming, crossed the Continental Divide at South Pass, and started across the high plains, those magnificent grassy landscapes that I had heard and read and dreamed about for so long. At cafés and rest stops we saw real cowboys: leather-skinned men in Stetsons and boots, their eyes squinty from a life lived in the sun. We saw other men who looked as if they might be Indians. They wore the same kinds of blue jeans and Stetsons that the cowboys wore, but they kept to themselves.

For me, it was all part of a great adventure. In that big open country, rolling mostly downhill now and chasing cloud shadows across the endless, open grasslands, as the fresh prairie wind blew through the open windows and into our faces, it was impossible not to feel exhilarated.

Even my father was in good spirits. Although it was he who bore the main burden of getting us safely to our destination with our unwieldy load, there he was, leading us in singing pioneer songs that we all knew from the *Burl Ives Songbook* — "Oh, Susannah," "Home on the Range," "Green Grow the Rushes, Oh," and

> *Did you ever hear tell of sweet Betsy from Pike?*
> *She crossed the wide prairies with her lover Ike.*

There were times, though, when I couldn't help but wonder what kind of crazy life we were leading. Rolling through some small, tree-shaded Nebraska town, I'd find myself wondering why on earth we couldn't just stop there and unhitch the trailer and stay put once and for all. Wasn't one place just as good as another?

We pulled into one such town at lunchtime, and I remember watching out the restaurant window as three boys rode their bicycles in easy companionship down the middle of the street. They were only a year or two younger than I was, and the sight of them started me wondering what it must be like to live in a place like that: to grow up in one house, to go to the same school year after year, to have the same friends, to know a place so well that each street and shop and sidewalk seemed to be your own.

But then another thought occurred to me: Didn't these people ever get restless, didn't they sometimes long for a different view out the window or wonder what lay down the road? And when lunch was over and we drove on, the town and the boys and my daydreaming vision of a small-town boyhood were left behind. As we headed out onto the open road, I realized I was glad we were leaving. Because if we had stayed, I might never get to find out what lay around the next bend and over the next hill. And I wouldn't have given that up for anything.

I was beginning to realize that it was not so bad to be on the move. As we shuttled around the landscape, dropping in here and there, we had adventures that no one else had. We lived in places and saw things and did things that we treasured at the time and were to remember vividly for years afterward.

The truth was, moving was getting in my blood.

16

GETTING OUT

"*H*onestly, Alice, I wish you and Walter would settle down," said Aunt Helen, up to her arms in dishwater. "My address book is getting to be such a mess."

Aunt Marcella, who was stacking glassware in the cupboard, sounded astonished. "You mean you write them in in ink?"

"Poor dear," said Aunt Pat with exaggerated sympathy. "No one ever told her she should only use pencil."

It was Thanksgiving at Gramma's house, the first family gathering since our return from California, and I had wandered into the kitchen looking for one last piece of pumpkin pie. Dinner was over, and my aunts were cleaning up the dishes and having a good time at my mother's expense, chattering and laughing.

Aunt Helen pretended to be hurt by her sisters' chiding. "Of course I use pencil," she said, pouting. "But with all that erasing, I've worn a hole right through the page."

All of my aunts laughed at that.

My mother forced a smile. "Sometimes I have trouble keeping track myself," she said quietly as she concentrated on drying a plate. I could tell she was embarrassed and angry, but she was trying to be a good sport.

I wondered why she didn't just tell them to shut up. At least Dad went places and did things, unlike their husbands, who never went anywhere.

Not that we weren't accustomed to hearing jokes about our frequent peregrinations. By now such barbs were part of the family repertoire. But since our California fling, everyone seemed to be having more fun than ever over the way we lived. I couldn't say which my mother hated more: the ribbing or the condescension that usually went with it.

Yet even after we returned to Wisconsin, my father couldn't stay put. He was like an old dog going around in circles, unable to find a comfortable spot in which to lie down. Scarcely had we unloaded the California U-Haul and seen the last of the desert dust washed off the Chevy by the sweet midwestern rain than we found ourselves packing up and moving on once more. The difference was that we never again moved very far. Having sampled life across the state line — first in Detroit, then in Sacramento — my father had apparently concluded that Wisconsin was where he belonged.

Wisconsin was familiar. It meant family instead of strangers, green fields instead of brown, and people and a way of life he understood, not like in California, where everyone seemed plain crazy to him, what with their fads and their divorces, their shocking clothes and their flashy cars. The weather was better, too. Winters were nasty, but at least the summer heat had an end to it and didn't just burn on until you thought you were going to shrivel up and turn to ash and blow away.

No doubt about it: for Dad, Wisconsin was God's country. "Yep, best place in the world," he'd say, putting on his country-boy act. "You betcha." Still, the question remained: Just where in God's country was home meant to be?

For the next few years Dad's search was confined to the area in and around Madison. Some years earlier we had visited the city as tourists. Awestruck, we had tramped through the grand marble corridors of the state capitol building and climbed to the dome to admire the views of the surrounding lakes and the distant rolling hills. Now my father decreed that Madison was to be our new home.

The main thing, Dad had explained during that Sunday afternoon meeting around the kitchen table in California, was that he was sure he could get work in Madison. Not only that, but Madison was the home of the state university. Joyce would be able to start college there in the fall. In another year I could do the same.

I nodded. Fine. Sure. Whatever you say, Dad.

But he wasn't done yet. The other advantage to Madison, he went on, was that Uncle Tad lived there. Steady, reliable Tad, who had generously offered to let us stay with him and his wife Roberta until we could find a place of our own. I glanced at my mother. Her jaws were clamped together. She was staring at a spot on the tablecloth. She said nothing.

Although it took only a few weeks for Dad to find us a place to live in Madison, it felt like months. Tad and Roberta had three children of their own, as well as assorted cats, dogs, gerbils, parakeets, and guinea pigs. We all did our best to get along, but there were just too many of us: two families crammed into a small suburban tract house that was barely big enough for one.

My mother was once again forced to play the role of the poor relation, dependent on the kindness of relatives — and Dad's relatives at that. She was sure that Aunt Roberta looked down her well-bred English nose at us. Maybe she did. But to give her credit, it can't have been easy having all of us underfoot.

Dad, meanwhile, was having more trouble finding work than he had expected. In fact, my sister and I enjoyed better luck than he. Almost immediately Joyce began clerking at Woolworth's, and I landed a job as stock boy at a bread bakery.

"Gee, now everybody's got a job except Dad," I announced cheerfully over supper at Uncle Tad's.

Poor Dad. I thought he was going to choke. The veins stood out on his neck. His eyes bulged. His face turned bright red. His fist tightened on his fork. Over the table a deadly silence fell.

Oops, I thought. I wasn't sure what had happened, but I knew it wasn't good.

If Dad had exploded then and there it might have been easier. At least it would have been out in the open. But before he could erupt in full fury my mother intervened, ordering me to leave the table.

"Why? What did I do?"

"Just go," she said. *"Now."*

I did as I was told. Only later, in the privacy of Uncle Tad's basement recreation room, did she set me straight.

"Don't you ever do that to your father again," she said. She punctuated each word with a finger jabbed at my chest. Since at seventeen I now towered over her by nearly a foot, my chest was at her eye level. But that did not stop her. Never had I seen her so angry.

"But all I said was —"

"I know what you said. And so do you. It was very hurtful and cruel. You should be ashamed of yourself."

I bit my lip. "I'm sorry. I didn't think —"

"That's right. You didn't."

I hung my head and felt suitably contrite.

But I felt something else, too: the secret thrill of discovering that my father was not the only one with the power to wound. In the ongoing guerrilla war that smoldered between us, he turned out to be as vulnerable to my sneak attacks as I was to his frontal assaults.

My mother must have understood this, otherwise why would she be here, chewing me out on his behalf instead of letting him do the job himself? In the past I had always imagined that she was protecting me from him. But something seemed to have shifted, and for one stunning moment I saw that it also worked the other way around.

My words had force. I had force. And even he could feel it — he, who until now had seemed invulnerable to any puny gesture of self-assertion that I might make, to any minuscule triumph that I might achieve.

The revelation was both exciting and frightening, and as quickly as I glimpsed it I turned away. To gaze at such a thing for too long seemed as dangerous as watching a solar eclipse straight on. But I had felt its power. I knew now that it was there. I could feel the chill of its shadow.

Dad eventually found a job — as a draftsman at Gisholdt, a machine tool company. Soon after that he also found us a house to live in. But it was only the first of half a dozen Madison addresses: half a dozen more smudges in Aunt Helen's book. For each house had some built-in flaw that made moving inevitable and that sent the various sisters and in-laws scurrying for their erasers.

The first place turned out to be too close to the Oscar Mayer meat-packing plant, which we discovered the first time the wind shifted to the north. Within six months we were gone, and none of us had any regrets.

Our next home was in one-half of an attached two-family house. The owners lived next door, and they seemed to be nice people. But Dad soured on them from the moment he first heard them using the shower and flushing the toilet on the other side of the common wall. If we could hear them, they could hear us, and if there was one thing my father hated it was the feeling that every move he made was being watched or overheard. He took to keeping the shades down during the day and avoided going out if he saw the owners in the yard. He also began looking for another house.

The next place was on a pleasant, tree-lined street that we soon discovered was the home turf of a hotrodding hood with an Elvis Presley hairdo. "That bum," Dad growled every time the guy revved his engine and went roaring down the street. Dad seemed convinced that the creep had been put on earth for no other reason than to annoy him. Well, he wouldn't have it. He'd pull up stakes first. And so he did.

Eventually I came to realize that there was probably no place on God's green earth where my father could feel content for very long. I have no doubt that if he had been dropped into the Garden of Eden itself, he would have found some reason to move on.

I can hear him now, complaining about the neighbors:

"Can you believe it, Alice! Those two are at it again. All they do these days is argue about forbidden fruit. I don't know why they can't at least keep their windows closed so the whole neighborhood doesn't have to listen to their yatata-yatata."

Or, shaking his head: "Will you look at that! Now we've got zebras and giraffes in the front yard! It's getting so you can't walk outside without stepping in some animal's mess!"

As for the landlord: "I'm sick of it, Alice. He watches every move we make. He ought to just mind his own business for a change. I'm telling you, I've had it. There's got to be a better place than this. Start packing. We're moving."

By the time I started college, I had lived in fourteen different houses and attended nine different schools. Looking back, I realized I could date my memories of past events by which house we lived in at the time and which school I was attending. The chronology of my life could be counted on an abacus of houses.

Once, when I told a psychologist friend about all the moving around we did, she asked if my father's father had been an alcoholic.

"I don't know. Maybe. Why?"

"Because according to some theories," she explained, "the constant need for change is typical of children of alcoholics." Trapped in a chaotic and frightening world beyond their control, those children are quick to flee to new places, and are just as quick to move on again before the new place, too, has a chance to become threatening.

Given what I knew about life in the home of my father's parents, the theory made sense. All I had to do was recall Uncle Leonard's story about how, as a small boy, he had cowered under the kitchen table and watched in horror as his father came close to braining his mother with a kitchen chair. Then, too, there was Aunt Laurie's casual references to Grampa's "social" evenings with his pals down at the speakeasies. Nor could I forget the shameful family secret that I had only ever heard referred to in whispers: that Grampa had been driven out of the house by his wife and eldest daughter.

In any case, whether or not the old man was actually a drunk, one way or another there was plenty of chaos and fear in that house, as my father himself once came close to admitting to me. I was a sophomore in college by then and still living at home. But I was finding the arrangement increasingly intolerable. The tension between my father and me was fierce and incessant. One day, as he was driving me to campus, I finally got up the nerve to confront him. I no longer remember how it started, but our dialogue had deteriorated as usual into acrimony and accusations.

"I can't talk to you," I finally burst out. "We never just have a conversation. You're always yelling."

"Yelling!" he yelled. "What's a little yelling? In the house where I grew up everybody was always yelling. A little yelling never hurt anybody."

By now we had arrived at my stop, a block from the campus. He pulled up to the curb.

"A little love never hurt either," I muttered.

"Love is something you earn," he shot back.

"Damn right," I retorted. Then, grabbing my green Harvard book bag, I got out, slammed the door, and stalked off down the street.

"Come back here," he shouted after me.

"Go to hell," I shouted back over my shoulder.

He got out of the car then, and for a sickening moment I was afraid he was going to come after me. I vowed that I wouldn't run. I'd fight him there in the street if I had to. But it didn't come to that. I kept walking and he stayed where he was, shouting and pounding his fist on the roof of the car. "You come back here. Damn it, do you hear me? Come back here."

But I kept going, and cursed the tears I could not hold back.

It was the end of my living at home. That day I found a furnished room to rent in a student slum. I went home just long enough to get my things.

My mother was distraught. "I wish you weren't going," she said as she stood in the doorway to my room and watched me pack.

I concentrated on folding my shirts. "I can't stay here anymore. You know that. Somebody's going to end up getting hurt."

I didn't tell her about the headlines I'd been writing as practice for my journalism classes:

AREA MAN BEATEN TO DEATH
BLOODY BASEBALL BAT FOUND AT SCENE
POLICE SEEK SON IN BRUTAL SLAYING

I even practiced writing the story, being careful to get in each of the six important points: Who, What, When, Where, How, and Why. The first five would be easy: names and addresses (but only the most recent), the time of day, a loving description of the murder weapon. It was when I thought about the Why that it got harder. Helpless rage. Hatred. The words seemed inadequate to describe what I felt. "Police quoted neighbors as saying they often heard raised voices . . . a long history of conflict between father and son . . ." Somehow, that didn't cover it.

"I just wish it didn't have to be this way," my mother said.

"Maybe you should tell *him* that." I heard how hard I sounded. But I was determined not to let my resolve be weakened by guilt or pity. I knew that if I stayed, things would only get worse. Besides, I was too excited at the prospect of finally being on my own.

With sad resignation my mother assembled a care package of leftover pots, pans, dishes, and linens to help me on my way. It was as if I was being packed off to camp, except that she and I both knew I would not be coming back.

As for my father, I'm sure he was as relieved to have me gone as I was to be going. Despite his swaggering insistence that a little family quarreling never hurt anyone, he literally had no stomach for conflict. Even a minor flare-up would send him running to the medicine cabinet for the Maalox. Anything really serious could put him in bed for hours with the shades drawn. By leaving, I'd be doing him a favor.

Only much later did I look back on that final quarrel in the car and realize that my father had inadvertently given me a hint of just how awful it must have been for him to grow up in a war zone. Was that what he was running from as he jumped from job to job and house to house? Did the sounds of battle still echo in his head like machine-gun fire? Somewhere deep inside did he fear that his family's demons might yet get their clutches on him and drag him down the way they had dragged down his father? Did he feel that his only chance of outrunning a similar fate was to keep on moving, always moving?

After I left home, I lost count of the places my parents lived. Whenever I returned for a visit, home was invariably someplace different from where it had been the time before. I, too, learned the wisdom of using pencil when writing Mom and Dad's address in my book. But then, they were soon doing the same for me.

London, New York, London again, then back to New York — my own dislocations had been no less frequent than theirs and my list of recent addresses no shorter. Stability, after all, had been low on my list of priorities, way behind experience, travel, adventure, ambition, and a cold determination to give the lie to my father's assumption that I would never amount to anything.

"You'll be thirty years old, and you'll still have to be told what to do," he was fond of telling me.

Part of me believed him. A larger part was set on proving him wrong. One day, I vowed, I would rise so high that his scorn would turn to envy. His sarcasm would bounce off of me like BBs off a suit of armor. I would stand taller and stride farther than he had ever dreamed of doing.

My first inkling of how that might be achieved had come to me in high school, when I discovered that there was something I could do well. I could write.

Since grade school I had lagged behind my sister, who had the irritating habit of getting A's in every subject that my father thought was important and practical, which meant math and science. Again and again, I was reminded of her success and my failure: "Joyce does so well, why can't you?" It did not seem to count that I invariably got top grades in English. Almost always my compositions were returned with A+ written in the margin. Often the grade was accompanied by a scrawled comment: "Good work!" or even "Excellent!"

On paper I was the whiz I never could be in person. Face-to-face with a verbal adversary, I was hopeless. I would stumble and grope. A half-witted parakeet could have talked circles around me. But give me paper and pen and a chance to work out what I wanted to say, and I became a different person: bright, confident, even witty.

My first high-school English teacher, Nana Schee, told me I had an "ear." I was not exactly sure what that meant, but I knew she thought it was a good thing to have.

When Miss Schee invited me to submit something to the school paper, I happily sat down and composed what I imagined was a wonderfully clever poetic satire on school life, borrowing the rhythms and meter of Poe's "The Raven." I included a gleeful poke at "our dreary science classes" and how they bored "all lads and lasses." I went on in that brilliant vein for six or eight verses. The pleasure I found in playing with rhymes and rhythms — the music of the words — was exceeded only by the sheer delight I felt when my sterling creation finally appeared in print. I hadn't had such a thrill since the time in gym when I caught a pop fly and heard my team cheering for me. There it was, my name in bold-face type, and under it, my own words, printed exactly as I had written them. All day long I kept sneaking peeks at the page, savoring the sight. Spotting a classmate who was reading the paper, I'd crane my neck to see if my poem was what he or she was reading. And often it was. Some of my readers smiled. Some even laughed out loud. A few came up and said things like "Good going" and "That was great!"

It seemed I had struck a chord. I had said in public what no one else had had the nerve to say, and I had put my name on it, so that even Mr. Schweiner could identify the culprit. I knew my science grade would probably suffer, but I didn't care. For the first time in my life I had done something recklessly brave and heroic.

As an added bonus my poem made a big splash with Judy Palomecki, whose attentions I had been secretly coveting. When the divine creature actually sought me out and told me how much she liked what I had written, I was elated. Writing had powers I had never imagined.

Success was addictive. Eager to repeat my triumph, I pumped out more satiric doggerel. I also began reporting on school events and waxing wise in editorials. Writing, I discovered, gave me license to speak up and to stick my nose where it didn't belong. I got front row seats at football and basketball games. I also had an excuse to talk to prom queens and leading ladies — girls who otherwise would not have given me the time of day. I might not be the leading man or the captain of the football team. But I could get my name in the paper whenever I wanted.

Gradually it dawned on me that writing might just be a way to make a living. I had never met any real writers. I did not know anyone who had. All the adult men I knew — my uncles, my friends' fathers, my own father — had "real" jobs. They were machinists, electricians, carpenters. A few were professionals, including Uncle Ed, who was a pharmacist, and Uncle Gene, my mother's oldest brother, who was a banker. They had practical, down-to-earth jobs that brought in steady paychecks. To them, the idea of anyone setting out to make a living at something as airy and uncertain as writing would have been incomprehensible, if not downright foolhardy.

I could just imagine them talking it over at a family get-together.

"A writer, huh? And how does he plan to pay the rent?"

"Hmmph. He doesn't like eating, I guess."

"Oh, isn't he the sensitive one though? Mr. Artsy Fartsy himself."

I could hear their voices, because I had the same words going around in my head, sowing doubts like weeds on my otherwise grassy landscape of hope. Yet I knew such a life was possible. Others had done it, so why not me? Who else but writers had produced all those books on the shelves of my mother's bookcase and in the school library? Who else but writers kept coming up with all those stories in the magazines and newspapers?

I was still in grade school when my mother introduced me to her collection of books by Richard Halliburton, that devil-may-care adventurer. In the thirties, Halliburton had charmed my mother and hundreds of thousands of other readers with accounts of his romantic escapades, including flying across the Sahara to Timbuctoo in a rickety biplane, climbing Mount Fuji in winter, swimming the Panama Canal lengthwise, and splashing by moonlight in the reflecting pool in front of the Taj Mahal.

In high school, when I chose Halliburton as the subject for a biographical term paper, Miss Schee steered me toward a loftier subject: Winston Churchill, no less. I dutifully took on the great man's story and was captivated. He, too, had been an adventurer and journalist, whose march to greatness began when he wrote about his escapades in the Boer War.

In the high school library — a wonderfully antique room with lots of dark wood and mullioned windows like a Tudor mansion — I had been discovering the works of other provocateurs of wanderlust: Lowell Thomas, who had visited the Dalai Lama in Tibet and ridden with T. E. Lawrence in Arabia; Hemingway, a midwesterner who had broken free and found fame and glamorous women by covering wars in Italy and Spain and turning out novels that stirred me to the core with their melancholy visions of passion and tragedy in distant places.

With the wide world in my sights, I enrolled in journalism school at the university. It seemed unlikely that I'd be able to earn a living by writing fiction. At least as a journalist I'd have a trade, and one that stood a chance of being more interesting than most. Who could tell? I might even get to be a foreign correspondent, wear a trench coat, and see some of the faraway places I had been reading about for so long.

My father, acknowledging the inevitable but wanting to inject a dose of reality into my daydreaming, suggested I think about audiovisual aids. "You could write film strips. It would be good steady work."

I rolled my eyes. How could I explain to him that what I had in mind was something far grander and more exciting?

That I came as close as I did to making the kind of life I had dreamed about surprised me as much as anyone. In the years after college I traveled widely. As a young reporter in London, I stood in the rain with a mob of other newshounds outside the home of my old friend Winston Churchill as the great man lay dying. I attended the press conference of Martin Luther King, Jr., when he was on his way to Stockholm to accept the Nobel Peace Prize. In New York, I covered the funeral of Malcolm X. I interviewed movie stars, reported on Pope Paul's visit to the United Nations, and covered the triumphal welcome-home parade of the first American astronauts to walk in space. I was a guest at celebrity-strewn parties on Central Park West and flew over the Everglades at twilight, en route to covering the grisly aftermath of a mass murder aboard a tramp steamer off Key West. I saw my byline printed in prominent publications, my articles reprinted in anthologies, my books reviewed in newspapers and bought by book clubs.

If I had a regret it was that I had not yet written a novel or made a splash in the literary world. Now and then, when the thought nagged, I'd roll a sheet into my typewriter and try a story. But then another adventure would present itself and off I'd run. Never mind art. This was life!

In my rush for glory, I surpassed my father — in education, in the amount of money I made, in the things I had seen and done. Was that why he kept sniping at me? Was that what his rebukes and sarcasm had been about all along: fear that I would someday outshine him? Or was it the opposite fear that kept him goading me and that kept me pushing harder, doing more: the fear that I would never measure up, that I might never amount to anything after all?

Meantime, I had the unexpected good fortune to fall in love with a dark-haired, dark-eyed girl who loved me back and to whom, by some miracle, my dreams did not seem outrageous. On the contrary, she encouraged them and was more than willing to share the adventures.

Equally miraculous, I became father to a son.

Time and distance had begun to heal some of the wounds that Dad and I had inflicted on each other over the years. But it was Jesse's arrival that made the biggest difference.

"Dad, I have a son," I told him, wiping my eyes as I stood at the phone in the lobby of New York Hospital within an hour of watching Jess being born. "I have a son. And, Dad, he's beautiful and he's healthy. And he's got dark, wavy hair, like yours."

His voice caught as he said, "That's wonderful, Tom. Just . . . wonderful." The catch came again, then: "God bless you, son."

Four small words. Words I thought I'd never hear from him. But then, I was calling at five in the morning and had awakened him from a sound sleep, so maybe it was just that he hadn't had a chance to dress his emotions in their usual reticence. From him, rebuke had always come easier than affection. Praise, if it came at all, showed itself in roundabout ways. When I graduated from college and later, when my work began appearing in magazines that for years had been family icons, he never said so much as "good job." Mom would tell me he was proud, but never a word of praise did I hear directly from him.

Four small words. I savored every one.

That they came so late no longer mattered. That they came at all was part of the miracle.

Only later did I realize how close I came to never hearing them. Although no one knew it, the time was not far off when he wouldn't even know my name.

PART III

Pass, world!: I am the dreamer that remains,
The man clear cut against the last horizon.

— Roy Campbell

17

TAPE

*T*he rest of the weekend I was the good son. I helped Mom shop and ran errands. I fixed the latch on the back door. On Saturday night I took her to dinner and a movie. I hoped to make up at least a little for the other fifty-one weekends of the year, when I was only a voice on the telephone.

On Sunday, after church, I drove us to the nursing home. By the time we got there, the nurses had already taken Dad down to therapy. We found him seated at a worktable, propped up in a high-backed wheelchair, with pillows tucked in beside him to keep him from slumping sideways. Spread on the table were colored blocks, rubber balls, and a few other toys and gadgets I could not immediately identify. A young woman in a white coat sat beside him.

"Why, Walter, look who's here," she said. "We have visitors."

Her name was Sandy, obviously because of her hair, and she spoke with the singsong cheerfulness of a kindergarten teacher. The toys on the table suggested that kindergarten was a fair description of what she taught. Still, it was irritating to hear her talking to Dad in that tone. Just because his memory was gone didn't mean he was a child.

I took his bony hand. It felt as light as a bird's wing. "Hello, Dad. It's Tom. Remember me? Your son Tom? How are you doing today?"

His head turned in my direction. Down the narrow tunnel of what was left of his vision, he struggled to focus. "Tom," he murmured, barely moving his lips.

"That's right," I said. "I'm Tom. I've come to see you."

Despite his saying my name, I wasn't sure he knew who I was. But I did not want to interrupt his therapy session by pushing him further. Instead, I pulled up chairs for Mom and me, then settled down to watch.

Sandy's specialty was small-motor coordination. What Joe's exercises had tried to do for Dad's larger muscles, Sandy's were designed to do for his smaller ones. The object was to get Dad to use his limbs, especially those on his left side, which had been most severely affected by his recent strokes. Movement would keep the blood circulating, strengthen the muscles, and restore his neurological awareness of his crippled left side.

Having pulled Dad close to the table, Sandy had strapped the lower part of his left arm to a triangular board that had swivel casters attached to its underside at each of its three corners. Dad's task was to use his good right hand to roll his left arm around on the tabletop. It wasn't easy. His head kept falling forward, and Sandy had to keep reminding him what he was supposed to be doing. To me, it looked like a hopeless effort. But, like Joe, Sandy professed to see some signs of improvement. I had to take her word for it.

Dad's next task looked even more difficult. A series of various-sized machine bolts had been mounted on a board. Dad's job was to sort through an assortment of nuts, match each one to the right bolt, and then screw it on. It was the kind of exercise that most three-year-olds could have managed easily. From what I had seen of Dad's condition, I doubted he was capable of handling anything this sophisticated. But he set to work.

He concentrated fiercely. He did not slump or nod off but stayed intensely focused, matching first one nut to a bolt, then another and another. Sweat broke out on his forehead. He seemed to be willing his ravaged body and brain to perform. Never had his will seemed more steely or determined. It was as if he were trying to prove to us — and perhaps to himself — that he was still in charge. As he confidently twisted the last nut onto its matching bolt, I found my eyes blurring and felt myself wanting to cheer.

"Walter, that's wonderful," Mom said.

"Terrific, Dad," I said, and I could swear I saw a little smile wrinkle the corner of his mouth.

"He's really doing very well today," the therapist said. "Better than he's done all week. I'm sure your being here is making a difference," she told me.

"I'm glad," I said, blinking to clear my sight. I was awed and elated. For the first time on this visit I had seen in that wasted shell a faint glimmer of the able, competent man my father had once been: the man who could fix anything, who knew which parts went together and which tool to use for which job.

In his hands those machine bolts and nuts seemed as familiar as a brush to a master painter or a chisel to a sculptor. Despite the devastation inflicted on him by strokes and disease, some trace of the old skills survived. And as he slumped back, exhausted, I couldn't help wondering whether in some dim corner of his ravaged brain he didn't feel at least some small sense of satisfaction, some flicker of pleasure, at being able to make his hands do such things again.

His slide had begun not long after Jesse was born. At first I did not know that's what it was. No one did. All I saw, when he and Mom drove out east to visit us that summer of 1973, was that he had gained a shocking amount of weight. As he got out of the car in the driveway of the Princeton mansion where we were house-sitting for the season, Dad looked as if he was carrying close to two hundred and fifty pounds on his six-foot frame. His belt was invisible under his sagging belly. Layers of fat rolled over his collar like melting candle wax. His multitude of chins shook when he talked, and he lumbered like a walrus as he walked to the house.

Still, once he was settled inside he made a wonderfully generous pillow for baby Jesse. Sunk into an overstuffed sofa, with his chins resting on his chest and his chest resting on his belly and his belly resting on his thighs, he looked as benign as a Buddha, and surprisingly tender as he cradled his grandson in his formidable lap.

It was a side of him that I was not used to seeing. Nobody was, except Mom. And sometimes even she was dismayed by his reluctance to openly display any signs of affection in public. What was especially frustrating was that "public" for him seemed to include his own family.

One evening, when Mom and I were having dinner at her favorite Wendy's and I was asking her about times past, she ruefully reminded me of the day Dad came home for a visit after being away in California for six weeks, trying out his new aerospace job. In twenty years of marriage the two of them had never been separated for such an extended period. Now he was flying home for a long weekend. Taking an airplane! No one in our family had ever taken an airplane before.

In anticipation of his return, Mom had permed her hair, made herself up with powder and lipstick, and put on a nice dress. For good measure she made sure that the house was filled with the aroma of pot roast. With Michael keeping watch at the front window, Mom fluttered around the house, now straightening the doily under the potted violets, now running a dust cloth one more time over the top of the upright piano. She just couldn't seem to stay still.

"He's here," Michael called at last. "He's getting out of a taxicab."

Dutifully we gathered in the living room to greet him. Personally I was a lot less enthusiastic about his return than everyone else. After all, I had been the man of the house for the previous six weeks and would now have to relinquish my newfound authority. But I knew I'd better put in an appearance, and I was there in the front room as he came up the walk.

I saw Mom check her hair in the mirror one last time. Then she straightened her back and threw open the front door.

"Welcome home, dear," she said.

"Welcome home," Joyce, Michael, and I sang out.

He stepped inside. "Hello, everybody," he said, smiling almost shyly through his beautiful tan. He stood there awkwardly, suitcases in hand, as if he didn't quite know what to do next. He was like a guest who had arrived late for a party and wasn't sure whether he was still invited.

Did he sweep Mom into his arms? Did he smother her with kisses? Did he reach out to give the rest of us a paternal embrace? That's the way it would have been on *Ozzie and Harriet* or *Father Knows Best*. But that was television. This was our house. This was Dad.

Setting down his suitcases, he reached out to Mom and . . . shook her hand. Then he moved on to the rest of us, shaking each of our hands in turn. Remembering it years later, Mom shook her head bleakly and said, "He might as well have been a vacuum cleaner salesman." While his children were in the room watching, he could not bring himself to let go even a little, not even with the wife he had not seen in a month and a half.

Now, in the plush living room of that turreted and sprawling Princeton mansion, I watched him cuddling his grandson and I thought that maybe, just maybe, something had changed. Being a grandfather to Joyce's five might have done it. He may also have been affected by hearing my accounts of how I was sharing in Jesse's upbringing.

Determined to be a different kind of father than mine had been, I had happily embraced every aspect of parenting. I took my turns changing diapers, bathing and feeding, and carrying the little guy around at night when he woke up crying. When we hiked into town or to the nearby park, it was I, as often as Ellen, who proudly pushed him in the stroller or carried him in the backpack. With the possible exception of the diaper-changing and the 2 A.M. strolls around the nursery, I relished every minute that I could spend with my son. And I had not been shy about relating my tales of fatherhood in my calls and letters to Mom and Dad. The truth was, I must have been insufferably smug about the whole business, almost as if the whole purpose was to let Dad know just how much better I was at it than he had ever been.

For whatever reason, Dad turned out to be surprisingly warm and cuddly with his newest grandson. I may have been flattering myself, but I liked to think Dad's burst of affection had something to do with the fact that Jesse was the only grandson who bore the family name. Suddenly Dad was being positively amiable with me, and for the first time I found myself regretting the geographic distance that kept us apart. I had needed that distance to make a life for myself, separate from his harsh judgments and his low expectations. Yet now, for Jesse's sake and for the sake of that newfound well of tenderness that Jesse's birth seemed to have plumbed, I wished there were not so many miles between us.

What I couldn't figure out was why Dad seemed compelled to keep stuffing himself — and why he had to be so sneaky about it.

It happened the first day of their stay. Ellen had made us all a substantial breakfast of pancakes, eggs, fresh fruit, and coffee.

"Come on," Dad said to me half an hour later. "We'll go for a drive."

As usual, it came out as a decree rather than an invitation, and normally I'd have bridled at his presumption. But this time his goodwill was evident, despite his choice of words. "Sure," I said. "I'll show you the town. We'll take one of the Saabs."

Running those two Swedish beauties a couple of times a week was among the more delightful chores I had taken on in exchange for the use of the house, and I was having fun playing lord of the manor.

My father, who was usually quick to sneer at anything he considered too fancy or pretentious, was nevertheless a sucker for fine machines and gave the cars an admiring inspection inside and out. Then, in our borrowed luxury sports coupe I gave Dad a first-class guided tour of the neighborhood. I showed him the battlefield where George Washington had fought the British after taking Trenton. I cruised through the grounds of the institute where Einstein had worked, then swung by the governor's mansion and circled the Princeton campus, keeping up a running narrative of local history and gossip.

Dad injected wry comments and seemed to be enjoying himself. But it wasn't until he spotted a coffee shop in town that he really perked up.

"Pull in here," he said. "We'll have coffee."

Inside, to my surprise, he ordered another full breakfast of eggs, toast, bacon, and greasy potatoes. How he managed it I didn't know. I was still too full from our first breakfast to do any more than sip coffee and nibble a piece of the toast he passed over to me. But he seemed voracious.

"There's, uh, no need to mention this to Mother," he said as he dug in.

I started to laugh. I thought he was being funny. But there was no humor in his eyes as he shoveled in the food. He seemed grim, determined, almost as if he were in a trance.

What's going on here? I wondered. But I said okay and later said nothing about our foraging stop. In fact, I put it out of my mind entirely and spent the rest of the day playing host, including organizing a croquet game on the back lawn.

But that evening, an hour or so after dinner, Dad decreed another drive, just the two of us. I didn't mind. It was a beautiful summer evening. Fireflies twinkled by the thousands, making the dark lawn look like a reflection of the night sky.

"Where to?" I asked.

This time he directed me to a diner he had seen on the highway.

There, as I watched in amazement, he tucked into an order of steak and french fries, which he followed with a slice of apple pie à la mode.

On the way home he again mumbled a request that I not say anything to Mom. He sounded like a kid who'd been caught sneaking cookies. Was he ashamed? Was he afraid of making Mom angry — him, afraid of her? I couldn't guess what was going on in his head, and I wasn't about to ask. But, although I complied with his wishes, I also refused to accompany him on any more of his binges. I was not about to become a co-conspirator in whatever self-destructive game he was playing.

But that did not stop him. Each day he would drive off in his own car and disappear for an hour or so, presumably to gorge himself on more food. It was puzzling and disturbing. At fifty-five my father seemed bent on eating himself into an early grave. It was as if he was turning a lifetime, worth of frustrations and anger in upon himself, committing slow suicide one meal at a time.

Something else was changing as well. Habits that we in the family had long regarded as mere quirks had begun to escalate to the level of compulsions and phobias. Over the years, for instance, he had developed a passion for taping things together. Among ourselves we joked that he had never met a tape he didn't like. Masking tape, electrical tape, cellophane tape, strapping tape — in the course of a year he probably used enough to cover a football field, or at least an end zone. You knew a letter was from him without looking at the handwriting or the return address: you could tell by the masking tape that ran around the edges of the envelope. Christmas or birthday packages that came in the mail were masterpieces of strapping-tape design, with double-reinforced corners and carefully sealed edges. The mat on his desktop was bordered in duct tape, as was the sheet of cardboard that he had stuck to the dashboard of the Chevy to cut down on sun glare.

None of this seemed unusual. It was just Dad being Dad. We'd joke among ourselves that he could make a lucrative living by hiring himself out as the 3M poster boy. My mother, laughing, once told him she guessed that he had been fibbing all along about his real identity: his middle initial didn't stand for "Thomas"; it stood for "Tape." Walter Tape Froncek.

At the time, he was still able to laugh about his odd foible. "Yeah,

213

well, you can accuse me all you want," he said, raising a mischievous eyebrow, "but you can't make it stick."

We groaned as expected, much to his delight.

Recently, however, what we always thought of as just another of Dad's quirks — funny but harmless — had begun to take on the aura of something more ominous, something obsessive. Tape began appearing on lampshades and around the handles of his briefcases; on telephone cords, window shades, countertops, and carpet edges; wrapped around pencils and the earpieces of his eyeglasses. It was almost as if he feared the world would fly apart if he didn't tape it down.

His fears seemed to be multiplying. At the first hint of an autumn chill he would bundle up as if it were deep winter, and if I happened to be visiting, he'd urge me to do the same. "You'll catch pneumonia," he'd say. If I announced I was going for an evening jog around the neighborhood, he'd recite a litany of the perils that lurked in the twilight streets: dogs, reckless drivers, potholes, uneven sidewalks.

I'd scoff at his fears. "I'll be fine," I'd assure him, and go trotting away, wondering as I went what had become of the adventurer he once was: the man who had loved nothing better than exploring back roads and leading us to new sights, new homes, new lives.

What made all this so puzzling was that by this time — in his middle fifties — he seemed to have attained so much of what he had always been searching for. For one thing, his current job suited him to a T. Having lost his last drafting position when his employer went bust, he was back in the classroom, doing what he loved best: teaching. No longer a white-shirted drone among drones, he was once again the one and only, the star performer, the leading man.

As before, he was teaching tool- and diemaking to apprentice machinists. But now, instead of being tied to one particular school, he rode a circuit of half a dozen vocational schools scattered over a hundred-mile radius of central Wisconsin. He still had a boss, of course: a supervisor in the educational bureaucracy. But on the road my father was his own man, as close to being independent as he had ever been in his life. That was what made the job such a good fit. He could drop in on a school, teach his class, then get out, before he could get ambushed by whatever personality conflicts or political intrigues might be skulking in the shadows.

And when the teaching day was over, he could get behind the wheel and drive and drive and drive, setting his own destination, stopping where he wanted, eating what he wanted, taking his time, talking to strangers, moving on — all of which, to him, was pure pleasure. It was also safe. For if he kept moving, no one could draw a bead on him. He was no one's sitting duck. For a man who needed to disappear almost as much as he needed to be the center of attention, it was the perfect setup.

Home, too, seemed about as close to perfect as it had ever been — at least from what I could see. Located near the geographic center of Dad's circuit, the place where he and Mom now lived appeared to offer every advantage that my father had ever gone looking for. True, the house itself was nothing special — an ordinary low ranch on a quiet street in a small tract development. But the setting was just about as pretty as they came.

To get there you drove north from Madison on I-94, then turned off after a while onto a series of small back roads that took you through rolling farm country, past picturesque red barns, trim white farm houses, and velvet green pastures where herds of black-and-white cows idled. It was the kind of scenery likely to bring to mind the music of Aaron Copland and the paintings of Grant Wood: all French horns and farmers in clean overalls.

Eventually the road wound down into the broad, flat bottomlands of the Wisconsin River valley, and to a tract development bearing the impossibly idyllic name of Harmony Grove. Mom and Dad's house was halfway down a wide street and set back on a broad lawn. Behind the house, a small channel led out to the river, and down at the water's edge there was a rickety little pier, to which was tied an aluminum rowboat complete with an outboard motor. There were neighbors next door and across the street, but not so close that Dad had to feel they were watching his every move. Likewise, the nearest town, which was five miles away, was well out of sight but still handy for shopping.

Waterfront, open space, blue sky, a job he enjoyed, children married and doing well — for my father the important things had finally fallen into place. He had every reason to feel contented and accomplished, or so it seemed when I brought Ellen and Jesse out for Thanksgiving in the fall of Jesse's second year.

Dad was still grossly overweight, and his eyes were now giving him trouble as well, so much so that he'd had to give up night driving. But otherwise he seemed in high spirits, even exuberant, as the house

215

quickly filled up with children and grandchildren. Joyce and Dick were there with their gang. Mike and Dee came up from Madison. There was laughter, excitement, kids running and chattering.

Dad bantered with Dick about the Badgers' chances for getting to the Rose Bowl — zero to none, in his estimation. Later, he led Michael and me on a tour of his basement workshop, where he had been tinkering with the boat motor. He told jokes, listened to mine, and laughed heartily at the punch lines.

"Come on, everybody," Mom called at last. "It's on the table."

Turkey, stuffing, sweet potatoes, cranberry sauce — it was all there. The kids poured in, full of excitement, squabbling over who got to sit where. When things settled down, prayers were said, toasts were offered, and the dishes began making their rounds.

But at the head of the table it was as if someone were pulling down a shade. Little by little Dad's mood began to darken. His face sank into a scowl. He grew silent and drummed his fingers impatiently on the tabletop. Great sighs emanated from deep inside.

Around the table everyone did their best to ignore him. The talk and laughter grew louder, as if we were all secretly determined to have a good time despite him. The children, oblivious, chattered away like a bushful of sparrows.

"Can't you keep them quiet?" Dad suddenly growled at Joyce.

An embarrassed silence ensued.

"Walter," my mother said, soothingly, "they're just being children."

"Yeah, yeah," Dad rumbled.

"It's okay," Joyce said, and quickly enlisted the older kids to take the younger ones, including Jesse, out of sight and hearing.

But even with the kids gone, Dad's dark mood continued to cast a pall over the table. The heavy sighs and the drumming fingertips continued. Instead of asking when he wanted a dish passed to him, he simply glowered at whichever item he wanted, waiting for someone to read his mind.

I was sitting at the other end of the table and so was too far out of range to be of any use. Besides, as far as I was concerned, if he wanted something, he could damn well ask for it like everybody else.

Joyce, sitting closer, bore the brunt, and nervously did her best to anticipate his wishes. "What would you like, Dad?" she'd ask with what I thought was disgusting solicitude.

"Bread," he'd mumble. Or: "Potatoes." No "please," no "thank you." Just demands. It was not hard to imagine him sitting in a high chair, pounding his fist and throwing pablum.

Finally he pushed back his chair, scraping the feet loudly on the linoleum, and left the table without a word. A moment later we heard his bedroom door slam down the hall. The rest of us were left to wonder what we'd done that had so annoyed him. Maybe we should have been quieter. Maybe we should not have come at all.

Mom, embarrassed, tried to explain. "He hasn't been feeling well," she said.

"Baloney," I shot back, only barely restraining myself from using a stronger word. I was royally fed up with being subjected to the tyranny of his moods. "The only problem was that he wasn't the center of attention. And guess what? Now he is. He won, didn't he? He always wins. He's out of the room, but he's still the only thing we're talking about."

But I was wrong. There was more going on with him than any of us knew — more, probably, than even he imagined.

Mom gave me the news over the phone a week later, after I had returned to New York with Ellen and Jesse. Driving home from one of his school assignments, Dad had blacked out at the wheel and swerved into oncoming traffic. Mom, who just happened to have accompanied him on that trip, had let out a shout and grabbed the wheel in time to yank the car back into its lane. Only her quick thinking had averted a collision.

Meantime, her shout had been enough to wake Dad out of his blackout so that he could get the car off the road. Then he got out and let Mom drive the rest of the way. I could still hear the terror in her voice a day later as she related the incident.

Bewildered, not knowing what was happening to Dad, she drove him to a hospital, where the doctor confirmed her own suspicions: Dad had had a stroke. What surprised her was that he also had diabetes, and had had it for years.

Diabetes. Suddenly it all made sense: Dad's eating binges, his obesity, his mood swings, the bottles of water he was always swigging from.

They were all diabetic symptoms. The maddening thing was that Dad himself had apparently known about his condition all along.

"He didn't tell you?" the doctor asked.

Mom could only shake her head and drop her eyes. It was humiliating. To have to admit such a thing to a stranger! What kind of marriage was it where the husband did not tell the wife about something so serious? What kind of wife was she that her own husband would not confide in her?

When she confronted him about it in the hospital, Dad fended her off. He hadn't wanted to worry her, he explained. Only after continued prodding did he finally confess to the real reason: he had been unable to bring himself to administer the insulin shots that might have brought the disease under control.

She could only nod in sympathy, aware as she was of his lifelong horror of illness and injury. Even so small a thing as Joyce's childhood tonsillectomy or me breaking my wrist when I was five had been enough to make him queasy, leaving Mom to do the nursing or to make the mad dash to the hospital. But understanding was one thing. What hurt was knowing that he had not been able to turn to her in his time of deepest need. If he had only confided in her, she was sure she could have helped him. Together they could have tackled the thing that had taken hold of him. But of course, before he could turn to her he would have had to admit his illness to himself, and that he had been unable to do. In his fear he had shut her out. Now not even he could deny the truth.

Grudgingly, Dad allowed Mom to do what he had been incapable of doing for himself. She gave him his shots and monitored his medication. Fearing another blackout behind the wheel, she drove him on his bi-weekly circuit. And since she now went everywhere with him, she was also able to keep an eye on his diet. Under her regime there were no more between-meal snacks of eggs and fries, Danish, and doughnuts.

That she was only trying to save him from himself did not make her demands for temperance any easier to bear. He was a sinner in the hands of a righteous angel, and his resentment was fierce. "Get off my back," he'd growl when she reminded him to take a pill or to forgo the fried onion rings. But gradually, though he grumbled, he acquiesced to her dictates, and this in itself was a mark of the change that had overtaken him.

As for Mom, it was as if in late middle age she had suddenly found a new career. Some years before, when Michael started high school, she had gone to work as a clerk typist in the local library. It was her first job outside the house since she'd been married, and she enjoyed it enormously. For the first time in her married life she had a paycheck of her own. She learned to drive, bought her own car, and overcame her shyness enough to make one or two friends with whom to share complaints about the boss and news of children and grandchildren.

The job had lasted for more than ten years, ending only when Dad insisted on moving yet again: away from town and traffic and too many people; back to the country one more time; back to blue sky and open fields, with the river nearby and an outboard tied up at the pier out back.

My sister and I wondered later if he didn't already sense that something was wrong — if, like an old elephant, he hadn't taken himself off into the bush to die.

Traveling with Dad every day, Mom began to notice something new. He began to have odd lapses of memory. Returning to his motel at the end of a day of teaching, he'd forget the number of the room where the two of them were staying. Or he'd forget which town they were in, or which school he was supposed to be teaching at the next day.

"What do you mean, which school?" she'd say, puzzled and secretly frightened. "You've been doing this same round for seven years."

"I forgot, that's all. Just tell me, will you? I don't need your hectoring."

His outburst surprised her, until she realized that he was as frightened and bewildered as she was by what was happening to him.

In fact, it was worse than she knew. As she heard later from Dad's supervisor, he had begun turning up in the wrong classroom. Other times, when he was in the middle of teaching, his students would point out that he had covered the same material weeks earlier.

To his students, his behavior must at first have seemed comical. I can imagine them smirking at his foolish mistakes, perhaps laughing outright. But eventually one of them must have sent word to the administration. Dad was put on notice: unless his sloppy performance improved, he would be terminated.

But Dad never saw that letter. By the time it arrived, Mom knew

219

there was no point in showing it to him. He had suffered another stroke, and this time it was clear that he would not be going back to work.

Tests were done. At first the doctors thought Dad's "memory deficits" might have been brought on by a series of strokes that were probably the result of high blood pressure. Months went by before a doctor came up with a name for the disease that was robbing my father of his mind and of his active life. It was called Alzheimer's, after the man who had first described it. It was a kind of senility.

This was in 1975, and no one in the family had ever heard of Alzheimer's.

"Senility?" I said when Mom told me the news over the phone. "How can he be senile? He's only fifty-seven."

"Apparently age has nothing to do with it," she told me. She sounded on the edge of tears. "Some people get it when they're still in their thirties and forties."

She was a good reporter. She had listened to the doctor well and taken careful notes. The disease, she told me, was caused by destructive plaques, or deposits, that latched onto the brain's nerve fibers, tangling them hopelessly and destroying the vital links between them. Deterioration was progressive and irreversible.

I almost could not bring myself to ask the next question. "How long before . . . ?"

"There's no way to tell. It could go quickly or it could last a long time. Statistically it's usually around ten years."

But statistics did not take into account my father's stubbornness. Five years passed, then seven, then eleven. During that time we watched the humiliating disease reduce an active, intelligent, and difficult man to a placid and acquiescent child.

The ironic thing was that, aside from what was going on inside his skull, Dad was healthier than he had been in years. Now that his diet and medication were in Mom's hands, she was able to get his weight and diabetes under control. His heart was strong and his circulation was good, which meant no limbs had to be amputated to prevent gangrene — a common side effect of adult-onset diabetes. Although he no longer had any choice about what he could eat or do, at the core his will seemed as strong as ever. He hung on and on. Sometimes I wondered if he wasn't determined to live forever, just so he could go on making Mom's life miserable.

Little by little, year by year, Dad lost one capability after another. His grandchildren grew up knowing their grampa as a shuffling old ghost with blankly staring eyes.

As Dad deteriorated, Mom's job got harder. Besides being his cook and housekeeper, she also became his full-time caretaker and nurse. When he could no longer cut up his food, she did it for him. When he could no longer find his mouth with his fork and food smeared his chin and dribbled down his shirtfront, Mom covered him with a bib and began feeding him herself. And after a while even that wasn't enough.

"Chew, Walter. Chew," she'd coach, prodding his cheek with her fingers to remind him that he had food squirreled away in there.

After he became incontinent, she had to be on constant alert to get him to the bathroom in time, even in the middle of night. If she slept through his pleas for help, there'd be accidents. Diapers helped. But she also learned the wisdom of keeping his mattress covered with a rubber sheet and his favorite lounge chair swathed in plastic.

"You okay in there?" I called to him as I stood outside the stall of a public restroom during one of my visits home. This was in the days when he was still mobile, and Mom and I had taken him on an outing to the county zoo, pushing him in his wheelchair past the bears and giraffes.

"You okay in there?" How often, I wondered, had he asked me the same question when I was a child and he was the one waiting outside the stall door?

"I'm done," came a small voice. Even as unaware as he was, this must still be as embarrassing for him as it was for me.

"Give it a little longer," I said. I had heard his water trickle out, but I didn't want to risk taking him away before he had a chance to do whatever else he needed to do, though I dreaded having to clean him up afterward.

A teenager came into the rest room, then a black man in shorts, a T-shirt, and a Brewers cap. Each of them glanced my way, probably wondering why I was lurking there. I turned to the sink and washed my hands, trying to look busy. I waited a few minutes longer, then went into the stall to rescue Dad. As I got him to his feet I chattered inanely, hoping to keep up the pretense that this indignity was not happening. "The zoo's great, isn't it? And what a beautiful day for a visit. Yes, indeed. Here, let me give you a hand with that."

As I helped him refasten his diaper, I tried to avert my eyes, wanting to preserve some shred of his privacy. But I could not help looking.

Until that moment I had never seen my father's nakedness. Even when I was a kid and found myself with him in a bathhouse at a beach or a pool, he would modestly keep himself turned away when he changed, or he would wait to change until I was done and gone. Now, as I bent to help him adjust his clothing, I came face-to-face with the root of his masculinity, and I was shaken to the core. The rest of his body might be shrunken and bent, but down there, below the sag of his belly, the root of his power was still startlingly thick and virile. Though it lay limp in its nest of flesh and black hair, its potential potency seemed undiminished.

I shivered involuntarily, and as quickly as I could I refastened his diaper, hoisted his trousers, and buckled his belt.

Later though, looking back, I wondered what it was that had left me so absurdly shaken. Clearly it was more than embarrassment at the mere sight of him. What was he, after all, but a man like any other, a man like myself? Yet it was almost as if I was afraid that, given this one vital root, the dying tree might yet send forth a new trunk and so return to full vigor and strength, to overwhelm me yet again.

Crazy notion. Totally irrational. The man was a shell — weak and failing in every aspect. His body was stooped. His memory was shot. His eyes were going. His legs barely worked. His bladder and bowels were beyond his control. He probably hadn't had an erection in years. Yet like some fairy-tale goblin that would not die, he still had the power to turn my knees to water and make my heart pound with dread in his presence.

I had to face it. His power over me no longer resided in him. By some demonic process of osmosis it had come to live somewhere deep within my own psyche, and I despaired of ever rooting it out so that I could be free of him once and for all.

For my mother, raising three kids had not been nearly as difficult as caring for Dad during those years. At least with kids you saw improvement. You saw growth toward independence and maturity. With Dad, she knew, there was no hope for improvement. The road he was on went in only one direction: downhill. And supporting him along that road was a full-time job. If she got distracted for even a minute, she might turn around to discover the front door open and him on his way down the street in his pajamas. Or she might find him teetering at the top of the basement stairs, having mistaken the basement door for the door to his bedroom.

Doors, the stove, objects on a shelf — suddenly the house became a perilous place, as full of dangers for him as it would have been for an active and curious two-year-old. To keep him from wandering away or from injuring himself on the basement stairs, Mom got out the toolbox and installed extra locks on any doors that might lead to trouble. She moved furniture to make sure he had a clear path to roam, so he could keep his legs exercised. The longer he could stay mobile, the easier it would be for her.

On call twenty-four hours a day, often exhausted from lack of sleep, Mom couldn't help but be overcome with frustration and anger.

"Sometimes I just want to scream at him," she'd tell me over the phone. "But how can I? It's not his fault that this has happened. It's not like he got sick on purpose."

"I wouldn't put it past him," I said, only half-joking.

"Now, you know that's not fair."

"Who said anything about being fair? You know what you should do? Try screaming into a pillow."

"Oh, I couldn't do that."

"Sure you can. I've done it. It helps. I know a guy who gets into his car when he can't stand it anymore and rides the interstate and screams his head off. And then he's fine. The thing is, you've got to get the anger out somehow or it's going to eat you alive."

She sighed. "I know," she said.

The sigh was the giveaway. That's when I knew she'd never do it. She was resigned. She'd swallow her frustration and shoulder her cross, all the while smiling sweetly and insisting that she was managing just fine. Meantime, her back would go out or her arthritis would kick in or she'd be felled by blinding headaches.

But she wasn't fooling anyone. The anger was in her and we all knew it. And now she had admitted it herself. She might surround herself with all the sweet-faced dolls in the world, and decorate her house with frilly curtains and cute pictures of cats and small children with big eyes. But given the chance, she'd rush off to the latest Charles Bronson or Clint

Eastwood movie, and the bloodier and more violent it was, the better she'd like it.

And who could tell? Maybe that was as good as screaming into a pillow.

Despite the horrible difficulties of coping with Dad's illness, the truth was that it made him a lot easier to be with, at least when the disease was in its early stages. Once critical and overbearing, he was now as complacent as a lapdog, willing to go wherever Mom led him and do whatever she said. At family gatherings, he'd sit quietly in his lounge chair while the conversation went on around him, sometimes surprising everyone by offering a wry comment but mostly just smiling benignly. It was almost as if the enemy enzymes that were sabotaging his synaptic links had launched their first assault against that corner of his brain that harbored all of his discontents and frustrations, leaving him at last at peace.

"It's so unfair," Joyce once told my wife with tears in her eyes. "Why couldn't my father have been this nice when he was healthy?"

Joyce, of course, had been bearing most of the burden of helping out, especially once Mom sold the house in Harmony Grove so she could be closer to Joyce and Dick. They became her mainstays, running errands, helping around the house, sitting with Dad while she went out to shop.

As for me, I was a thousand miles away, torn between guilt at not being able to do more and relief at not having to. Once a year I'd drop in for a visit. Then I'd quickly find out what I'd been missing — like the time Mom asked me if I'd mind looking after Dad for a couple of hours, while she went shopping.

"Of course I won't mind," I said with grand generosity. I was glad of the chance to do something to help, especially something so easy. "Go ahead, get out of the house for a while. Take your time. Enjoy yourself. Maybe there's a Bronson matinee playing."

"Where is Alice?" Dad asked almost as soon as she was out the door.

"She went to the store, Dad," I said over my newspaper. "She'll be back soon."

"I'm sorry," he said. "I'm sorry."

"That's okay, Dad."

There was silence for about a minute. Then he asked again: "Where is Alice?"

"I just told you. She's gone to the store."

"I'm sorry. I'm sorry."

"That's all right. Stop apologizing. There's no need."

"I'm sorry."

Half a minute later it was a new question. "What time is it?"

"It's just after two, Dad."

"When do we eat?"

"We just had lunch, Dad."

"I'm sorry." Pause. "Where is Alice?"

"At the store, Dad. I told you. She's at the store."

"I'm sorry. What time is it?"

And so it went, on and on, over and over. It was like being locked in a room with a runaway cuckoo clock. Ignoring him didn't work; it was like trying to ignore a dripping faucet. What I had imagined would be a relaxing stint of baby-sitting — a way to discharge my obligation with a minimum of hassles — was turning into an afternoon in hell.

His repeated questions went on unremittingly. After an hour and a half I began to think I would either strangle him or run screaming out of the house.

But even then he managed to surprise me. I was walking him to the bathroom. "Come on along," I said, holding on to his arm. That's when, inside his head, something connected. Suddenly it was as if Dad were on-stage again. My words were a cue, and for a brief moment his old man's shuffle was replaced by the light-hearted skip of a young hoofer as he croaked out the next line: "And listen to . . . the lullaby of Broadway."

There was a glimmer of delight in his eye as he looked up at me over the tops of his glasses and grinned in simple pleasure at his small triumph of memory.

Apparently the killer enzymes had not yet reached the synaptic pathways leading to the place where the old show tunes were stored. In the darkening corridors of his brain, where so much else had been obliterated, the words and the music still echoed.

18

BRIDGES

When we brought Dad up from therapy, his roommate was not in his bed. We had the room to ourselves, which was fine with me. I couldn't shake the feeling that this might be the last visit I'd ever have with my father, so I welcomed the privacy.

I wheeled Dad over to the window, while Mom checked the dresser drawers to make sure he had enough clean clothes and that no one had stolen his socks. Wintry sunshine poured in, but it did nothing for my spirits.

Saying good-bye should have been easy. I'd had plenty of practice at walking away without batting an eye. Regrets, letters to follow, reunions: not my style. Once a chapter was over, that was it. There was no looking back. I had no gift for old ties. The future, what came next — that was what mattered. Too many good-byes had left me immune. The future was my antibiotic.

But this time the future offered no refuge. This time all there was was the weight of the past, this sterile room, this withered figure in a wheelchair.

I looked out into the afternoon sunshine. At the end of the block I could see the snow-covered park and, beyond, a cold blue slice of Lake Michigan. But what dominated the view was the hospital complex across the street, especially the windowless brick building in the foreground. I guessed it was the hospital's furnace room or power plant, because from it rose an enormous smokestack. The thing must have been a hundred feet high.

I couldn't help smiling. The symbolism was so absurdly obvious that I was surprised I hadn't noticed it before. That towering chimney was like the handiwork of some demonic set designer with a warped sense of humor. Who else would have had the nerve to erect just there, outside my father's window, such a taunting evocation of lost power and potency?

But for me, there was more than symbolism to be found in that image. There was history, too.

"Look, Dad," I said. "That smokestack over there, does it remind you of anything?"

He squinted into the sunlight, stared blankly. "No," he murmured.

"Lakeside Power Plant? Where you worked when we were kids? You took us on a tour once. I couldn't believe how high the chimneys were. How many chimneys were there? Eight or ten, wasn't it? And those big piles of coal — remember? To me they seemed like mountains."

No flicker of comprehension showed in his face.

"He doesn't remember," my mother said wearily. "I doubt if he can even see across the street."

She was probably right, but against all reason, and without knowing quite why, I wanted my father to see what I saw. I wanted him to remember, as I remembered, a time when vigor and mastery were still his.

He had been in the nursing home for just over a year now, ever since his latest stroke had robbed him of the use of his left side, rendering him unable even to shuffle along with a walker. From then on, he had needed a wheelchair to get around. But getting him in and out of the contraption was more than Mom could manage on her own. A nursing home became inevitable.

It was a hard transition. Mom had been nursing him for almost twelve years. More than once during that time she had secretly — and guiltily — yearned to have the house to herself, even if only for half an hour. Now, without him, the loneliness was unbearable. Her house felt as empty and used up as an old tin can. Now she yearned only to have Dad back again.

Instead, she visited him every day, stopping at the nursing home about lunchtime and staying for hours. She fed him, shaved him, brushed his teeth, clipped his fingernails and toenails, and kept his hair combed. She took away his dirty clothes and brought him clean ones. She decorated his bulletin board with seasonal trimmings and greeting cards and with family photographs. She pestered the nurses endlessly, making sure that they treated Dad's bedsores, kept him on the right diet, and got him to the exercise room on schedule.

Yes, she understood that this place was merely a way station, the last stop before the end. She knew as well as I did that after this there'd be only one more move for Dad — and it wouldn't be with a U-Haul. Until that time came, though, she was determined that his days would be as normal and comfortable as she could possibly make them.

Still, her devotion to Dad was taking an enormous toll. My sister and brother and I could hear it in the strain in her voice, could see it in the dark circles under her eyes. Each of us in turn had urged her to take time off, to give herself a break now and then.

"Why don't you come out for a visit?" I told her once. "The people at the nursing home can manage perfectly well for a few days. You won't do Dad any good if you're so strung out all the time. You've got to take care of yourself, too, you know."

"I know." She sighed. "Joyce tells me the same thing."

Finally she did agree to visit. But she was with us for only two days when the nursing home called with the news that Dad was in the hospital. One of his kidneys had failed. He needed an operation immediately.

"I knew it," Mom said, wringing her hands. "I just knew something like this would happen."

We put her on the next flight home. She had not dared another trip. Since then, no day had gone by that she wasn't at his side.

Now, as I sat with Dad by the window, she finished arranging his dresser drawers and collecting his laundry. Next she checked under his bed and retrieved a missing slipper. Then she came over and began tucking pillows under Dad's arms to keep him from slumping sideways in the wheelchair. While she did, she spoke to him with patience and profound tenderness. It was as if all the years of anger and frustration had never happened.

When she had Dad propped up the way she wanted, she kissed him on the top of his head, then went off to look for a nurse. She was not happy with the coming week's menu, she said. She was going to get the staff to change it, or she'd know the reason why.

Left alone with Dad, I groped for something to say. Inarticulate with him as ever, I babbled on about how glad I was that I had come and how good it was to see him and how I hoped the nurses were taking good care of him.

"But I guess they haven't got any choice, eh? Not with Mom cracking the whip."

Joke. Was that a smile at the corners of his mouth? Or just the random twitching of a nerve?

He was peering at me over the tops of his glasses, which had slid down his nose again. Reaching over, I pushed them back up in front of his eyes. Whether they did him any good I had no idea. But they were part of him and he would have looked undressed without them, which surely was why Mom kept him wearing them.

"I'll be going home after this," I told him. "I live out east now, you know. Near New York City. Remember? You and Mom came to visit sometimes. You came just after Jesse was born. Remember Jesse? Your grandson? He's in high school now. Hard to imagine, isn't it?"

He stared at me, said nothing. Was he listening, or was his mind somewhere else? There was no way to tell.

"I've been living out east for almost twenty-five years," I rambled on. "That's longer than I lived out here. It's strange, though. Sometimes I still wonder where home is, where I really belong. You know? I mean, I've been in the same house and the same job for ten years now. That's the longest I've ever been in one place in my life. It should feel like home, right? But then I come out here and I think maybe this is where I should be. This country, the fields, the hills. It's so beautiful. You know, sometimes I even dream about it. Especially about the house you built. Funny, isn't it? It still turns up in my dreams. Do you ever dream about it, Dad? About that house?"

Nothing.

I wanted to weep. It was as if a great chasm lay between us. The gulf that separated us years ago had been bad enough, born as it was of mistrust and resentment and hostility. But it was hardly a dent in the earth compared to the Grand Canyon across which we now surveyed one another. Corroded by disease, the bridges that might have connected us were crumbling by the score, by the hundreds. Those few that remained were no wider than a neural filament, and across them I was now feeling my way, groping for some link, some common ground that we might share while there was still time.

"It was amazing," I told him, "but when I flew into Milwaukee the other day I could actually see the house from the airplane. Did I tell you?"

My eyes were suddenly blurry, and I blinked to clear them.

"We were coming in for a landing and the plane circled right over it. It was right there below me. And I could tell just which one it was because of the way it sits on the property . . . at an angle. . . . You know? . . . Do you remember it, Dad? Do you remember the house you designed and built?"

His eyes changed. Was something registering inside that head of his? Were his eyes narrowing in concentration? Or was he only squinting from the glare of the sunlight?

Hopeful, I tried again, thinking I might yet tease a memory out of him.

"What was the name of the road it was on? Can you help me, Dad? What was that road called?"

But there was no glimmer of recognition.

Despairing, I wiped my eyes and got up from the chair and turned to the snowy landscape outside the window. I contemplated again the absurdity, the insult, of that goddamn smokestack across the street.

"Rawson?"

The word was as raspy as sandpaper, barely a whisper.

I turned back, my heart lifting. "That's right! Dad! It was Rawson Avenue. You do remember!"

And this time I was sure that he smiled.

I sat again and took his hands in mine. I leaned close and peered into his brown eyes. "Do you remember the house, too? There was a fireplace in the living room, with knotty pine bookshelves and cupboards on either side. And a big porch out back that you planned to close in someday."

But the light in his eyes was fading again. He had expended his last effort. If he remembered any more of that place and of the dream that had made it happen, I could not tell. For all I knew, the memories might

230

still be in there, as vivid for him as they were for me. But if so, they were beyond my reach.

Mom returned then. I checked my watch. Time to go. I wanted to make sure we had time to drive past the house on the way to the airport.

I bent to plant a kiss on the parchment-thin skin of his forehead, and from somewhere in the recesses of my own memory sprang out one of the few Polish phrases I knew: *"Dae me buzi, Tata."* Give me a kiss, Papa.

I put my cheek close to his mouth until I felt the pressure of his lips, the scratch of his beard.

"Good-bye, Dad. I'll see you soon. I'll be back for another visit. I promise."

"Bye," he said, peering up at me, maybe seeing me, maybe not.

I turned away and walked out of the room.

Depression descended on me as my mother and I left the nursing home and got into the car. It was not just saying good-bye and knowing that my next visit was likely to be for his funeral. It was not just the way he looked, shriveled and staring and helpless. It was all of that, but it was also realizing finally how little his life had amounted to. Even the house, which had once been such a momentous and all-consuming part of him, even that had come down to no more than a flicker of memory, a mere synaptic blip, like a harbor light glimpsed briefly on some distant shore, then winking out in the darkness, never to be seen again.

No place in the world had meant so much to him. He had considered it his greatest accomplishment, and part of him regretted ever afterward having left it behind. Not that he ever said so, of course. Admitting to regrets would have been too much like admitting to having been wrong. But why else did he keep returning to that place? Whenever we were nearby — usually on the way to Racine, to visit Laurie or Busha — he would leave the highway to turn down Rawson and have a look at "our house." He was like a soldier returning to the scene of past battlefield glories. Cruising slowly past, his neck craned over the steering wheel, he would note where a new tree had been planted on the front lawn or how a lamppost and carriage light had been added alongside the driveway. He'd recall putting on the roof, or laying the footings.

"Yeah, and remember winter in the cabin," one of us would say.

"And hiking through the snow to the outhouse?"

"Mom's outhouse!"

"Boy, it was cold out there!"

Once, driving past, he came to a stop to stare in amazement. "Well, will you look at that!" he exclaimed. On the porch over the garage there was now a glassed-in sun-room, just as he had drawn it in his plans.

"Looks real good." he said. "They did a nice job."

"Come on," my mother said, her eyes straight ahead. "Let's go. We'll be late." Even then, she'd had no time for nostalgia about what she had lost. Remembering only made her angry all over again.

What had gone wrong? The question would not leave me alone. Oh, Mom had given me reasons: Dad's long commute; night school; the burden of keeping up with two and a half acres of lawn and gardens, much less finishing the house. Who knows? Maybe it was everything combined.

Still, I couldn't dispel the growing conviction that something else may have been at work, something deeper. Wasn't it possible — even likely — that in his secret heart my father had balked at the prospect of his dream actually becoming a reality? What if he finished the house and it turned out not to be everything that he had wanted it to be? What if it failed to live up to expectations — his and everyone else's? Then what? He would have had to live with the knowledge that he had failed. Better to leave the thing unfinished, for then it could not be tarnished by the possibility of inadequacy or disappointment.

"The first, best country is home," wrote Oliver Goldsmith, and he might as well have been talking about that piece of Wisconsin prairie where my father first paced out the boundaries of his house. In most ways those years were the best years of his life. He was in his prime: young and healthy, happily married, with two rambunctious children and a third on the way. He had a steady job, and he was reaching for the thing he wanted more than he had ever wanted anything.

And I, his son? In those years, in my child's eyes, all the world was new and my father was a god: the bold and daring master of all, who was capable of imagining and doing the most extraordinary things — like raising a house out of a hole in the ground. To me, in those years, he was not a man who had ever been defeated.

Surely it is all of this that has kept me returning in my dreams and imagination to that "first, best country." Looking back, that place and that time seem bathed in a golden glow. In comparison, so much of what followed for us seems out of register, like a sloppy color engraving, where the colorplates never quite match up. In every place afterward we were more like tenants than residents. We were visitors in other people's houses, other people's dreams. We were forever passing through on the way to someplace else.

In some sense, of course, this could serve as a fitting description for the trajectory of most lives. A philosopher might consider our constant uprooting and starting anew to be not so much an aberration as a metaphor for the changes that affect every life. Still, there's a difference between appreciating a metaphor and being dragged through one by a discontented autocrat.

The fact was, as I looked back on the years that came after that place on Rawson, all I could see of my father's life was a succession of failures, false starts, and self-defeats. Gloomy thoughts. But they were what filled my mind as I walked out of the nursing home and got behind the wheel of Mom's car. When she was settled on the passenger side, I put the car into gear and headed north toward the airport.

I drove for a time in morose silence. I had no artificially upbeat comments left in me.

"God, what a waste," I said at last, unable to shake my mood.

"What's that?" Mom asked. "What are you talking about?"

"Dad's life. I mean, look at what it amounted to. All the dead ends. All the things left unfinished, the jobs that never went anywhere. All the moving just for the sake of moving. It all seems like such a futile journey. I mean, for God's sake, he wasn't stupid. He was a smart guy. But it was like he could never get a handle on his life. He could never quite make it come out right."

"No," she said quietly. "You're wrong. It wasn't a waste."

I took my eyes off the road long enough to look at her in amazement. "It wasn't?" I asked.

She replied with utter conviction. "Not at all. He did everything he wanted to do."

I was incredulous. Was it possible that I had misunderstood him so completely?

But as I thought about what she said, I began to see the truth of it. I also began to see why I hadn't understood it sooner. Determined as I was to rise above his meager expectations of me, I had long ago set my sights on what I smugly assumed were loftier ambitions than his. In my most deliciously vengeful imaginings, fame and wealth and glamour would be mine. I and my work would be known and respected. I would win awards. I would be invited to speak on important occasions. My name and picture would turn up in national publications. I would appear on television. In my final apotheosis I would rise so high that he would not be able to touch me or pull me down. I would be invulnerable. And in comparison to my fabulous successes, his own life would be revealed for what it was: petty and insignificant and dogged by defeat.

In reality, of course, I had not climbed nearly as high as in my grandiose fantasies. Not that I had done all that badly. But Mom's comment made me realize that when it came to my father's life and ambitions, I had missed the point entirely. By measuring him against my vengeful and unforgiving yardstick, and by remembering only his failings, I had failed to see just how far he himself had come.

The son of struggling immigrants, he had begun his working life in a factory. Unsatisfied, determined to better himself, he studied hard, became an apprentice, then a journeyman, then a master machinist, then a tool-and-die man, a draftsman, and a teacher.

Pursuing a dream of green fields and open space for himself and his children, he bought a house in the country and raised ducks and planted vegetables. Having conceived a dream of building his own house, he went and did exactly that. Later, yearning to live on a lake and own a boat, he did that too. He wanted to try California. We lived in California. He had come through the uncertainties of the Depression and the war. Yet he had managed to make a decent life for his wife and his three children, and to bring some adventure into our lives. And none of us had turned into junkies, alcoholics, loafers, or philanderers.

"My father never had any dreams," a friend once told me when I was proudly relating the story of the house Dad built. My friend's father had been a postal worker all his life. Like my father, he was the child of immigrants and had come through the Depression and the war. For him, the most important thing in life had been security: a life of steady paychecks and regular routine. The thought of trying something different apparently never occurred to him. And who can say that he was wrong? But to have lived without dreams? To me, this seems like the saddest of epitaphs.

Despite everything, I felt deeply grateful that no such summing up could ever conceivably be applied to my father. His dreams may have been different in kind and scale from mine, and his world may have seemed impossibly small to me in the days when, as a young man, I was busy launching myself into a wider one. But those dreams had made all the difference in his life. Change, uncertainty, and discontent had taken their toll, but they had also carried him — sometimes despite himself — further than probably even he had ever imagined.

True, he was not comfortable with where his yearnings had led him. Part of him always believed that the machine shop was where he really belonged, and all the rest — the white shirt and tie, his skill, his artistry — was just a pretense and a fraud. "What do I know? I'm just a poor working slob," he'd say when his opinion was challenged, or when he caught a whiff of pretension (usually mine). It was pure melodrama, of course, and sometimes he played the line for laughs. But it recurred so often that I came to suspect he was describing the man he truly thought he was. Even so, he did not let this deter him from boldly reaching for the next dream, and the next, and the next.

To imagine something better and then to have the persistence and will to make it happen: this is no small gift for a parent to pass on to a child. And I had grasped it with both hands. Though I may have had no comprehension of the extent to which my father's dreams and discontents were shaping our lives, along the way I had absorbed the knowledge that change was not only possible but inevitable, and that hopes and dreams were worth pursuing, even when the chances of success were far from guaranteed. After all, you never could tell what wonderful thing might turn up around the next bend.

It is true that I have grown fond of the place where I work, the village where I live, the house I come home to at night. I think now that it's not such a bad thing to stay put, to belong somewhere.

And yet, every now and then I catch a whiff of something in the air — autumn leaves, the damp earth of spring — and I feel an incredible yearning, an overwhelming urge to pack up. To move on. To start over. To try something new . . .

*   *   *

235

We left the interstate, followed the ramp, and drove west on Rawson. Once there had been wide open fields along this stretch of road. Now a suburban wilderness of sprawling condominium developments spread out on either side. I winced at the sight. Is it all going to be changed? I wondered. Will I recognize anything?

But as we drove farther along, I was delighted to see that some important things were the same. The woods that had been my wild frontier had been spared the bulldozer and were now a county nature preserve, marked by a handsome and permanent-looking rustic signpost. What had been the neighborhood tavern was now the park's headquarters, and as I drove slowly past, I thought I caught a glimpse of a trail marker just off the end of the parking lot. My secret places were apparently still intact, waiting to be discovered by other young frontiersmen.

I drove on, slower now, knowing we were close. We passed the park's western border, then one more house, and there it was.

It still looked much as it did in the old photographs and in my memory: compact, fairly ordinary in proportions and design, but of course smaller than I remembered. What made it distinctive — so much so that I had been able to spot it from the airplane — was the way it sat on the land: well back from the road and turned at an angle to its neighbors, letting all the world know that its builder was too proud and independent to do things the way everyone else did them.

There had been changes since the last time I was there. The house, once white, was painted a dreadful shade of pale blue, and an ugly metal awning projected over the front door, like a bookkeeper's eyeshade. But the shape of the house had not been tampered with. And yes, that sunroom on the back looked just fine.

It was the yard that surprised me. A careful landscaper had obviously been at work, because the place looked vastly improved over what it had been when we lived there, almost like an extension of the park. A large and shapely fir tree graced the front yard, and I could see other new trees out back. The lawns were impeccable, and there were handsome flowerbeds near the front door and along the driveway.

I pulled the car to a stop on the edge of the road and shut off the engine.

"What are you doing?" my mother asked anxiously. "We should go. You'll miss your flight."

I reached for my camera. "I just want to get a picture."

I got out, crossed the road, and began shooting. Verticals, horizontals, long shots, close-ups. But my telephoto was not powerful enough to bring me as close as I wanted, and I found myself inching up the driveway and across the lawn.

I was firing away, trying to get the best shot I could, when the front door opened and a man came out and stood on the stoop, under the metal awning. "Can I help you?" he called.

I was suddenly aware of how I must look to him: a stranger with a camera, walking up his driveway: a real estate agent, perhaps, or a tax inspector. Or worse, a housebreaker. I realized I should count myself lucky that he didn't have a shotgun slung over his arm.

Lowering my camera, I gave him a cheerful greeting and a friendly wave. "I used to live here," I explained. "I just stopped by for a look."

"Is that right?" he said, still wary.

"Yup," I said in my best folksy dialect. "Matter of fact, my dad built this house when I was a kid."

With that, his manner changed completely. "No kidding," he said, smiling now. "When was that anyway? I've always wondered."

By this time I had reached the stoop. Careful not to set foot on his steps, I stretched a hand up to him and introduced myself. He looked a few years older than I was, but with less hair and bigger jowls.

"He started it in forty-eight," I said, "but it took him about a year to get it to the point where it was livable. While he was building it, we lived in a little one-room cabin that stood over there, just about where that tree is."

"Well, what do you know about that," he said, shaking his head in wonder. "Not long after we moved here, the people next door told us about that cabin. They said a whole family had lived in a tiny little shack while the house was going up."

"That was us," I said proudly. Apparently our pioneering days had become part of the local folklore, and the thought pleased me. What amazed me was that the neighbors he was referring to were still there all those years later. They had not moved in all that time. Not even once. It was hard to imagine.

"You know, you're not the only one who's come back to see this place," the man told me.

"I'm not?" I thought he must be talking about Joyce or Michael.

"No. Now and then the kids of the people we bought the house from come back to have a look. Their folks bought it from your Dad, I believe. There were four children and they all grew up here. They lived here seventeen years before we bought it. And the kids still come back to see it, and some of them bring their kids. They were real happy here."

I grinned. "My dad would be glad to hear that. So you've been here . . . ?"

"Eighteen years this last fall. We raised our three here. We've enjoyed it. It's been a good house. A happy house."

We chatted a few minutes longer. Then, worried about my plane, I thanked him and said good-bye.

As I walked backward down the drive, trying to take the place in, to recapture all that it meant to me, I realized I had more reason to thank the man than he knew. In his few words, he had given me a great gift.

Not for our family alone had this place been the first, best country. My sister and brother and I were not the only children who had shared in the dream that my father had brought into being. For two other families as well, his house had been a happy place, a place to revisit and remember.

That, I thought, was no small legacy for any man to leave behind.

And as I drove away I had a feeling that for once Dad would not have contradicted me. Instead, I imagined, he'd have looked at me over the tops of his glasses and grinned proudly and said, "You betcha."

ACKNOWLEDGMENTS

My father was a pack rat. He saved everything: playbills, scrapbooks, report cards, bills, receipts, résumés, medical records, letters to prospective employers, early sketches of the house he eventually built, bills from contractors and lumberyards, builder's handbooks, and carpentry manuals. He also took countless still photographs and many reels of 8-millimeter home movies. On our frequent moving days, when I was carrying cartons of my father's archives out to the U-Haul or up the steps into a new house, I often wondered why he kept all that stuff. As far as I could tell, he never did anything with it. I never imagined that my father's archives — to give a dignified name to those random hoardings — would one day be more useful to me than they probably ever were to him. In the writing of this book, they not only sparked my memories; they often helped me to establish chronology and details that would otherwise have been impossible to reconstruct.

While this memoir is drawn largely from my personal recollections, I am deeply indebted to many others for generously sharing their memories with me. Although I have sometimes taken liberties in creating scenes and dialogue, in every such case these sections are based upon direct recollections of myself or others.

For sharing their recollections I wish first of all to thank my mother, who patiently endured my impertinent probing into matters she would just as soon not have dredged up. Thanks also to my sister, Joyce, and my brother, Michael, for sharing their stories and perspectives. Often they surprised me. They remembered things I did not, and they did not remember things that were enormously important to me. Sometimes, indeed, I had to wonder if we had grown up in the same family, so different were our various recollections of the same events. And yet enough common threads ran through our experiences to assure us all that we were indeed bound in blood and bone.

My thanks also to those aunts and uncles who so generously offered their time and hospitality as they imparted their memories to me: Laurie Hibicki, Leonard Froncek, Tad Froncek (now deceased), Marcella Beyma, Pat West, Ed West, and Norb Schemanski.

For professional assistance, my first and best debt of gratitude belongs as always to Bill Reiss, agent and counselor, who got the train on the track, kept it fueled with advice and encouragement, and guided it safely into the station.

Thanks also to Dana Adkins for her perceptive editorial insights and encouragement at the outset; Tracy Brigden, whose enthusiasm carried me over many rough stretches; Marjorie Palmer, who listened and encouraged; Barbara Morgan, for her judicious good counsel; and Sally Arteseros for her very helpful comments and suggestions. I count myself lucky to have had such pros in my corner.

Thanks to Dick and Jeannette Seaver for their faith in the book, for their dedication to quality, and for their great good sense in employing a superb editor, Cal Barksdale, whose judgment and taste have been impeccable throughout the editing of this book.

Thanks to Stan Lieberfreund, counselor and friend, for his unfailing support and guidance. Baseball's loss was our gain.

I'd say thanks, too, to Ellen, but *thanks* is too small a word to embrace all that I owe to her — my wife, partner, and best friend. Her loving and caring, her endless patience, and her unflagging faith sustained and strengthened me during the often difficult and sometimes painful process of writing this memoir. She didn't let me off the hook as often as I'd have liked, and the book is better for it. She has been my sail, rudder, and compass through the whole voyage of our life together.

Most of all, I thank my father, for the house he dreamed and built and for the memories he left me. We had our rough times, he and I, but there was love, too, hard as it was for either of us to say the word. May he rest in peace.

ABOUT THE AUTHOR

Thomas Froncek lives with his wife, Ellen, and their son Jesse in a hundred-year-old house in New York's Hudson River valley. Although the author has no current plans to build a house, he is handy with tools and has been known to construct bookcases, repair leaky faucets, and replace bathroom tiles and fallen plaster. On occasion he has also installed attic insulation and hung sheetrock. However, he studiously avoids electrical work, the more serious aspects of plumbing, and anything having to do with concrete. A writer and editor, Mr. Froncek is the author of numerous books and articles. His most recent book, *Take Away One*, was a selection of Reader's Digest Condensed Books, in which form it was published internationally in eight languages.